- 在文化中习得语言
- 在语言中了解文化

感悟加拿大文化

英语趣味会话 （第4版）

Understanding Canadian Culture through English Conversations

李桂山 吕嗣鹏 ◎ 著

机械工业出版社
CHINA MACHINE PRESS

图书在版编目（CIP）数据

感悟加拿大文化：英语趣味会话 / 李桂山，吕嗣鹏
著. -- 4版. -- 北京：机械工业出版社，2024. 11.
--（英语文化驿站系列）. -- ISBN 978-7-111-77185-2

Ⅰ. H319.9

中国国家版本馆CIP数据核字第2024E1T573号

机械工业出版社（北京市百万庄大街22号　邮政编码100037）
策划编辑：杨　娟　　　责任编辑：杨　娟
责任校对：张晓娟　　　责任印制：邸　敏
三河市宏达印刷有限公司印刷
2025年1月第4版第1次印刷
169mm×239mm・19印张・1插页・389千字
标准书号：ISBN 978-7-111-77185-2
定价：69.80元

电话服务　　　　　　　　　网络服务
客服电话：010-88361066　　机 工 官 网：www.cmpbook.com
　　　　　010-88379833　　机 工 官 博：weibo.com/cmp1952
　　　　　010-68326294　　金 书 网：www.golden-book.com
封底无防伪标均为盗版　　　机工教育服务网：www.cmpedu.com

前　言

我于1976年至1978年由国家选派，作为留学生在加拿大麦吉尔大学（McGill University）留学，并于1990年2月获得加拿大研究专项奖，应加拿大政府外交部的邀请再次赴加拿大，进行加拿大社会与文化方面的实地考察和研究。

作为访问学者，在过去的40多年里，我多次赴加拿大和美国进行学术研究、讲学、访问，并进行国际教育合作等多项工作。在此期间，结识了许多加拿大和美国各界人士，与这些新朋老友进行了广泛交谈。我从与美、加朋友交谈中获取了大量的有关加拿大社会与文化的背景知识，同时也学到了许多诙谐的英语习语，使我深感英语习语纷繁浩瀚。英语习语的妙用所营造的那种轻松愉快的气氛使我记忆犹新。我的体会是，习语使用得恰如其分，习语掌握得纯熟流利，就可以增强语言的表达能力，好比锦上添花。

本书通过对话的形式，记录了我与美、加朋友们的交谈内容。它介绍了北美，尤其是加拿大的风俗、社会、民族特点等文化背景知识。

本书自2008年1月第一次公开出版以来，时至今日已连续两次修订。本次为满足众多读者的需求，我对之前的内容重新修订再版。全书共分36个单元，每个单元都有一个中心话题作为背景知识，采用中英对照的形式，目的是方便读者学习英汉互译。这些背景知识向读者介绍了加拿大的历史、社会、文化、大学生活、独立自主、平等意识、少数民族、多元文化、枫糖文化、饮食习惯、户外运动、行为准则、文学作品和教育制度等，内容丰富、语言生动易懂，对我们进一步了解加拿大社会发展过程中的趣闻轶事很有帮助，也是我们了解加拿大社会与文化的宝贵资料。

此外，本书每个单元都设计了一个诙谐的对话，对话后还附有一些必要的词汇和注释，以供参考。其中，对部分理解起来比较有难度的生词、短语或者句子，在给出汉语释义的同时，也用英文进行了注释。每个对话中含有5~10个英语习语，它们都是加拿大和美国朋友在和我的交谈中自然运用的习惯用语。为方便读者学习，我们对每一处习语均做了简明的英汉释义，并列举了两个或三个例句进行补充说明。

　　课后的习语例句的汉译英部分和每课背景知识的英译汉部分是由廉晋萍老师和朱柯冰老师共同完成的。作为新世纪赴加拿大留学的研究生，吕嗣鹏（Wood）同学根据自己在加拿大三年的生活和学习经历，对本书进行了新视野下的有效修订，从而丰富了对话内容，拓展了加拿大社会与文化方面的知识。

　　在本书的编纂期间，天津摩尔培训学校刘铎（Andy）校长和天津理工大学离退休工作处的各位领导提供了诸多支持和帮助，特此向他们表示衷心的感谢。

　　本书再版前有幸得到了加拿大西三一大学(Trinity Western University)副校长菲利普·莱尔德（Philip Laird）博士的认真指导和审核。在此谨向他表示衷心的感谢。

　　本书同样得到了加拿大尼亚加拉瀑布大学（University of Niagara Falls）校长辛迪·麦克劳德（Cyndi Mcleod）女士的审校和帮助。在此谨向她表示衷心的感谢。

　　同时，本书有幸得到了加拿大康考迪亚大学（Concordia University）英语应用语言学教授帕尔默·艾奇逊（Palmer Acheson）博士的校阅，并提出了宝贵建议。在此谨向他表示衷心的感谢。

李桂山

Preface I

Throughout my 25+ years as a Senior Leader and Administrator at 5 universities across 4 different countries, I have been lucky enough to have many opportunities to work with partner institutions in China. Throughout the years those partnerships have become stronger and resulted in long-standing friendships. I have always been both impressed and inspired by the commitment of Chinese students to learning English as a second language, something that I find sadly lacking here in the West.

My own experience of learning new languages has always been to embrace any and all opportunities to practice conversation. Not only does this enhance listening skills but it also helps you understand the broader culture of which the language is a key part. Understanding the local culture helps to understand the language.

This book is an innovative, inspiring and, often, humorous way for students (of all ages) to learn about Canadian culture, history, and society whilst also developing conversational English. I'm sure we have all experienced the fact that language used in conversation is often very different from the written language and is much more challenging to understand. The 36 different conversations are all great examples of authentic spoken conversational English, both here in Canada but also in the United States and the United Kingdom.

As I always tell my students, learning should be a fun experience, and this book is a great way to learn about Canadian culture and conversational English whilst having fun doing so.

Professor David Gray
Provost & Vice-President (Academic)
University of Niagara Falls Canada

在我为4个不同国家的5所大学担任高级领导和行政管理人员的25年多的时间里，我有幸能够与中国的合作伙伴一起共事。多年来，这些合作关系不断加强，使得我们的友谊地久天长。这期间，我一直对中国学生学习英语作为第二语言的决心印象深刻，并深受鼓舞。而这种学习精神在西方是少见的，很令人遗憾。

我自己学习新语言的经验就是抓住一切能抓住的机会练习对话。这不仅可以提高听力技能，还可以帮助你理解语言作为其中关键组成部分的更加广泛的文化知识。而了解当地文化，反过来也有助于加深理解语言本身。

这是一本对学生（包括各个年龄段的人）领悟加拿大文化、历史和社会的一本佳作。是一本以诙谐、幽默的方式来提高英语会话能力的具有创新、令人鼓舞的杰作。我们肯定都经历过这样的事实：对话中使用的语言往往和书面语言相比有很大的不同，而且更难以理解。这本书中36个不同的对话单元都是地道的口语会话，同时也是英语口语的绝佳范例，它们不仅适用于加拿大，也适用于美国和英国。

正如我经常告诉我的学生的那样，学习应该是一种有趣的体验，而阅读这本书就是在开心快乐中学习加拿大文化并提高会话英语能力。

大卫·格雷教授
教务长兼副校长
加拿大尼亚加拉瀑布大学

Preface II

This is a light-hearted offering, written in the hope that it contributes toward a better understanding of the Canadian culture.

It is intended for students, tourists, managers, teachers, traders and all the English learners. They will certainly get a better understanding of Canadian society and culture by reading this book. The readers would certainly learn about Canadian history, its people, its resources and prospects and they could get an over-all view of the material grandeur of Canada.

This book, through 36 different topics and the witty conversations, introduces the background knowledge of Canadian society and culture.

Mr. Li Guishan has visited Canada many times in more than forty years and has the honor of making the acquaintance of Canadian people in all walks of life. The valuable information in Mr. Li's *Understanding Canadian Culture through English Conversations* is all derived from dialogues and communication that he overheard or participated in while he was in Canada. This book has introduced Canadian history, society, culture, college life, independence, equality, ethnic groups, multiculturalism, the culture of maple syrup, camping in nature, Canadian etiquette, literary works, and educational system, etc. Another highlight of the book is that he naturally and freely concentrates on the many idioms that fill in the 36 different dialogues. And the spoken English in the dialogues are quite reflective of modern, conversational, informal English. This book does contain good witty idiomatic expressions that are frequently used in everyday life.

Over the last 36 years, I have learned several foreign languages successfully and recently began studying Chinese and Japanese. For the past 27 years, I have also been a teacher of languages and a trainer of language teachers. It has been my experience that one of the most effective and efficient ways of learning the spoken variety of languages is to study increasingly complex conversations. Words and sentences in isolation are easily forgotten, but conversations usually have a beginning, a development, and an end, and are much more memorable than odd snippets of languages.

I am sure that intermediate and advanced-level Chinese learners of English will find this book of dialogues to be a useful way of increasing their knowledge of idioms. It should prove to be a best-seller.

Palmer Acheson, Ph. D.
Professor of Applied Linguistics
Director, Undergraduate Programs
Center for Teaching English as a Second Language
Concordia University
Montreal, Quebec, Canada

这是一份倾情献礼，希望能为弘扬加拿大文化贡献力量。

本书适用于学生、游客、管理人员、教师、商人和所有英语爱好者。阅读这本书，他们一定会对加拿大社会与文化有更深刻的了解。读者能够从中学习到加拿大的历史、风土人情、自然资源和发展前景，感受到一个庄严宏伟的加拿大。

本书通过36个中心话题和诙谐幽默的对话，向读者介绍了加拿大社会与文化背景知识。

本书作者李桂山先生在过去的40多年里多次访问加拿大，他幸运地结识了加拿大各界朋友。根据在交往中的所闻、所用，他撰写了这本《感悟加拿大文化——英语趣味会话》。书中介绍了加拿大的历史、社会、文化、大学生活、独立自主、平等意识、少数民族、多元文化、枫糖文化、户外运动、行为准则、文学作品和教育制度等多方面的知识。本书另一个亮点是自然而流畅地将丰富的英语习语贯穿于36篇对话中，语言饶有现代气息，朗朗上口，通俗易懂。这本书的确包含了许多日常生活中诙谐幽默的惯用妙语。

在过去的36个春秋里，我成功地学习了数种外语，近来我又开始学习汉语和日语。我执教已有27载，曾从事语言教学工作，培养语言教师。积多年之经验，我认为循序渐进地学习一些内容丰富的会话是训练语言表达能力最富有成效的途径。单独的词汇语句易于忘记，而会话往往有始有终，有情节发展过程，因此比只言片语更容易记住。

　　我相信，那些学有所长的中国英语爱好者会发现，此书对他们增长英语习语方面的知识大有裨益。它必将会是一本畅销书。

帕尔默·艾奇逊博士
应用语言学教授
大学研究项目主任
英语作为第二种语言教学中心
康考迪亚大学
蒙特利尔，魁北克省，加拿大

目 录

前言
Preface I
Preface II

Unit 1	**Finding a Place to Stay 住宿**	... 001
	Dialogue　Let's Keep Our Fingers Crossed	... 004
Unit 2	**Vancouver 温哥华**	... 007
	Dialogue　We Finally Stand Face to Face	... 009
Unit 3	**Working Mothers 工作的母亲**	... 015
	Dialogue　I'm Running Myself Ragged	... 018
Unit 4	**Monetary Circulation 货币**	... 023
	Dialogue　Kill Two Birds with One Stone	... 026
Unit 5	**Native People 本土人**	... 031
	Dialogue　Indian Paintings Are on Display	... 034
Unit 6	**Government 政府**	... 037
	Dialogue　You Have It in You to Be an Expert of Canada	... 039
Unit 7	**Time Zones and Time Differences 时区和时差**	... 044
	Dialogue　You're Laying It on Thick	... 047
Unit 8	**National Parks 国家公园**	... 051
	Dialogue　You Can Say That Again	... 053
Unit 9	**Employment and Vacation 就业及休假**	... 058
	Dialogue　He's Tight-Fisted	... 061
Unit 10	**Canadian Writers 加拿大作家**	... 065
	Dialogue　They're Selling like Hot Cakes	... 069
Unit 11	**CN Tower and Cable TV 加拿大国家电视塔和有线电视**	... 073
	Dialogue　I'm in a Bind	... 076
Unit 12	**The Group of Seven of Canada 加拿大七人画派**	... 081
	Dialogue　This Idiom Baffles Me	... 085

CONTENTS

Unit 13   Women and Children 妇女和儿童 ... 091
    Dialogue   The Pot Calling the Kettle Black ... 093

Unit 14   Leisure Activities 休闲活动 ... 099
    Dialogue   They Were Absolutely Breathtaking ... 102

Unit 15   Looking for a Job 找工作 ... 106
    Dialogue   This Job Gets Me Down ... 109

Unit 16   Friendliness 友善 ... 114
    Dialogue   We're on the Same Wave-length ... 117

Unit 17   Fitness Craze 健身热 ... 121
    Dialogue   I've Got Two Left Feet ... 123

Unit 18   Food and Drink 饮食 ... 128
    Dialogue   I Can't Tell Them Apart ... 131

Unit 19   Shopping 购物 ... 136
    Dialogue   I Finally Picked out a Good One ... 138

Unit 20   Maple Syrup Festival 枫糖节 ... 142
    Dialogue   You Couldn't Beat That Deal with a Stick ... 145

Unit 21   College Life 大学生活 ... 150
    Dialogue   I'm on Top of the World ... 153

Unit 22   Gatherings 聚会 ... 158
    Dialogue   She Drew Me out of My Shell ... 160

Unit 23   Concept of Equality 平等的观念 ... 166
    Dialogue   Out of the Blue ... 168

Unit 24   Royal Canadian Mounted Police 加拿大皇家骑警 ... 173
    Dialogue   Mind Your Own Business ... 176

| Unit 25 | Multiculturalism 多元文化主义 | ... 181 |
| Dialogue | Like a Fish out of Water | ... 184 |

| Unit 26 | Niagara Falls 尼亚加拉瀑布 | ... 189 |
| Dialogue | Get a Bird's-eye View of the Falls | ... 192 |

| Unit 27 | Quebec 魁北克 | ... 198 |
| Dialogue | Fancy Meeting You Here | ... 200 |

| Unit 28 | Education in Canada 加拿大教育 | ... 204 |
| Dialogue | I Got off to a Flying Start | ... 207 |

| Unit 29 | Weather Conditions 气候状况 | ... 211 |
| Dialogue | I Was Frozen Stiff | ... 213 |

| Unit 30 | On Our Own 独立自主 | ... 219 |
| Dialogue | We Don't Usually See Eye to Eye on Many Things | ... 223 |

| Unit 31 | The Meech Lake Accord 米其湖条约 | ... 229 |
| Dialogue | Smooth Things Over | ... 231 |

| Unit 32 | People and Land 国土和人民 | ... 236 |
| Dialogue | They'll Come in Handy | ... 240 |

| Unit 33 | Camping in Nature 大自然野营 | ... 243 |
| Dialogue | We Canadians Love the Great Outdoors | ... 246 |

| Unit 34 | Privacy 隐私 | ... 252 |
| Dialogue | I'm Really Fed up | ... 255 |

| Unit 35 | The Happy Life of Seniors 老年人的幸福生活 | ... 260 |
| Dialogue | I Was Completely Captivated by Shanzhige Performances | ... 262 |

| Unit 36 | The Roots of Canadian English 加拿大英语的根 | ... 268 |
| Dialogue | I'd Better Stop Talking Shop | ... 273 |

后　记　论加拿大英语的特点　　　　　　　　　　　　　... 277

索　引　　　　　　　　　　　　　　　　　　　　　　... 288

Unit 1
Finding a Place to Stay
住宿

It is not difficult for a visitor to find a place to live in Canada. Places to stay may be called hotels, motels, inns, lodges, resorts or homestay.

Canadian law says that the landlord cannot refuse to rent a place to people by their race, skin color, age, nationality, religion, sex, marital status, or disability. A landlord can refuse to rent to pet owners and people who smoke.

When you agree to rent a house or apartment, you and the landlord are making a contract. It can be a written or spoken agreement. If you sign a lease, it means that you will stay in the apartment for the time period specified in the lease. If you want to move out before the lease expires, thereby breaking the lease, you will need to compensate the landlord. On the other hand, the landlord cannot ask you to move out before the lease expires. He is also breaking the lease if he does. The law says the landlord must make the repairs if the roof leaks or the toilet doesn't work or there is no hot water.

Motels have plenty of parking spaces and are usually near freeways and highways. Inns are usually like motels. Lodges and resorts are in the mountains, on the coast, or near the lakes. Lots of hotels have special facilities for conventions—large and small meeting rooms, banquet rooms.

Motels or hotels all have smoking rooms and non-smoking rooms. Sometimes, the price depends on how many people in one room. Canadian Automobile Association (CAA) has travel books which list most of motels and hotels with prices, facilities, contact information and directions.

Motels and hotels always have check-out time, such as before 12:00 at noon. Staying beyond the check-out time may result in additional charges. Some hotels and motels charge paid movies, but most of them have a free movie channel.

Electricity in North America is 110 volts, not 220. You cannot use your hair dryer or your electric razor unless you can change it to 110 volts. When telephoning from your hotel room, you will often have to go through the hotel switchboard, especially for long distance calls. These calls can be quite expensive, because the hotel usually adds a high service charge to the calls you make. On the other hand, local calls can generally be made from your room by dialing directly. You can also ask the hotel receptionist to give you a wake-up call in the morning. Phone cards are available in Canada and in the United States. It is inexpensive and convenient to use phone cards to make long distance calls.

If your hotel does not have a laundry service, maybe you can find a laundromat nearby, which might even be open 24 hours a day. You will need exact change to operate the washing machines and dryers. You will always find soap, towels and linen in hotels and motels in Canada.

Most universities and some colleges provide student residences (sometimes called dormitories or dorms). Many residences offer food services or cafeterias, while others provide small kitchens for student use. The social atmosphere of living in residence can be a definite advantage to a newcomer. It is one of the best places to meet people and make contacts. On the other hand, if you are a person who needs privacy, residence may not be for you. There are often more shared (or two-person) rooms than single (or one-person) rooms available.

The housing offices or foreign student offices at the universities may tell you of possible places. Or you may also see an ad in a newspaper. While you are talking with the landlord on the telephone, ask as many questions as you can. Before renting a house or an apartment, you need to pay a deposit, which is usually equivalent to one month's rent fees, as a guarantee for fulfilling the contract and not damaging the property. If there is no damage, and you clean the apartment, the landlord will give you back all the money, plus interest.

译 文

　　对一个游客来说，在加拿大找一个住宿的地方并不困难。提供住宿的地方被称为宾馆、汽车旅馆、客栈、小屋、度假村或家庭住宿。

　　加拿大法律规定，房东不能以种族、肤色、年龄、国籍、宗教信仰、性别、婚姻状况或残疾的原因拒绝出租房屋。但是房东可以拒绝出租房屋给饲养宠物的人和吸烟者。

　　一旦你承租一所房子或一套公寓，你和房东就签订了租赁合同。这个合同可以是书面的，也可以是口头协议。如果要签约，那你就要住满规定的时间。提前搬走，叫做毁约，要赔偿房东。但另一方面，房东也不能让你提前搬家，如果是这样，他也是毁约。法律规定，如果屋顶漏雨、马桶有故障或者没有热水，房东必须负责修葺。

　　汽车旅馆有足够大的停车场，而且通常临近大路或高速公路。路边客栈类似汽车旅馆。在山上、海边或湖畔建有住宿和度假的小屋。许多宾馆还为会议准备了专门的设施：大、小会议室和宴会厅。

　　汽车旅馆和宾馆都分有可吸烟房和禁止吸烟房。房价有时和一个房间的床位多少有关。加拿大汽车协会出版旅游书，里面列有大多数汽车旅馆和宾馆的房价、设备、联系电话和路线。

　　汽车旅馆和宾馆都有退房时间，比如中午12点前。过了退房时间可能要多收钱。有些宾馆和汽车旅馆看闭路电影要额外付费，但多数有一个免费的闭路电影台。

　　在北美，电压为110伏，而不是220伏。你只有把电吹风或电动剃须刀的电压转换为110伏时，才可以使用。当你在宾馆房间拨打外线特别是长途电话时，需要通过总机转接。这样的电话费用会很高，因为宾馆通常要附加一些高额服务费。另一方面，本地电话只需要从你的房间直接拨打就可以了。你还可以要求宾馆服务员在清晨为你提供电话叫早服务。加拿大和美国可以使用电话卡，这对打长途电话来说既方便又便宜。

　　如果你所入住的宾馆不提供洗衣服务，你可以在附近找一家自助洗衣店，也许还是24小时营业的。你必须用正好的零钱操作洗衣机和烘干机。加拿大的宾馆和汽车旅馆一般都提供肥皂、毛巾和床单。

　　多数大学和一些学院提供学生住宿（有时被称为宿舍），许多提供餐饮服务或自助餐厅，而有些则为学生提供小厨房。住宿的社会环境的确有利于新生，这是结交朋友和建立联系的最好场所之一。另一方面，如果你需要私人空间，学生宿舍可能不适合你。学校还提供许多合租房间，双人间的数量比单人间多一些。

　　大学里的住宿办公室或留学生办事处可能会告诉你一些可住宿的地方，或者你也可以查阅报纸上的广告。当你和房主通电话时，一定要尽可能地多问问题。在入住前，你需要支付押金，通常相当于一个月的租金，作为履行合同和不损坏财产的保证。如果没有任何损坏，而且你还清扫了房间，房东会把押金以及利息都还给你。

Let's Keep Our Fingers Crossed

(Li has got a Canadian Studies Academic Scholarship and he is leaving China for Canada soon for his teaching and research activities. However, he is a bit at loss.)

Tom: You don't look cheerful today. You look exhausted.

Li: That's right! As you know, I'm leaving for Canada in two days. But I haven't found a place to stay in my first stop in Vancouver.

Tom: You could stay a few days at my mom's. You will be certainly greeted with a warm and friendly welcome.

Li: Thank you very much. How generous you are! Tom, could you give me some ideas on how I *go about* finding a place to stay after a few days at your mom's?

Tom: My pleasure. There are several ways to find housing. The housing office or foreign student office at the university may tell you of possible places. Or you may also see an ad in a newspaper. While you are talking with the landlord on the telephone, ask as many questions as you can. You need $300 to $500 or more at once as a down payment when you first rent the apartment.

Li: I've learned from our special orientation that you usually have to pay some extra money when you move in. Right?

Tom: Correct. The landlord keeps this money as a damage deposit until you move out. The landlord can use some of this money to pay for any damage there is. If there is no damage, and you clean the apartment, the landlord will give you back all the money, plus interest.

Li: Thank you very much for your info. Can I come to visit you tonight? You could give me the introductory letter to Professor Mike Jefferson.

Tom: *Drop in* at any time tonight. I'll phone my mom first and then you take my letter to my mom. Remember, phone my mom if anything unusual *crops up* when you are in Canada, or you find yourself in a difficult situation; no one

Unit 1 Finding a Place to Stay 住宿

to meet you at the airport, no place to stay and nothing to eat...

Li: ...and tramp the streets. Are you going to talk to me like this?

Tom: Oh, no, I'm just kidding. I'm sure you will be taken good care of by Canadian friends. Let's *keep our fingers crossed*.

Li: Thank you very much for what you have done for me.

Tom: My pleasure.

Vocabulary and Notes

- How generous you are!
- orientation

- If there is no damage, and you clean the apartment, the landlord will give you back all the money, plus interest.
- tramp the streets

你太慷慨大方啦！

定向，定位；情况介绍；（出国前的）培训

如果没有损坏，而且你把房间打扫得干干净净，房东将把所有的钱并且加上利息归还给你。

流落街头

Idioms for Everyday Use

go about (doing something)
着手干、做（某事）

start working on (doing something)

Could you give us some brief ideas of how you **go about** building a boat?
你能给我们简单地介绍一下你们是如何造船的吗？

Tom didn't have any good ideas of how to **go about** finding a better job.
怎样才能找到一份较好的工作，汤姆没有什么好办法。

drop in (on someone)
顺便拜访（某人）

pay a casual visit to a person or to visit someone informally

A: Why don't you **drop in** and have a glass of beer with me?

B: Sorry, I'm in a hurry to get to my yoga class and we'll dine out when I'm back.

A: 到我房间来喝杯啤酒好吗？

B: 对不起，我要赶着去上瑜伽课，等上完课我们一起出去吃饭。

Please **drop in** on me whenever you have time. I'm available most evenings.

你什么时候有时间，就什么时候来。我几乎每天晚上都在家。

crop up
突然发生或出现

happen unexpectedly

- A: Sorry, something has **cropped up** again and I won't be home tonight till late.
  B: I'm not surprised. That would be abnormal if you came back home early.
  A: 对不起，又发生了一点意外的事情，今晚我要很晚才能回家。
  B: 我并不感到惊奇。如果你早回家那就不正常了。

- A: Something unusual has just **cropped up** at the office, Helen. So I'm afraid I won't be able to meet you for lunch.
  B: I don't know! Whenever you arrange to take me out to lunch, something always **crops up**. What is it this time?
  A: 海伦，办公室里刚才突然发生了不寻常的事情，所以我想我不能和你一块儿去吃午饭了。
  B: 我真不理解！每次你安排好带我出去吃午饭，总有意外的事发生。这次又出什么事了？

- Some difficulties have **cropped up**, so we must work late to deal with them.
  突然出现了一些困难，因此，我们必须加班来处理这些问题。

keep one's fingers crossed
祈求好运（交叉一只手的两个手指以祝好运，但愿不要出什么问题）

cross two fingers of one hand for good luck; make a wish that nothing goes wrong

- He **kept his fingers crossed** while I took the exam.
  他祝我考试走运。

  I think our volleyball team will win the match but I'm **keeping my fingers crossed**.
  我想这次比赛我们的排球队准赢，但愿不要出什么意外。

- A: I hope I could get the permission from the department office to go to Trinity Western University.
  B: Good for you. Let's **keep our fingers crossed**.
  A: 我希望系办公室能够准许我前往西三一大学。
  B: 一定会被批准的。祝你好运。

Unit 2
Vancouver
温哥华

The city of Vancouver was named after Capt. George Vancouver, who had explored and mapped the west coast of north America for England in the 1790's.

The Port Metro Vancouver is the largest port all along the entire Pacific Coast of North and South America. Vancouver's downtown is surrounded by water on three sides and you can walk along the water around almost the whole of downtown.

As the chief Pacific Coast railway terminal, the Port Matro Vancouver has a large ocean trade with the Orient. It has vastly expended shipping since the opening of the Panama Canal in 1915, and is now Canada's largest port.

Most of Canada's grain, lumber, pulp and coal leave from the Port Metro Vancouver. And it's where the manufactured goods from Asia arrive.

The biggest university in Vancouver is University of British Colombia (UBC). The Museum of Anthropology housed at UBC has one of the world's outstanding collections of Pacific Northwest aboriginal artifacts, including totem poles, carvings, jewelry, masks, baskets, tools and musical instruments.

Science World in downtown Vancouver gives kids a hands-on experience of physics, chemistry, biology and zoology—and a whole lot of fun. The teachers from primary and secondary schools are usually taking their children to Science World to have open-door schooling. The city's Stanley Park, on a peninsula in English Bay, is a 400-hectare green area (6,000 Chinese Mu) and that is the favourite place for locals and visitors to relax spiritually and physically. That is the place to provide with sports fields, trails, hills, beaches and plenty of flowers. The Vancouver Aquarium is in Stanley Park and features many wonders in water. Downtown, Robson Square is known as the city center, which makes up three blocks of offices, restaurants, shops and theaters. The Vancouver Art Gallery and Public Library are right in the city center.

Chinatown in Vancouver is North American's second largest after San Francisco. The Chinese Cultural Center provides guided walking tours and visits to the Chinese Museum and groups may participate in hands-on cultural workshops. Vancouver's Chinatown is the place to visit for a taste of Chinese culture. Boasting one of the largest Chinese communities in North America, Vancouver is also home to a variety of other ethnic communities from Europe and Asia.

Situated between the mountains and the sea, Vancouver is an attractive city. There are more than 100 parks there. Thanks to the warm winds from the Pacific, Vancouver has a mild climate, so that the flowers bloom all year round along the Pacific coast. There is a great deal of rain in the city. Since the weather along the Pacific coast is quite pleasant all the year round, tourists from all over the world can be seen in all seasons.

In the warm Pacific climate of Vancouver, the temperature rarely drops below freezing. It seldom snows in the city, but when it does snow, it transforms the city into a picturesque winter wonderland, albeit briefly. The surrounding mountains, easily accessible from the city, offer ample opportunities for skiing, snowboarding, and other winter sports, making Vancouver a perfect base for those seeking both urban and outdoor adventures during the winter season. Vancouver rains a lot in April, so people there often say, "April showers bring May flowers." You will enjoy the beautiful flowers around there in May.

温哥华市是以乔治·温哥华船长的名字命名的。18世纪90年代，出于为英国勘测并绘制北美西海岸沿海地图的目的，他来到此地探险。

温哥华港口是南北美洲整个太平洋沿线最大的港口。温哥华的市中心三面环水，你可以沿着几乎环绕整个市区的河畔散步。

作为加拿大主要的太平洋西海岸铁路沿线的终点,温哥华港口和亚洲国家进行着大量的海上贸易往来。自从1915年巴拿马运河开通以来,温哥华港口的转运能力大幅提升,如今这里已是加拿大最大的港口。

加拿大大部分的粮食、木材、纸浆和煤炭都从温哥华港口出口,这里也是亚洲产品的进口港。

温哥华最大的大学是不列颠哥伦比亚大学(UBC)。校内的人类学博物馆藏有世界著名的太平洋西北土著石器,包括图腾柱、雕刻、珠宝、面具、篮子、工具和乐器。

温哥华市区的科技馆为孩子们传授着物理、化学、生物和动物学方面的知识,并寓教于乐。老师们经常带着小学生和中学生到科技馆进行教学实地考察。坐落在英吉利湾半岛上的斯坦利公园是一片占地400公顷(6000亩)的绿洲,是本地人和游客放松身心的最佳去处。那里有运动场、原野、山丘、海滩和大量的鲜花。温哥华水族馆位于斯坦利公园里面,有好多珍奇的水生生物。在市区,罗伯逊广场被认为是这座城市的中心,那里的办公楼、饭店、商场和剧院占地面积有三个街区。温哥华艺术馆和公共图书馆就在城市的中心。

温哥华的中国城是继旧金山之后北美第二大中国城。中国文化中心提供旅游及参观中国博物馆的指南,团体游客还可以参加文化实践活动。温哥华的中国城是体验中国文化的好去处。温哥华以成为北美最大的中国社区为荣,它也包容了来自欧洲和亚洲的其他民族社区。

位于高山和海洋中间的温哥华是一个充满魅力的城市。那里有100多个公园。受到太平洋暖风的影响,温哥华气候宜人,太平洋沿岸全年鲜花盛开。城市雨水充沛。由于太平洋沿岸全年气候宜人,来自世界各地的游人一年四季络绎不绝。

身处太平洋温暖气候的温哥华,气温基本在零摄氏度以上,很少下雪,但一旦下雪,整个城市便会被装扮成银装素裹的冬日仙境,尽管是短暂的。从城市出发可轻松抵达周边的山区,为滑雪、滑板和其他冬季运动提供了充足的机会,使得温哥华成为那些在冬季既想享受城市生活又想体验户外探险的人们的理想之地。四月里的温哥华经常会下小雨,因而人们常说"四月雨催五月花"。五月到处可见美丽的鲜花。

We Finally Stand Face to Face

(Peter is at the International Airport in Vancouver, meeting his Chinese friend, Li. Li's waving his hand at Peter and coming up to him.)

Li: Hey! Peter! It's wonderful to see you again.

Peter: (shaking hands, giving his friend a bear hug) That's super! Welcome back to Canada. After ten years of corresponding, we finally **stand face to face**. Look, we both are **getting along in years**. How did you recognize me?

Li: Well, your long beard made you **stand out** from the others, so I recognized you at first glance.

Peter: Li, I just can't tell you how happy I am to see you again. But let's do something about your luggage first. Why don't you **stick around** and **keep an eye on** your stuff? I'll bring my car up here.

Li: (in the car) Peter, how come it's drizzling even in April? Is this typical Vancouver weather?

Peter: You know what they say: "April showers bring May flowers." You will enjoy the beautiful flowers around here in May. Well, Li, fasten your seatbelt. Let's **hit the road**. Look at all this traffic. I hope we won't be held up by a traffic jam.

Li: I'm so surprised to see all these cars, so many different colors, and different sizes.

Peter: You've got a boiling sea of bicycles in China and we've got a boiling ocean of cars in Canada. Every family here has a car, or two or even three. Statistics shows that more than half the population knows how to drive an automobile and have licenses to drive.

Li: I hear that nowadays in Canada the major part of your traveling is done in cars.

Peter: It makes sense. Many Canadians own cars not only for business but also for pleasure traveling. *The Vancouver Sun* says that the average Canadian car owner drives his car 2,000 miles each year on vacation trips alone.

Li: I see. But I think the air must be polluted as a result of the exhaust from so many cars.

Peter: Yeah, sometimes they're more trouble than they're worth. But cars do play an important role in a country like ours. Well, look! That's my apartment. My wife is preparing dinner for us. I've got plenty of food; you can certainly **eat and drink your fill**.

Li: Hope she's cooking some Chinese food.

Peter: You're probably right. She says she's trying to stir-fry shrimp with cucumber and sweet and sour fish. My daughter loves Chinese food.

Li: How old is your daughter now?

Peter: Nine. Here's a photo of her.

Li: (looks at the photo) Very pretty. With her curly hair and big eyes, she seems to *take after* you.

Peter: But in her character she's more like her mother. Well, Li, here's my house. Look! My daughter's coming to see us.

Li: Peter, thank you very much for everything you've done for me.

Peter: Don't mention it. *It's all in a day's work*.

Vocabulary and Notes

• wave one's hand	招手
• give someone a bear hug	give someone a rather rough, tight hug 紧紧拥抱某人
• That's super!	太棒了！太令人高兴了！
• after ten years of corresponding	10年的通信往来
• recognize	认出；辨认
• beard	hair of the lower part of the face 络腮胡子；胡须
• drizzle	下蒙蒙细雨，下小雨
• April showers bring May flowers.	四月雨催五月花。
• fasten the seatbelt	系好安全带
• be held up by a traffic jam	被交通阻塞截住
• a boiling sea of bicycles	自行车的海洋
• license	(Am.) an official paper, card, etc., showing that permission has been given to do something; (Br.) licence 执照；特许证
• driving license	驾驶执照
• exhaust (*n.*)	排出的气（或水等）

- they're more trouble than they're worth | If you say something is more trouble than it is worth, you mean that it takes a lot of time or effort and you do not achieve or gain very much in return. 与其说得到好处，还不如说带来麻烦；得不偿失
- stir-fry shrimp with cucumber | 虾仁炒黄瓜
- sweet and sour fish | 糖醋鱼

Idioms for Everyday Use

stand/be/come face to face with someone
与某人面对面相遇，和……碰面

meet and can talk to someone or look at someone directly

- He went into the library and found himself **face to face with** the president of the school.
  他走进图书馆，发现自己和校长碰个正着。
- A: I was shopping the other day and suddenly **came face to face with** Helen in the crowd.
  B: That's a fancy meeting.
  A: 那天，在购物时我和海伦突然在人群中相遇了。
  B: 那可真是奇遇。

get along in years (常用进行时态)
老起来了（指年纪）

grow or become older

- My father is **getting along in years** and doesn't see too well any more. But his movements are still quick.
  我父亲逐渐老起来了，眼神不像以前那么好了，可是他的动作还很敏捷。
- The Chairman of the Art Department is **getting along in years**, and that's a big place for an old man to handle.
  美术系的主任上了年纪，那么一个重要的职位老人家是难以应付的。

stand out
很显眼，突出

can be easily seen or noticed

- Red **stands out** against a white background.
  在白底上红色显得特别醒目。

Unit 2　Vancouver　温哥华

▮ Kevin was very tall and robust, and **stood out** in the crowd.
高大强壮的凯文在人群中特别显眼。

▮ *Farewell, New York City* in the *30 Selections of Foreign Culture* **stands out** from all the others.
《外国文化30篇》中的《别了，纽约城》这篇文章在其他那些文章中显得与众不同。

stick around/about (常用于一般时态)
为等候某人或某事而待在附近；不走远
| stay where you are, often because you are waiting for someone or something

▮ A: I've been here waiting for him for a good hour. I'd better go.
B: **Stick around** for a while longer—he may show up soon.
A: 我在这儿等了他整整一小时了。我最好还是走吧。
B: 请再稍等会儿——他马上就会来的。

▮ **Stick around**. I'll buy some fruit for your grandpa and I'll be back in five minutes.
站在这儿别动，我去给你爷爷买些水果，五分钟我就回来。

keep an eye on (something or someone)
照看；照管
| watch them and make sure that they are safe

▮ A: Will you please **keep an eye on** my books? I'll be back in about five minutes.
B: Where are you going? I'm going to attend my yoga lesson in a few minutes.
A: 请给我照看一下书好吗？我大约五分钟后回来。
B: 你到哪儿去呀？几分钟后我可要去参加瑜伽班课程。

▮ We asked our neighbors to **keep an eye on** the house while we were away on vacation.
外出度假时，我们让邻居照看我们的房子。

▮ A: Can you **keep an eye on** the baby while I go shopping?
B: OK, but please come back as quickly as you can. I'm going to a movie at seven.
A: 我这会儿出去买东西，你给我照看一下孩子好吗？
B: 可以，不过你得尽快回来。七点我要去看电影。

hit the road
开始旅行；出发；上路
| set out on a journey; leave

▮ A: Tom and Jennifer have already packed the car, and they are ready to go.
B: Good. Take the camera and let's **hit the road**.
A: 汤姆和詹妮弗已经装好车，准备出发了。
B: 好的，让我们带上照相机上路吧。

- We decided we'd **hit the road** very early the next morning.
  我们决定明天一大早动身。

eat/drink one's fill
尽量吃；尽量喝 | eat/drink as much as someone can

- You can **eat your fill** in the strawberry fields, but if you want to take any strawberries home, you have to pay for them.
  在草莓地里你可以尽情地吃。但如果你想把草莓带回家去，就得付款。
- He had not touched a drop for two days, and then he could no longer control himself. He took off his coat and **drank his fill**.
  他两天滴水未沾，此时再也控制不住自己了。他脱掉大衣，喝了个痛快。

take after
容貌或性情上像（长辈） | look or behave like (an older relative)

- A: Tom **takes after** his father in everything but his nose.
  B: I don't think so. He doesn't have the same chin as his father's.
  A: 除了鼻子外，汤姆其他地方长得都像他的父亲。
  B: 我不这样认为。他的下巴长得不像。
- The boy **takes after** his father; he has the same red hair, blue eyes and big feet.
  这个男孩长得像他的父亲，也是红头发、蓝眼睛和一双大脚。

(It's) all in a day's work
分内的工作；不客气，应该做的 | not mind doing the work although it is difficult; with pleasure

- A: I very much appreciate your kind help, otherwise, I couldn't get the work done today.
  B: Oh, that's nothing. **All in a day's work**.
  A: 非常感谢你的帮助，不然的话，今天我就完不成这项工作了。
  B: 这没什么，我应该做的。
- I thanked him deeply for the proofreading of my manuscript, but he smiled and said that it's **all in a day's work**.
  我深深地感谢他为我校对书稿，可他笑了笑说不必客气。

Unit 3
Working Mothers
工作的母亲

More Canadian women are preparing for better-paying jobs. However, the earnings of men and women are not yet equal for several reasons. As of 2023, Canadian women earn on average about 87 cents for every dollar earned by men. Many Canadian women are still working in traditional female jobs. Many are teachers or nurses or work in offices or stores. These jobs pay less than traditional male jobs. At the same time, many working women are already mothers. These women are struggling to meet all the demands of jobs outside and family chores. To do both, these working mothers often have to choose to work less than the normal 40 hours a week. This is another reason why they earn less.

In order to retain working mothers, many Canadian companies have made new rules to make it easier for them to balance work and family life. More and more companies now offer part-time jobs and some companies also provide child-care centers for the children of their employees.

The remarkable change in recent years has been the increased number of mothers who have young children and work outside their homes. A record 75 percent of mothers in two-parent families with children under age six are now in the paid labor force, while 55 percent of single-parent mothers with young children are in the same situation.

Women have an active involvement in all aspects of Canadian life. In 1918, after a long struggle, they won the right to vote in federal elections. In 1929, less than 4 percent of women worked outside the home and by the early 1990s, 65 percent were in the labor force. Today, around 82 percent of women aged 25 to 54 are part of the labor force.

Despite these advances, working women still shoulder a disproportionate share of household chores. According to recent studies, women who work full-time spend an average of 135 minutes a day on housework, while their husbands spend only 65 minutes. Part-time working wives spend 110 minutes daily caring for their children, compared to 30 minutes by their husbands. Men also enjoy more passive leisure time, spending 140 minutes a day on activities like reading or watching television, whereas their working wives spend only 95 minutes.

"Wives in Canada who go to work still do the chores at home. Men with wives who work full-time outside the home spend less than half as much time as their wives on housework, " said Robert Chouchman, executive Director of Toronto's Family Service Association.

Another change in family life in the last few years has been an increased awareness of the role of the father. Fathers are spending more time with their children. Most hospitals allow a father into the delivery room so that he can be there to see his children come into the world. From birth, through diaper changing, to nursery school and after-school activities, today's father participates in his children's upbringing.

More and more husbands are sharing the burden and willingly taking on some difficult chores. In such cases, husband and wife become equal partners, both working outside, both pushing the vacuum cleaner. However, when the equal partnership is a fact, it does not always work well. The marriage can be destroyed when the wife is more successful in her profession than her husband in his, particularly when she earns more than he does. Sociologists see in this situation one of the main reasons for the increase in the divorce rate.

"The younger generation of fathers is doing much more child care," Benjamin Schlesinger, a professor of social work at the University of Toronto who has done extensive studies on the Canadian family, said in an interview. "These men tend to marry women who grew up with the tremendous influence of the

Unit 3　Working Mothers　工作的母亲

women's movement, who are unwilling to take on the formal role of mother and kitchen helper."

Being a working mother can be difficult. Getting home after a hard day's work they have to do the chores and find some time to spend with the kids. It's an uphill battle.

译　文

如今，越来越多的加拿大女性正在为收入更高的工作做准备。然而，由于几个方面的原因，男性和女性的收入还不平等。截至2023年，加拿大男性每挣1美元，女性平均挣87美分。许多加拿大妇女仍然从事传统的女性工作。许多人是教师或护士，或在办公室或商店工作。这些工作的收入低于传统的男性工作。与此同时，许多职业女性已经成为母亲。这些女性正在努力满足外面工作和家庭琐事的所有要求。为了做到这两点，这些职业母亲往往不得不选择比正常的每周工作40小时更少的时间。这是她们挣得少的另一个原因。

为了留住职业母亲，许多加拿大公司制定了新的规定，让她们更容易平衡工作和家庭生活。现在越来越多的公司提供兼职工作，一些公司还为员工的孩子提供托儿中心。

近年来一个显著的变化是，越来越多的有年幼孩子的母亲会选择外出工作。在有6岁以下孩子的双亲家庭中，有75%的母亲现在参加了有偿劳动，而有年幼孩子的单亲母亲中有55%的人处于同样的境地。

妇女积极参与加拿大生活的各个方面。1918年，经过长期的斗争，她们赢得了联邦选举的投票权。1929年，只有不到4%的女性外出工作，而到20世纪90年代初，有65%的女性加入了劳动力大军。如今，在25岁至54岁的女性中，约有82%的人是劳动力。

尽管取得了这些进步，但职业女性仍然承担着不成比例的家务劳动。根据最近的研究，全职工作的女性平均每天花135分钟做家务，而她们的丈夫只花65分钟。兼职工作的妻子每天花110分钟照顾孩子，而丈夫只花30分钟。男性也有更多的被动休闲时间，每天花140分钟在阅读或看电视等活动上，而他们有工作的妻子只花95分钟。

多伦多家庭服务协会的执行董事罗伯特·考曼调查后讲道："加拿大的已婚全职女性仍然要做家务，而已婚全职男性所做的家务却连他们妻子做的一半都不到。"

近几年来，加拿大家庭生活的又一变化是父亲的责任感正在日益增长。父亲们拿出更多的时间来陪伴孩子。大部分医院允许父亲进入产房目睹孩子的出生。从出生、换尿布、上幼儿园到课外活动，今天的父亲陪伴着孩子们的成长历程。

越来越多的丈夫分担着家务的负担，自愿承担一些艰巨的家务。在这种情况下，丈夫和妻子成为平等的伴侣，都外出工作，都推吸尘器。但是，当夫妻真正实现了平等，情况也有不妙的时候。当妻子在事业上比丈夫更成功,特别是妻子比丈夫赚得更多时,婚姻有可能会破裂。社会学家在这里看到了离婚率上升的其中一个主要理由。

"在照看小孩方面,年轻一代中的父亲们花的时间要多一些。"多伦多大学社会工作教授本杰明·施莱辛格对加拿大家庭做了广泛的调查研究,在一次会见时说道,"这些男人往往会娶受过女权运动影响的那些女性为妻子,因为她们不愿只担当母亲或厨房帮手的角色。"

作为一名在职母亲要面对很多困难。上班辛苦了一天,到家还要做琐碎的家务,还要抽时间和孩子们相处。真可谓是艰苦的战斗。

Dialogue

I'm Running Myself Ragged

(Peter gave a welcome dinner for his friend Li from China. After they finished their meal, they chatted.)

Li: (to Alice, Peter's wife) Just a wonderful meal! The chicken was really tender, and the fish you cooked had a Chinese flavor.

Alice: It's what you call "sweet and sour fish". I used my tried and true recipes. The fish was fried first, and then the sauce was poured over it—the sauce is made of vinegar, sugar, chopped garlic and ginger.

Peter: Alice, you're **showing off** in front of the expert. I still remember the dishes Li cooked for me ten years ago. Li, you're still a fabulous cook, aren't you?

Li: That'll be for you to decide. I've got several new dishes that I want to try out on you tomorrow.

Alice: I'll **take you up on** that. We're not conservative in our food tastes, and we especially like Chinese food.

Peter: Because of the number of different ethnic groups in Canada, we've learned to appreciate many different kinds of cuisine. A Canadian family may enjoy Chinese food one night, Italian food the next—then Greek, or Ukrainian.

Li: Oh, I see. You certainly enjoy a great variety of meals. Well, do you think Canadian food is complicated? I sometimes can't recognize the names of foods.

Peter: Certain types of Canadian food may cause you some confusion. For example, a hamburger is made of ground beef, not ham; and a hot dog contains a sausage that may be made of pork or beef. If you don't recognize the name of a food, you *don't know the first thing about* cooking.

Alice: Li, look at all my different cookbooks. We've been trying our hands at different kinds of foods. It's fun, but also a lot of work.

Li: I agree. My wife does most of the cooking. She's had *a tough row to hoe*, doing the housework and looking after our daughter these years.

Alice: I'll bet! Being a working mother can be difficult. I'm *running myself ragged*—getting home after a hard day's work and then trying to do the chores and find some time to spend with the kids. It's an uphill battle.

Li: It's hard if both partners don't pitch in around the house. Peter, try to give her a hand. Didn't you tell me in your letter that you're splitting the chores, and trying to be a good husband?

Peter: Yes, I'm trying. In fact, I'm going to wash the dishes, because the dishwasher is *on the fritz*.

Vocabulary and Notes

- tender — very soft and easy to chew or cut 嫩的；柔软的；容易嚼或容易切的
- tried and true — well-tested 经实践证明是好的
- recipe — 菜谱；烹饪法
- vinegar — 醋
- garlic — 大蒜
- ginger — 姜
- fabulous cook — 出色的厨师
- That'll be for you to decide. — 由你来做出判断（决定）。
- conservative — 保守的；守旧的
- ethnic (=ethnical) — 种族的
- appreciate many different kinds of cuisine — 品尝许多种不同的饭菜

- Greek　　　　　　　　　　希腊的；希腊人
- Ukrainian　　　　　　　　乌克兰的；乌克兰人
- ground beef　　　　　　　碎牛肉
- I'll bet.　　　　　　　　　What you are saying is true. 你说得对/没错。那还用说。
- do the chores　　　　　　做家务
- It's an uphill battle.　　　这是一件艰难（费劲）的工作（任务）。
- pitch in　　　　　　　　　help, work together 帮忙，合作
- It's hard if both partners don't pitch in around the house.　　如果夫妻二人不配合做家务，那是很困难的。
- split the chores　　　　　It usually refers to the husband and the wife who share the housework.（一般指丈夫和妻子）分担家务
- dishwasher　　　　　　　洗碗机

Idioms for Everyday Use

show off
炫耀，在别人面前显示、卖弄

behave in a way that makes your skills, abilities too obvious in order to impress people

A: I think Mary visited us just to **show off** her new car and her new dress.
B: That's all right. I would do the same if I won the lottery.
A: 我认为玛丽来看我们只是为了炫耀她的新车和她的新衣服。
B: 那有什么。如果我赢了彩票，我也会像她一样。

Philip is **showing off**. He is talking about how rich he is in order to impress his friends.
菲利普在自我卖弄。他在讲他多么有钱，想得到他的朋友们的钦佩。

Pamela speaks Chinese well, and, whenever the opportunity arises, she likes to **show off** in front of the strangers.
帕梅拉能讲一口漂亮的中文，一有机会就喜欢在别人面前显示自己。

take someone up on (something)
接受别人的邀请

be willing to accept (a promise or offer) made by someone

A: Come to my place during the Spring Festival, and I'll make you the best spring pancakes.

Unit 3　Working Mothers　工作的母亲

　　I can make spring rolls, too.

B:　I'll **take you up on** that.

A:　过春节时到我家来，我给你做最好吃的春饼。我还会做春卷呢。

B:　那我一定去。

He said he'd buy me a drink, so I **took him up on** it and ordered two bottles of beer.
他说他给我买喝的，我没推辞，要了两瓶啤酒。

| **not know the first thing about (something)**
对某事一窍不通；什么也不知道 | have not the slightest idea about (something) |

I **don't know the first thing about** doing business, so please ask Catherine of the market in Canada—she knows the ropes.
我对做生意的起码知识都没有，因此请向凯瑟琳讨教有关加拿大的市场——她很在行。

A:　Then why don't you take the American Literature course? I can lend you some literature books.

B:　But I **don't know the first thing about** American Literature.

A:　那么你为什么不选"美国文学"这门课程呢？我可以借给你一些文学书籍。

B:　可我对美国文学一无所知。

I **don't know the first thing about** geopolitics.
我对地缘政治学一窍不通。

| **a tough/hard/long row to hoe**
生活中困难重重；艰巨的工作 | a life full of difficulties; a very hard job to do |

A:　I hear her husband died yesterday. It seems that the doctors could do nothing about his illness.

B:　That's too bad. She has **a hard row to hoe** with four children.

A:　听说她的丈夫昨天去世了。看来大夫们对他的病已经无能为力了。

B:　太可惜了。带着四个孩子，她的日子更难熬了。

I'd like to be a surgeon, but I know it's **a long row to hoe**.
我想当一名外科医生，但我知道这不是一件容易的事情。

| **run someone ragged**
过度的劳累使某人精疲力竭 | make someone do so much that someone becomes exhausted; tire someone out very much |

A:　Sandra has now four children, works full-time, and takes courses at night. She gets up at 6:00 in the morning and doesn't go to bed until after midnight. She is **running herself** ragged.

B: Poor Sandra. I'm afraid that she would burn herself out or break down.

A: 桑德拉现在有四个孩子，白天全天工作，晚上又上夜校。她每天早上六点就起床，过了午夜才能睡，她已是筋疲力尽了。

B: 可怜的桑德拉。我担心她会耗尽体力或者把身体搞垮。

A: How's your work in that primary school?

B: I love teaching, but the children are so active that they run me ragged.

A: 你在那所小学的工作怎么样？

B: 我喜欢教书，但孩子们活泼有余，以至累得我精疲力竭。

Her work, children and housework were running her ragged.
她的工作、孩子们和家务事把她搞得精疲力竭。

on the fritz
发生故障；坏了

out of order; broken

A: You finished your washing?

B: Oh, no! Bad luck! The machine has gone on the fritz. I think I need a new one.

A: 你洗完衣服了？

B: 没有！真倒霉！洗衣机出了毛病。我想我该买一台新的了。

A: The television camera is on the fritz again. Could you come and look at it?

B: No problem. I'll take care of it after lunch.

A: 摄像机又出毛病了。你来给看看好吗？

B: 没问题，吃完午饭我来修理。

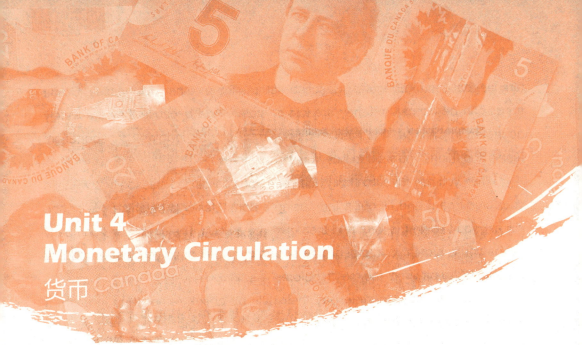

Unit 4
Monetary Circulation
货币

Canadian people use two kinds of money: coins and bills. Coins are made of metal, and each coin has a picture on it. There are five kinds of coins in circulation in Canada. They are the one-cent coin; the five-cent coin, the nickel; the ten-cent coin, the dime; the twenty-five cent coin, the quarter; the one-dollar coin. Canadian people call a one-dollar coin a loonie because it has a picture of a loon on it. A loon is a large water bird that lives in Canada. It has bright red eyes and a strange cry. People in Canada at present also use a two-dollar coin, which is called "toonie".

The Bank of Canada is responsible for issuing banknotes, which come in denominations of $5, $10, $20, $50, and $100. The banknotes feature notable Canadian historical figures, such as:

-$5: Sir Wilfrid Laurier, the seventh Prime Minister of Canada.

-$10: Viola Desmond, a Black Nova Scotian businesswoman who challenged racial segregation.

-$20: Queen Elizabeth II.

-$50: William Lyon Mackenzie King, the tenth Prime Minister of Canada.

-$100: Sir Robert Borden, the eighth Prime Minister of Canada.

Canadian people do not carry a lot of cash with them. They always say the best way to carry money is to have a major credit card like Visa or Master Card. Credit cards are issued by department stores, banks, credit-card companies, airlines, car-rental agencies, gasoline companies or other businesses. Credit cards can be canceled if they are lost or stolen. And because they are widely accepted in Canada, it is easy to use them to pay for lodging, transportation, meals and things you want to buy from larger stores.

When you pay for something with your credit cards, the salesperson will take your credit card and fill out a form using a computer or a machine. He or she will ask you to sign the form and then give you a copy. The credit card company sends you a monthly statement that shows the purchases you made and any balance left to pay from the month before.

In Canada, most people pay their bills by check rather than in cash. It is more convenient and the cancelled check is a receipt of payment. A bank willingly cashes a check for you and is ready to change large bills for you. If you have an account in a bank, you can get a check cashed without any charge. If you want a special check, the bank will give you the check for a small fee. The bank will also sell you traveler's checks which are good when you travel overseas. Traveler's checks can be cashed in most overseas hotels and banks.

Traveler's checks are insured. If they are lost or stolen, you will get your money back. Of course you can't get along without cash, but you don't need to carry much with you.

Don't carry large amounts of cash with you when you're traveling. We have a rule of thumb: "Never carry around any more cash than you can afford to have stolen." To be on the safe side, you'd better ask for smaller denominations: $20 or $50.

If you use traveler's checks, they must be countersigned in the presence of the clerk in a shop, and make sure you sign your name the same way you signed it when you purchased the checks.

Canadian people have many cards with them. The cards start with their social security number card, driver's license, ATM card, and go on to credit cards (not only one kind), insurance card, medicine card, student ID card, library card, and frequent flyer card. The list goes on. If you are not careful, you sometimes mix up all the similar size cards.

译 文

　　加拿大人使用两种货币：硬币和纸币。硬币由金属制成，每枚硬币上都有图案。加拿大市面上流通五种硬币：1分硬币、5分硬币或叫做镍币、10分硬币或叫做一角银币、25分硬币或称之为1/4元、1元硬币。加拿大人把1元硬币称为"卢尼"（潜鸟），因为硬币上带有一只潜鸟的图案。潜鸟是一种生长在加拿大的大型水鸟，有一双明亮的红色眼睛，叫声很奇特。现在加拿大人也使用2元硬币，也被称为"图尼"（北极熊）。

　　加拿大银行负责发行钞票，面额有5元、10元、20元、50元和100元。钞票上印着加拿大著名的历史人物，比如：

　　—$5：威尔弗里德·劳雷尔爵士，加拿大第七任总理。

　　—$10：维奥拉·德斯蒙德，一位挑战种族隔离的新斯科舍省黑人女商人。

　　—$20：女王伊丽莎白二世。

　　—$50：威廉·莱昂·麦肯齐·金，加拿大第十任总理。

　　—$100：罗伯特·博登爵士，加拿大第八任总理。

　　加拿大人不会随身带很多现金，他们总是说携带钱财最好的方法就是拥有一张主信用卡，比如维萨信用卡或万事达卡。信用卡由商店、银行、信用卡公司、航空公司、汽车租赁公司、汽油公司或其他商业机构发行。如果丢失或被盗，可以申请作废。由于信用卡被广泛认可，所以使用便捷，可以用它来支付住宿费、交通费、餐费，以及在大型商店购物。

　　当你使用信用卡付款时，售货员会拿着你的卡通过电脑或是机器填写一张单子，然后请你签字并给你回执。信用卡公司每月寄给你账单，上面有你的每一笔消费记录以及需要在月底之前付清的金额款项。

　　在加拿大，绝大多数人用支票而不是用现金来支付他们的账单。使用支票非常方便，而且盖销后的支票就是付款收据。银行愿意为你兑付支票、兑换大面值的钞票。如果你在该银行开有账户，在兑换支票时就不用支付任何费用。如果你需要特别支票，银行也会给你，但要收取一点服务费。银行还能卖给你旅行支票，为你到国外去旅游提供了很大方便。绝大多数国外宾馆和银行都能兑现旅行支票。

　　旅行支票有保险。如果丢失或被盗，你会获得补偿。没有现金当然不能生活，只是别随身带太多。

　　旅行时别带过多的现金。经验告诉我们："切莫随身多带现金，多了你可丢不起。"为了安全起见，你最好携带小面额纸币：20元或50元的。

　　如果使用旅行支票，就必须在商店店员的监督下签字，同时你要确定你的签名和购买支票时签名的字体一样。

　　加大拿大人身上有很多的卡。从社会安全号卡、驾照、自动取钱机卡开始，然后有信用卡（不仅是一种信用卡）、保险卡、医疗卡、学生证、图书证、飞行历程累计卡。没完没了。如果你不小心，你有时会被这些形状大小差不多的卡给弄懵。

 Dialogue

Kill Two Birds with One Stone

(The Chinese visitor Li is on his second day in Vancouver. His friend Peter asks Li if he needs some help.)

Peter: Anything I can do for you, Li? I'd like to help you in some way if I can.

Li: I can't think of anything at the moment, but I know there is something important I have to do today. It just **slipped my mind**!

Peter: Well, it will **come to** you eventually. Maybe I could **run some errands** for you or something.

Li: Ah! I remember! I need to cash a check because I'm going on a trip to Vancouver Island next week. Actually, I want to buy some traveler's checks. You can drive me to the bank if you have time.

Peter: You arrived in Vancouver just **in the nick of time**. The Easter holidays have just ended, and the banks opened only this morning.

Li: Do you think it's a good idea to buy some traveler's checks?

Peter: Definitely! Don't carry large amounts of cash with you when you're traveling. We have **a rule of thumb**: "Never carry around any more cash than you can afford to have stolen." To be **on the safe side**, you'd better ask for smaller denominations: $20 or $50.

Li: I was told that if you use traveler's checks, you don't countersign the check until the clerk in the store is watching you.

Peter: Yes, you've got it! The checks must be countersigned in the presence of the clerk in a shop, and make sure you sign your name the same way you signed it when you purchased the checks.

Li: Thanks for your advice. I have some questions to ask you concerning health insurance, too. And maybe you could **clue me in** on Canadian tax laws too.

Peter: No problem. Actually the health insurance business is also done at the bank. Let's go. We can **kill two birds with one stone**. At the bank, you'll be asked to fill out an application form for health insurance. The simplest one is called "Blue Cross" insurance. They will explain everything to you.

Li: So the bank here can do a lot of things. Let's go.

Vocabulary and Notes

• eventually	at last; in the end 最后；终于
• cash a check	exchange a check for cash 兑支票
• traveler's check	check issued by a bank for a specified amount and signed by the buyer, who may use it as cash 旅行支票
• Never carry around any more cash than you can afford to have stolen.	随身带钱要适量，丢了也不要紧。（随身带的钱以丢了也不要紧为标准。）
• denomination	（度量衡、货币等的）面值 （money of small denomination 小额货币）
• You don't countersign the check until the clerk in the store is watching you.	你要当着商店售货员的面签字。
• in the presence of	在……面前；当着……的面
• health insurance	医疗保险
• fill out an application form	填一份申请表格
• Blue Cross	（美、加）蓝十字会（一种非营利性质的健康保险组织，对投保者提供医疗卫生等福利）

Idioms for Everyday Use

slip one's mind 使某人一时想不起来；忘记某事	escape one's memory; someone forgets something

  A: Get ready, guys! Let's hit the road for Big Buffalo River.
B: I hope we didn't forget anything important. Did you remember to pick up the bait, Tom?
C: Oh no. It completely **slipped my mind**.

B: Are you crazy? How could you forget the most important thing for fishing?

A: 伙计们，准备好了吗？我们上路直奔大布法罗河。

B: 但愿我们没忘记重要的东西。汤姆，你记着带鱼饵了吗？

C: 哎呀忘了。我把鱼饵忘得一干二净。

B: 你疯了吗？你怎么能忘记钓鱼用的最重要的东西呢？

A: Did you remember to bring the book you promised me?

B: I'm sorry. It completely **slipped my mind**. I'll bring it tomorrow.

A: 你记着带来你答应给我的书了吗？

B: 对不起，我全给忘了。我明天带来。

(something) come to someone
某人想起某事；（思想意识等）到某人脑子里 | (something) occur to someone; strike someone

A: I just can't remember the name of that French professor.

B: Take it easy. It will **come to you** sooner or later.

A: 我怎么也想不起来那位法国教授的名字。

B: 别急，早晚会想起来的。

The idea **came to him** when he saw a workman slide the jar of wine from one end to the other. The chief craftsman suddenly jumped up, speaking loudly that they could skate the gigantic Bell along on top of the ice.

当他看到一个工匠把那坛子酒从一端滑到另一端时，他想起了一个主意。工匠的首领突然跳起来，大声说，他们可以把大钟沿着冰面滑过去。

go on/run errands
跑腿；为某人办事；出差 | go on a short trip in order to do something for someone or deliver a message

These boys supplemented their pocket money by **running errands** for the neighbors.

这些孩子们靠帮邻居跑腿来增加些零用钱。

It's the children's job to **run errands** for the parents.

为父母跑跑腿是孩子们应该做的事情。

in the nick of time
恰好；正是时候 | just in time; at the necessary moment

A: How did you take him to the hospital?

B: Well, fortunately, an ambulance passed **in the nick of time**, and we got him away to the hospital.

A: 你是怎么把他送到医院的？

B: 幸运的是，正好那个时候有一辆救护车经过，我们便把他送进了医院。

A: I've been waiting here for nearly half an hour now. Tom, and there still isn't a bus in sight. It's beginning to rain.

B: Here comes the bus. I hope it's bus No. 18.

A: Yes! That's it. Just **in the nick of time**.

A: 汤姆，我已经在这儿等了几乎半个小时了，还是看不到公共汽车的影子。马上就要下雨了。

B: 公共汽车来了。但愿是18路。

A: 没错！就是18路，来得正是时候。

(a) rule of thumb 单靠经验或实践得来的方法；粗略而简便的方法	a way learnt by practical experience; a quick and not very exact way of doing something

I never measure rice and water when I'm cooking—I just do it by **rule of thumb**.
我做饭时从不量米量水——只凭经验。

He was never trained for making furniture, but he can make pretty furniture by **rule of thumb** as well as any trained carpenter.
他从没学过做家具，但是他能凭借经验做出很漂亮的家具来，不亚于正式木匠。

on the safe side 为了稳妥起见；以防万一；安全地	take a precaution in order to avoid a risk or loss; just to be sure

I got seriously sick while I was in Detroit. Luckily I had some medicine with me. I always carry it whenever I'm traveling, just to be **on the safe side**.
我在底特律时病得很厉害。幸运的是我带了一些药品。旅行时我总是带着药，以防万一。

You'd better make a copy of the passport, just to be **on the safe side**.
你最好把护照复印一份，以防万一。

Although the sun was shining the other day, my father took the umbrella with him to be **on the safe side**.
虽然那天阳光明媚，我父亲还是带上了雨伞以防不测。

clue someone in 向某人提供必要的情况；使某人对情况有所了解	give someone necessary information for understanding something or finding an answer

- I'm a new-comer here. I would very much appreciate it if you could **clue me in** on the library of the school.

  我新来乍到。如果你能给我介绍一下学校的图书馆，我将不胜感激。

- Since I was absent from our last negotiation, I would like to have you **clue me in** on what happened.

  由于我没有参加上次的谈判，请你给我介绍一下上次谈判的情况。

kill two birds with one stone
一箭双雕；一举两得 | do two things at the same time

- A: If you are going to London on business next week, you could **kill two birds with one stone** and do your Christmas shopping at the same time.

  B: I'm planning of doing that.

  A: 如果你下星期去伦敦出差，你可以一举两得，同时在那儿购买圣诞礼物。

  B: 我是计划着那样去做的。

- A: Where are you off to, Fred?

  B: I'm going to pick up some more beer.

  A: Hey, Fred. There's a great pizza place right next door to the beer store. Why don't you **kill two birds with one stone** and pick up some pizzas?

  A: 弗雷德，你到哪儿去？

  B: 我想去再买些啤酒来。

  A: 嘿，弗雷德，在啤酒店旁边就有个不错的比萨饼店。何不买些比萨饼来？这是个一举两得的事儿。

- A: Since you're going to pick up Nancy from the fitness class, why don't you **kill two birds with one stone** and pick up Peter after his ballet class?

  B: OK, no problem.

  A: 你既然去健身班接南茜，那你顺便一举两得把上完芭蕾舞课的彼得接回来好吗？

  B: 可以，没问题。

Unit 5
Native People
本土人

The name "Indian" was given to natives of the New World by Columbus in 1492 when he wrongly assumed that he had landed in the land of India. These first inhabitants of the New World are believed to have come from Asia. Some anthropologists claim that Indians have been in North America for more than 30,000 years. There were many different groups in the migration, and the Indigenous People of Canada are divided into twelve distinctive language groups. In 1994 there were approximately 380,000 people registered as Indians under the *Indian Act*, of Canada.

Whenever I talk with Canadian Indigenous women, it is so natural that their faces spark in me the memory of the old aunties with whom I spent blizzardy nights on the Inner Mongolian prairie. I thought, it must be true, then, when historians and anthropologists point out that the ancestors of the Native Canadians were from Asia.

Many people in the world imagine that the Indigenous People of Canada are living in deep forests, using bows and arrows, wearing feathers on top of their heads, and hunting for survival. On the contrary, the Nations are located by the side of the highways. The plain-looking houses are made of wood or are covered with clay, much like a village in northern China. I visited Indigenous families many times and although the facilities inside seemed simple and crude compared with the homes of modern cities, the homes do not lack a television, gas, a heater, electronic appliances or a standard bathroom. Nowadays, most residents of reservation are old people who make and sell handicrafts. Younger Native Canadians seek jobs in urban areas after graduation, blending into modern society.

The Inuit are generally considered a branch of North American Indians. They lived off the sea, fishing and hunting seals and whales. Often the Inuit would eat the meat raw, which led to the name "Eskimo". That is an Indian word meaning "Eaters of raw meat". The Eskimos called themselves Inuit. Both mean "people". They are mainly coastal dwellers. For most Canadian Inuit, the snowmobile has replaced dog team travel.

Today, the Indigenous People of Canada are proud to be called the country's Indigenous people. The Inuit and Indigenous life-styles in northern Canada have undergone much change with the influence of technology and culture from southern Canada. The government has also built towns for them where they can get training in many kinds of jobs and where their children can go to school.

Encouraged by the Federal Government, Canada's native peoples are seeking to adopt the practical elements of modern society that best suit their needs while maintaining many aspects of their traditional way of life.

The Indigenous People of Canada enjoy favorable policies, such as economic subsidies from the government and self-governing status. The ancient Indian culture has become the national treasure. Caves and log cabins previously inhabited by Indians have become national relics, and Indian artifacts are displayed in various museums in Canada.

Totem Poles: For generations, native peoples of the northwestern coast carved wooden totem poles to record which animal their family belongs to, such as the raven, the frog or the wolf clan. The animals carved on the totem poles are symbols of the family's ancestors. Totem poles often guarded doorways to village homes.

Canadian history tells us that totem poles were sculptures considered to be works of art. It's considered top-notch woodcarving in Canada.

A totem pole is a long wooden pole with symbols and pictures carved and painted on it. North American Indigenous People made them long ago. You can buy some totem photos there. Some students wait on the visitors in the exhibition shop.

译 文

"印第安人"是哥伦布1492年发现新大陆时对当地人的称呼,因为他错误地认为到了印度。这些最早的新大陆居民被认为是来自亚洲。一些人类学家宣称印第安人在北美居住了3万多年。移民由很多群体组成,加拿大的印第安人被划分为12种不同语言的群体。1994年,根据加拿大《印第安人法》规定,大约有38万人注册为印第安人。

每当我和加拿大印第安妇女交谈时,她们的容貌就让我自然而然地想起当年在内蒙古草原共度风雪夜的老阿妈们。看来,历史学家和人类学家考证的印第安人祖籍在亚洲一点不假。

很多世人想象加拿大印第安部落是在密林深处,头插羽毛的印第安人手持弓箭以捕猎为生。其实不然,现在他们实际上就住在公路旁。那些木制的房屋或用黏土抹墙的房屋看上去显得质朴敦实,很像中国北方的村落。我多次拜访过印第安人家庭,与加拿大现代城市相比,屋内陈设显得简陋凌乱,但是电视、煤气、暖气、各种家电、卫生间洗澡设备一应俱全。如今部落里大多是老年人看家,做些工艺品出售。年轻人从学校毕业后便到城市里去闯天下,融进了现代社会的洪流中。

通常,因纽特人被认为是北美印第安人的分支,他们在海边生活,捕鱼、猎取海豹和鲸。因纽特人经常吃生肉,因而被称为"爱斯基摩人"。这是印第安词语,意思是"吃生肉的人"。爱斯基摩人则把自己称为因纽特人。这两种称呼都是"人"的意思。他们大体上都是沿海居民。对大部分加拿大的因纽特人来说,他们已经由使用机动雪橇取代了狗拉雪橇。

如今,加拿大的印第安人非常自豪能被称为这个国家的本地人。在加拿大南部技术和文化的影响下,加拿大北部的因纽特人和印第安人的生活方式发生了很大改变。政府也为他们建立了城镇,给他们提供接受各种工作培训的机会,而且他们的子女可以在那里上学。

在联邦政府的鼓励下,这些加拿大本地人正在慢慢接受现代社会的实用元素,在尽可能满足他们的需要的同时还保留了许多传统的生活方式。

政府对加拿大印第安人实行了很多优惠政策,经济上给予补助,政治上允许自治。印第安人古老的文化成了加拿大的国宝。印第安人居住过的岩洞和木屋成为国家的保护文物。印第安人的工艺品也被展览在加拿大大大小小的博物馆里。

图腾柱——多少年以来,西北沿岸的本土人雕刻木制图腾柱,用以记录他们所属的家族,比如乌鸦族、青蛙族或狼族。图腾柱上雕刻的动物是家族祖先的标志。图腾柱经常被放置在村舍的入口处用来保卫家园。

加拿大历史告诉我们图腾柱是雕塑,是艺术,是加拿大的最高水准的木雕。

图腾柱是一根长长的木制柱子,上面刻有符号和图案并被着色,它们是北美印第安人很久以前制作的。你可以在展览店里买到图腾照片,那里有一些学生为游客提供服务。

Dialogue

Indian Paintings Are on Display

(Li is working on his lecture notes. John, his friend, asks him to go to the exhibition.)

John: Hey, Li, what are you *racking your brain* over?

Li: I'm preparing the lecture for next week.

John: You've been working indoors the whole morning. Why don't you go out and have a change of air. The Native Indian Paintings are *on display* in the exhibition hall of our university, and there are also some arts and crafts to be seen.

Li: Well, sounds good, but my lecture on Chinese Culture starts next week. Look at these materials here; I have to read them over. I'm barely *keeping my head above water.*

John: Take it easy. I could help you this afternoon if necessary. I think you should go to the exhibition, and we probably could meet some native Indians this afternoon.

Li: Can we also see the totem poles there?

John: Definitely. I guarantee that I'll let you *feast your eyes on* them. You haven't seen Canadian totem poles before, have you?

Li: No, only in books. Canadian history tells us that totem poles were sculptures considered to be works of art. It's considered *top-notch* wood carving in Canada.

John: That's right. A totem pole is a long wooden pole with symbols and pictures carved and painted on it. They were made by North American Indians long ago. You can buy some totem photos there. Some students *wait on* the visitors in the exhibition shop.

Li: I don't have to spend money on pictures. I've always been something of a shutterbug. This will be a good chance for me to practice. I'll take my camera.

John: Good idea. Get ready and let's go.

Vocabulary and Notes

- exhibition   展览；展览会
- indoors   室内的；在屋里

stay indoors	待在家里，不外出
go indoors	进屋里
• go out and have a change of air	到外面换换空气
• arts and crafts	the arts that are concerned with making objects by hand 工艺美术
• material	材料；资料；素材
• guarantee	保证；担保
• totem pole	图腾柱（北美的印第安人所竖立的一种着色的木刻圆柱，柱上所刻的每个动物都是有意义的）
• sculpture	雕刻；雕塑
• wood carving	木刻
• symbol	sign; a shape or design that is used to represent something 象征；符号；记号
• shutterbug	someone who likes taking pictures （俚）摄影爱好者，摄影迷

📖 Idioms for Everyday Use

rack one's brain
绞尽脑汁，冥思苦想

try very hard to think of something; make a great mental effort

A: What are you scratching your head for?
B: I've been **racking my brains** all morning trying to remember the name of the company that produces the portable computers, but in vain.
A: 为什么事在那儿抓耳挠腮呀？
B: 我绞尽脑汁想了一上午，试图记起那个生产手提式计算机公司的名字，可就是想不起来。

Terry **racked his brain** during the exam trying to solve the problem.
在考试时，特里绞尽脑汁想解决那个问题。

on display
陈列着；展览着

being shown publicly

The paintings of the Canadian Group of Seven are **on display** at the art gallery.
加拿大七人画派的绘画正在美术馆展出。

More than one hundred models of the cars are **on display**. Let's go and have a look.
一百多种式样的小车正在展出。我们去看看吧。

keep one's head above water
免遭灭顶之灾；凑合着过日子；保持不欠债；还能工作下去 | prevent failure; remain financially solvent; be able to deal with work

- The cost of living is now so high that you need to earn a good income just to **keep your head above water**.

  现在生活消费这么高，得多挣钱才能过得去。

- I've got so much work to do this month that I don't know how I'm going to **keep my head above water**.

  这个月我有许多事要做，我不知道怎么才能应付得了。

feast one's eyes on (something)
尽情地欣赏；一饱眼福 | look at something for a long time with great attention; enjoy it very much

- The guests from France **feasted their eyes on** the ancient structures.

  法国客人用赞美的眼光欣赏着这些古老的建筑物。

- He **feasted his eyes on** those beautiful engravings.

  他尽情地欣赏着那些优美的版画。

top-notch
最佳的；上等的；一流的 | of the highest quality; first rate

- A: We're going to the carpet factory tomorrow. Want to join us?
- B: Definitely! I've heard a lot about it. It produces **top-notch** carpets.
- A: 明天我们要去地毯厂。想和我们一起去吗？
- B: 当然了！我对那个厂多有耳闻。它生产一流的地毯。

- His performance of Lu Xun was **top-notch**.

  他扮演的鲁迅特别出色。

wait on/upon
在商店或饭馆里服务 | serve in a store or restaurant

- The old writer remembers his own youth, when he was a poor servant **waiting on** the rich.

  老作家想起了自己的青年时代，当时他是一个伺候富人的穷佣人。

- A very pleasant young woman **waited on** me in Lozynsky's yesterday.

  昨天在劳辛斯基的饭馆里，一位举止文雅的姑娘招待了我。

- Susan has a summer job **waiting on** a sick person. So she doesn't want to attend the three-week intensive English course.

  苏珊有一份暑假工作，即照料病人。所以她不准备参加为期三周的英语强化班了。

Unit 6
Government
政府

The roots of Canada's parliamentary system lie in Britain. It is based on the British model. "Parliament" actually comes from the French word "parler" and it means "to speak". The Canadian people try to solve their problems by talking them over. In keeping with traditions handed down by the British Parliament, the Canadian Parliament is composed of the Queen / King (who is represented in Canada by the Governor General), the Senate and House of Commons.

The Senate, also called the upper House, is patterned after the British House of Lords. Its 104 members are appointed not elected, and are divided essentially among Canada's four main regions of Ontario, Quebec, the West and the Atlantic Provinces. The Senate has the same powers as the House of Commons, with a few exceptions.

The House of Commons is the major law making body. It has 295 members, one from each of the 295 constituencies or electoral districts. The members of the House of Commons are elected. The Canadian Constitution requires the election of a new House of Commons at least every five years.

There are four major political parties in the House of Commons. The Liberal Party is the government now. The Conservative Party of Canada is the official opposition party. The New Democratic Party is the third party and the Bloc Quebecois is the fourth party in the House. The Prime Minister has the right to choose the Cabinet members, and they make government policy.

Canada's political system is characterized by a first-past-the-post electoral system, where the candidate with the most votes in a riding (electoral district) wins a seat in the House of Commons. Federal elections are held approximately every five years, although they can be called earlier. The party that wins the most seats typically forms the government, with its leader becoming the Prime Minister.

Like Britain, Canada is a monarchy. The official head of state is the King, who is also the King of Great Britain, Australia, New Zealand and other former British colonies. Because the King does not live in Canada, he is represented by an official called a governor-general. When the government officials of the other countries visit Canada, they will first be greeted by the Governor-General before being welcomed by the Prime Minister. Both the King and Governor-General occupy roles which are largely ceremonial. And while the King and his family are regarded with affection by most Canadians, the monarch bears little relevance to the governing of modern Canada.

King Charles, King of England, is also Canada's King, and sovereign of a number of realms. In his capacity as King of Canada, he delegates his powers to a Canadian Governor General. Canada is thus a constitutional monarchy: the King rules, but does not govern.

Canada has three levels of government: federal, provincial and municipal. The federal government is responsible for the country's immigration, defense, the nation's economy, foreign policy, currency and postal services. Provincial governments look after education, highways, health care, natural resources and hospitals. Municipal governments take care of fire protection, recreation, the building of parks, city libraries, city streets and other local matters. The three levels of Canadian government share the responsibilities and they cooperate with each other.

Two official languages are used by Canada's Federal governments instead of just one. The two official languages are English and French. This bilingual practice is confirmed by the passing of the *Official Language Act* of 1969 and the *Constitution Act* of 1982. These languages are recognized in all the institutions of Parliament and the Government of Canada.

译 文

加拿大议会制度起源于英国，是基于英国模式建立的。parliament实际上来自于法文parler，意思是"演说"。加拿大人试图通过商议解决问题。为了保持英国议会传统的惯例，加拿大议会由女王/国王（在加拿大由总督代表）、参议院和下议院组成。

参议院也被称为上议院，是模仿的英国的上议院。其104名成员是指派的，而不是选举的，他们分布在加拿大的四个主要地区：安大略省、魁北克省、西部和大西洋区域。除了有些特殊情况，参议院与下议院行使同样的权力。

下议院是主要的立法机构，有295名成员，分别来自295个选区。下议院成员是通过选举产生的。加拿大宪法要求至少每五年选举一届新的下议院。

下议院有四个主要政党。现在自由党当政，保守党是官方的反对党，新民主党是第三党派，魁北克集团是第四党派。总理有权挑选内阁成员，由他们制定政府制度。

加拿大的政治制度的特点是简单多数制选举制度，即在一个行政区（选区）获得最多选票的候选人赢得下议院的一个席位。联邦选举大约每五年举行一次，不过也可以提前举行。赢得最多席位的政党通常组成政府，其领导人成为总理。

像英国一样，加拿大是一个君主立宪制国家。国家的最高官方首领是国王，同时也是大英帝国、澳大利亚、新西兰和其他英国殖民地的国王。因为国王不住在加拿大，他的权力便由总督代替执行。当其他国家的政府官员访问加拿大时，在总理接见他们之前会首先被总督接见。国王和总督的职责基本上是礼节性的。国王和王室虽然受到大多数加拿大人的爱戴，但他们对治理现代的加拿大几乎不起什么作用。

查尔斯三世是英国国王，同时也是加拿大和其他一些国家的国王。作为加拿大国王，他把权力交付给加拿大总督，加拿大因此成为君主立宪制国家，即国王管辖但不统治。

加拿大有三级政府：联邦政府、省政府和市政府。联邦政府负责移民、国防、经济、对外政策、货币和邮政服务；省政府负责教育、公路、健康、自然资源和医院；市政府负责防火、娱乐、公园建设、城市图书馆、街道和其他地方事务。三级政府既各司其职又互相合作。

加拿大政府有两种官方语言，即英语和法语。1969年的《官方语言法令》和1982年的《宪法法令》通过了这种双语体制。这两种语言均被加拿大国会和政府所有的机构认可。

You Have It in You to Be an Expert of Canada

(Li has just finished his Canadian Studies class and meets his friend, Jane, on campus.)

Jane: So, how are your Canadian Studies classes going, Li?

Li: Not too bad. I **keep plugging away**, though I had some difficulties at first. The professor speaks too fast in class, but I think I've **jotted down** most of what the professor said.

Jane: What have you learned so far?

Li: Well, the general facts of Canada: there are 9.9 million square kilometers, the second largest country in the world, more than forty times the size of Britain, or eighteen times the size of France; 10 provinces and three territories; two official languages, English and French; 25 million people, and 90% of Canada's population live in the Southern part of Canada and within two hundred miles of the U.S. border...

Jane: Didn't you learn the Canadian Parliamentary system?

Li: Oh, yes, but the lecture on the system of government was **cut short** since the time was limited. However, I've got the idea that the Canadian Parliamentary system is based on the British model.

Jane: Yeah, that **makes sense**. Canada is also ruled by parliament. "Parliament" actually comes from the French word "parler" which means "to speak". The Canadian people try to solve their problems by **talking them over**.

Li: Are the members of Parliament and the Senators elected?

Jane: Let me put it this way—the Senators are not elected. They are appointed by the Governor General on the advice of the Prime Minister. But the members of the House of Commons are elected.

Li: That's very interesting. Well, what's the relationship between the Quebec Provincial Government and the Federal Government at present?

Jane: That's a difficult question. You may ask professor Downey. He really **gets to the heart of** the Quebec problem.

Li: Thank you very much for your info. I've also got some idea of the four major political parties in the House of Commons—the Liberal Party, the Conservative Party, the New Democratic Party and the Bloc Quebecois. The Prime Minister has the right to choose the Cabinet members, and they make government policy. Right?

Jane: Well, *off the top of my head*, I'd say you know more about Canada than I do.

Li: Oh, no. Don't flatter me. You are a Canadian, and you definitely know much more about Canada than I do.

Jane: Well, Li, any time, if you need any help, don't hesitate to ask me.

Li: That's very kind of you.

Vocabulary and Notes

- 9.9 million square kilometers — 990万平方公里
- 10 provinces and three territories — 10个省和3个地区
- two official languages — 两种官方语言
- Parliamentary system — 议会民主制
- be based on the British model — （加拿大的议会制）是以英国模式建立的
- the House of Commons — 下议院
- the Liberal Party — 自由党
- the Conservative Party — 保守党
- the New Democratic Party — 新民主党
- the Bloc Quebecois — 魁北克集团
- the cabinet members — 内阁成员

Idioms for Everyday Use

plug away (or keep plugging away)
不放弃；不灰心；拼命地干着（某项困难工作）
| not to give in or become discouraged; work with the will to complete (a difficult job)

A: When the teacher told Jim that he had failed the course, Jim kept **plugging away**. He has now putting all his energy into his studies.

B: That's what I'm expecting him to do.

A: 当老师告诉吉姆他这门功课不及格时，吉姆没有气馁。他现在把所有的精力都放在学习上了。

B: 这就是我所希望他要做的。

A: Hello there, Henry. Say, how are your German lessons coming along?
B: Well, to be honest, I still haven't made much progress. It seems to me that the classes are not worthwhile.
A: Don't be discouraged. Keep **plugging away**, and I think you'll eventually make a lot of progress.
A: 喂，亨利，德语课程进展如何？
B: 坦率地说，我还是进步不大。对我来说这门课程似乎是白费力气。
A: 别灰心，加劲学呀，我想你迟早会取得进步的。

Even though there was little chance of success, he kept **plugging away**, and he finally won.
尽管成功的机会极小，但他坚持不懈，终于成功了。

jot down (something)
匆忙写下，快速记笔记

make a quick note of (something); write (something) down hastily on a piece of paper or in a notebook

I must **jot down** that telephone number before I forget it.
我得马上记下这个电话号码，免得忘记。

A: The professor spoke too fast in class. I couldn't write down the names of the books he mentioned.
B: Don't worry. I **jotted down** all the names of the books he was talking about.
A: 课上这位教授说得太快。我没能把他提到的书名记下来。
B: 没关系。我已经把他谈到的所有的书名都记下来了。

cut short
截短；缩短；使提早结束

bring to an end before the usual or natural time

A: Shall we go up the mountain and gather some more mushrooms?
B: I'm afraid we must **cut** our visit **short**. Remember, we want to get home before dark.
A: 我们上山再采些蘑菇好吗？
B: 我想我们应该到此为止。记住，我们要在天黑前赶回家呢。

Professor McPherson **cut short** his lecture in order to give the students more time for group discussion.
为了给学生更多的时间进行小组讨论，麦弗森教授缩短了他讲课的内容。

make sense
有意义，讲得通；合情合理

have a clear meaning; sound reasonable or logical

The explanation in this book **made no sense**, because the words were too difficult to understand.
这本书的解释让人看了莫名其妙，因为文字太难以致无法理解。

- His arguments have never **made much sense**.

  他的论点立意不清。

talk (something) over
讨论（某事），商量（某事）

try to agree about or decide by talking; discuss

- A: What else did you discuss at the meeting yesterday?
- B: We also **talked over** the new plan, and the Program Administrator put forward some suggestions.
- A: 昨天你们在会上还讨论什么了？
- B: 我们商讨了新的计划，项目负责人还提出了一些建议。

- You'd better **talk it over** with your wife and give me your answer tomorrow.

  您最好还是和您夫人商量一下，明天再给我个答复。

get/go to the heart of something
抓住某事的核心，抓住最重要的实质，抓住问题的所在

find the central meaning or most important facts of something

- After a long introduction of background information, the novel **gets to the heart of** the matter.

  在一段冗长的背景介绍之后这部小说才抓住问题的核心。

- A: Tom is looking so depressed all day. I can't figure out what problems he has after all.
- B: You can only **get to the heart of** his unhappiness by letting him talk.
- A: 汤姆一整天情绪很低落。我不明白他到底有什么问题。
- B: 你只能让他开口说话，才能找出他不愉快的症结所在。

- The manager didn't waste any time at all—he **went** directly **to the heart of** the matter.

  经理一点儿也没有浪费时间——他一下就抓住了事情的要害。

off the top of one's head
即席地；脱口而出；未经仔细思考地

if you say something off the top of your head, you say it without thinking very much about it before you speak

- A: Just give me a rough estimate.
- B: Well, **off the top of my head**. I'd say it'll cost about eighty-thousand dollars.
- A: 你就大概估个价吧。
- B: 我随便说说吧。我想它值八万美元。

- A: How was the lecture this afternoon?
- B: Well, he didn't prepare his lecture beforehand and only talked **off the top of his head**.
- A: 今天下午的讲座怎么样？
- B: 他事先没有做准备，在演讲时，他只是想到哪里就讲到哪里。

Unit 7
Time Zones and Time Differences
时区和时差

If you are making a trip around the world, you would of course have to be aware of important time zone differences. It is important for business people and travelers to understand international time differences. For long flights and international phone calls may cross many time zones.

When it is 12:00 noon in Montreal or Toronto, it is 5:00 pm in London, England; 6:00 pm in Paris, France or Rome, Italy, 8:00 pm in Moscow, Russia; 10:30 pm in Calcutta, India, 3:00 am of the following day in Sydney, Australia and 12:00 midnight in Beijing, China.

The earth rotates once every 24 hours. As the earth turns, it passes through 15 degrees of longitude every hour. Therefore, the world has been divided into 24 segments that represent time zones. In Newfoundland, Canada, the day begins much sooner than it does in British Columbia.

Time Zones of Provincial and Territorial Capitals and Time Differences

Capital	Time Zone	Time
St. John's. Nfld.	Newfoundland	1:30 pm
Halifax. N.S.	Atlantic	1:00 pm
Charlottetown. P.E.I.	Atlantic	1:00 pm
Fredericton. N.B.	Atlantic	1:00 pm
Quebec. Que.	Eastern	12:00 noon
Toronto. Ont.	Eastern	12:00 noon

Unit 7 Time Zones and Time Differences 时区和时差

(continued)

Capital	Time Zone	Time
Winnipeg. Man.	Central	11:00 am
Regina. Sask.	Central	11:00 am
Edmonton. Alta.	Mountain	10:00 am
Yellowknife. N.W.T.	Mountain	10:00 am
Victoria. B.C.	Pacific	9:00 am
Whitehorse. Yukon	Yukon	9:00 am
Iqaluit. Nunavut	Central	12:00 am

Canada is such a vast country that people in Newfoundland can be eating their lunch while people in British Columbia may be having their breakfast. It is said that when it's 12:00 noon Atlantic Time in Newfoundland, it's 7:30 am Pacific Time in British Columbia.

Because of the time difference, both people travel to Canada and Canadian people come to China suffer from the headache problem of sleep. I experienced personally the mental agony many times and some of my colleagues even snored during the welcome ceremony in Canada; and the delegations from Canada were sleeping soundly in the elevator in China.

In order to adjust the jet lag, you'd better take some sleeping pills with you, take two tablets so that you can have a sound sleep. Keep doing that for several days, and then you could adjust the time difference completely. When you feel drowsy and your eyes heavy with sleep, you must bestir yourself even it is the midnight in China.

Another note: Daylight Saving Time (DST) in Canada involves moving clocks forward an hour in the spring and back an hour in the fall, providing an extra hour of daylight at night during warmer months to make better use of daylight and save energy.

Daylight saving Time begins on the second Sunday in March, when clocks are moved forward one hour at 2:00 am. By the end of the first Sunday in November, set the clocks back one hour at 2:00 am. Most provinces and territories, including British Columbia, Alberta, Ontario and Quebec, observe daylight saving time, while Saskatchewan and some areas of British Columbia, Ontario, Quebec and Nunavut do not.

The benefits of daylight saving time include extended nighttime daylight and potential energy savings, although the practice can disrupt sleep patterns and circadian rhythms, leading to short-term health effects and complicating coordinating schedules across time zones.

译　文

　　如果你环游世界，你肯定会发现重要的时区的差异。了解国际时差对商人和游客来说十分重要，因为长时间的飞行和国际电话可能要跨越很多时区。

　　当蒙特利尔或多伦多在中午12:00时，英国伦敦却是下午 5:00；当法国的巴黎或意大利的罗马是下午6:00时，俄罗斯的莫斯科却是晚上8:00；当印度的加尔各答是晚上10:30时，澳大利亚的悉尼已是转天早上3:00，而中国的北京正在午夜的12:00。

　　地球每24小时自转一周。地球转动每小时经过15个经度。因此，地球被划分为24个时区。在加拿大的纽芬兰，这里的每一天都要比不列颠哥伦比亚早开始很多。

省级和地区首都时区以及时差

首都	时区	时间
圣约翰斯　纽芬兰省	纽芬兰	下午 1:30
哈利法克斯　新斯科舍省	大西洋	下午 1:00
夏洛特敦　爱德华王子岛省	大西洋	下午 1:00
弗雷德里克顿　新不伦瑞克省	大西洋	下午 1:00
魁北克　魁北克省	东部	中午 12:00
多伦多　安大略省	东部	中午 12:00
温尼伯　马尼托巴省	中心	上午 11:00
里贾纳　萨斯喀彻温省	中心	上午 11:00
埃德蒙顿　阿尔伯塔省	山区	上午 11:00
耶洛奈夫　西北地区	山区	上午 10:00
维多利亚　不列颠哥伦比亚省	太平洋	上午 9:00
怀特霍斯　育空地区	育空地区	上午 9:00
伊奎特　努纳武特地区	中心	中午 12:00

　　加拿大幅员辽阔，当纽芬兰的人吃午饭时，不列颠哥伦比亚的人们可能在吃早餐。当纽芬兰大西洋时间是中午12:00时，不列颠哥伦比亚太平洋时间却是早上7:30。

　　由于时差的存在，不管是去加拿大的游客，还是到中国来的加拿大人，都难免遭受睡眠的头疼问题。我本人也多次体验过这种精神方面的痛苦，我的一些同事曾在加拿大的欢迎仪式上打起呼噜来，来自加拿大的代表团在中国的电梯里愣是睡着了。

　　为了调整好时差，你最好带一些安眠药，吃上两片，能睡上个好觉，坚持几天就能完

Unit 7 Time Zones and Time Differences 时区和时差

全调整过来。当你感觉昏昏欲睡或者眼睛疲惫的时候，就必须使自己打起精神，哪怕是在北京时间的深夜。

另一个值得注意的是：加拿大的日光节约时间（DST）包括在春季将时钟调快一小时，在秋季将时钟调慢一小时，这样可以在温暖月份的晚上提供额外的一小时日光，以更好地利用日光并节约能源。

夏令时从3月的第二个星期日开始，在凌晨2:00将时钟拨快一小时；到11月的第一个星期日结束，在凌晨2:00将时钟拨慢一小时。大多数省和地区，包括不列颠哥伦比亚省、阿尔伯塔省、安大略省和魁北克省，实行夏令时，而萨斯喀彻温省和不列颠哥伦比亚省、安大略省、魁北克省和努纳武特的一些地区不实行夏令时。

夏令时的好处包括延长夜间日光和潜在的节能，尽管这种做法可能会扰乱睡眠模式和昼夜节律，导致短期健康受影响，并使协调不同时区的时间表变得复杂。

Dialogue

You're Laying It on Thick

(Li is back from his Canadian Studies seminar and is talking about the time differences with his Canadian friend Cindy.)

Li: You know what impresses me most today is the time zones. It's interesting to know that the country has been divided into six different time zones.

Cindy: Yes, that's right. Canada is such a vast country that people in Newfoundland can be eating their lunch while people in British Columbia may be having their breakfast.

Li: Yes. The professor says that when it's 12:00 noon Atlantic Time in Newfoundland, it's 8:00 am Pacific Time in British Columbia.

Cindy: That's correct! Well, Li, it's quite interesting to learn about Canada. Do you know how Canada got its name?

Li: Yes, I read an article about it before, but I'd better make a **double check** in the presence of a Canadian. When Cartier discovered Canada, to be exact, when he discovered the great river—St. Lawrence, he spent a winter in an Indian village near the site of present-day Quebec. The chief of the tribe showed him the beautiful land. He waved his hand and shouted, "Kanada". Cartier thought "Kanada" was the name of the Indian village. However, from that time on, Cartier always called the vast land on both sides of the St. Lawrence River Canada. So we call this country Canada.

Cindy: Sounds perfect! You're really doing well in Canadian Studies. I'm confident that you *have it in you* to be an expert of Canada.

Li: Thank you for your encouragement. But, you are *laying it on thick*. I'm only able to *scratch the surface*. Listen, I've got to go now. I want to *read up on* the chapter of Canadian Families in preparation for the next seminar.

Cindy: I'm very proud of you, Li. You're *burying yourself in* your studies almost everyday. Why don't you come with me tonight and have a drink with me.

Li: That might be a good idea. See you tonight.

Vocabulary and Notes

• time zone	时区
• ...people in Newfoundland can be eating their lunch while people in British Columbia may be having their breakfast.	……当不列颠哥伦比亚的人们吃早饭时，纽芬兰的人们在吃午饭。
• Atlantic Time	大西洋时间
• Pacific Time	太平洋时间
• in the presence of...	在……面前
• Jacques Cartier	雅克·卡蒂埃（1491—1557），法国海员。他是第一个发现加拿大的欧洲航海家，当时登陆的地方就是现在的魁北克市。1534年，他受法国国王弗兰西斯一世派遣去北方探险，寻找黄金和香料，勘探通往亚洲的航道。在印第安人的帮助下，到达魁北克，后来到达蒙特利尔。1541年，法国国王再次派卡蒂埃等探险家来到北美这片新发现的土地上，并建立了殖民地。
• St. Lawrence River	圣劳伦斯河
• I'm confident that...	我相信……，我有信心……
• encouragement	鼓励，鼓舞
• I want to read up on the chapter of Canadian Families...	我要去看看"加拿大家庭"那个章节（为下次听课做好准备）……

Idioms for Everyday Use

double check
仔细检查，反复核实（以防错误）

a careful second check to be sure that everything is right; check twice in order to be certain

- Look! The policeman is coming. Let's make a **double check** on whether we are on the right road.

  看！警察过来了。咱们再问问他我们走的路是否对。

- I think you'd better make a **double check** with Air Canada on the reservation of the ticket.

  我想你最好和加航再核实一下预订的机票。

have it in someone
有能力或勇气干某事

have the capacity, ability, to do something

- I think Susan **has it in her** to be a great concert violinist.

  我相信苏珊有能力成为一名出色的音乐会小提琴家。

- A: The Ravens are my favorite team. I think they **have it in them** to play good football.
- B: Well, I don't think so. We'll see about that! I think the Lions morale is high. So I say they're going to win.
- A: 我最喜欢"乌鸦队"。我相信他们打橄榄球会出奇制胜的。
- B: 我不那么认为。咱们到时候看吧！我认为"雄狮队"的士气高。所以我说他们会赢的。

lay/put/spread it on thick
过分夸奖某人；恭维别人以给他人留下好印象；言过其实

praise someone too much; exaggerate a statement in order to try to impress people; stretch the truth

- You're **laying it on thick** to call him an English expert. Are you trying to get him to help you with your English studies?

  你称他为英语专家，也太过奖了。你是不是想让他在英语方面帮你的忙呢？

- A: Hello, Naomi. There's a really good movie on at the Colin, twenty-five dollars for a ticket.
- B: Aren't you **laying it on a bit thick**? I'm sure the price wasn't quite as high as you say!
- A: 喂，内奥米，科林影院正在上映一部好电影，每张票25美元。
- B: 你是不是说的有点儿过分了？我敢肯定票价不会像你说的那么高！

scratch the surface
只接触……的表面；对……没有深入的研究；略知皮毛

learn or understand something only superficially; have limited knowledge of something

- A: Lawrence is really a remarkable literature expert! There's very little he doesn't know.
- B: I totally agree. Whenever you ask him questions, he doesn't just **scratch the surface**, but always gives you the detailed explanation.
- A: 劳伦斯真是个了不起的文学专家！他的知识实在渊博。
- B: 我完全同意。每当你向他请教问题时，他从不做肤浅的解释，总是解释得很透彻。

She thought she knew all about life in America, but when she went to live there for 6 months, she realized that she had just **scratched the surface**.
她自以为很了解美国的生活，但她到那儿住了六个月后才知道自己只是一知半解。

read up on
仔细研究，专门研究

make a special study of a subject

I must **read up on** Nelson for the history exam.
我为准备历史考试得专门研究一下纳尔逊的生平事迹。

- A: How come you've collected the book reviews of *the Sound & the Fury*, *Barn Burning* and *Intruder in the Dust*?
- B: Oh, I'm now **reading up on** William Faulkner and my graduation thesis will be focused on it.
- A: 你为什么收集关于《喧哗与骚动》《谷仓着火》和《坟墓闯入者》的书评？
- B: 哦，我现在正在研究威廉·福克纳的作品，我的毕业论文以此为题。

bury oneself in (something)
埋头于或专心致志于某事

involve oneself in or concentrate deeply on something

In the evenings he **buries himself in** his books.
每天晚上他都埋头读书。

- A: Hey, you've been **burying yourself in** the book for about a week. What's up?
- B: Well, even though I'm reading like hell, I've only finished even half of the reading assignment, besides; I've still got a composition to write.
- A: 嗨，一周来你一直埋头读书。你怎么了？
- B: 呃，即使我拼命读书，我才刚刚完成一半，而且，我还有一篇论文要写。

Unit 8
National Parks
国家公园

Canadians live in a land rich in natural beauty. When Cartier discovered Canada, to be exact, when he discovered the great river—St. Lawrence, he spent a winter in an Indian village near the site of present-day Quebec. The chief of the tribe showed him the beautiful land. He waved his hand and shouted, "Kanada". Cartier thought "Kanada" was the name of the Indian village. However, from that time on, Cartier always called the vast land on both sides of the St. Lawrence River Canada. So we call this country Canada.

There are many national and provincial parks in Canada. The Parks Canada Policy encourages public understanding, appreciation and enjoyment of the natural heritage so as to leave it unimpaired for "future generations". National park staff informs the public about the parks, either through first-hand experience or through educational programs designed to bring knowledge of the parks to people in their homes.

The Canadian Rockies are one of the world's largest blocks of mountain parks. In 1984 the United Nations declared four contiguous National Parks—Banff, Jasper, Yoho and Kootenay—to be a 20,160 sq km World Heritage Site. Adjoining Mt. Assiniboine, Mt. Robson and Hamber Provincial Parks were added in 1990.

This is a place where you can watch the peaks from a luxurious dining room, and you can watch golf past grazing elk. You can ride a gondola or ski lift to a summit view, take a tour boat up a glacial lake or take a snowcoach onto a glacier, explore easy walks and fabulous viewpoints. Or you can leave civilization far behind on a trail to the real wilderness. These mountains rejuvenate tired souls.

The Province of British Columbia has nearly 400 provincial parks and five national parks. Many of these are very large and have beautiful forests, mountains, rivers and lakes. People visit the parks for hiking, camping, fishing, boating, skiing and canoeing. Most national and provincial parks have campground and picnic sites. Campgrounds usually have campsites with picnic tables, fire pits, and space for a tent or camper. People can camp overnight there for a small fee. Private campgrounds are common in all parts of the province. People can usually make reservations for a private campground.

Stanley Park is an oasis in the center of Vancouver, and there are lots of things to see there: many trees, flowers, groups of totem poles; the Aquarium, the zoo, the dolphin performances. The Vancouver Aquarium inside the park is one of the largest and most popular aquariums in North America.

In trying to protect park environments, allow them to serve the needs of visitors, park agencies face many management problems. Some of the problems facing park managers in recent years include maintaining fish stocks, preventing forest fires, littering and vandalism, protecting visitors from bears, eliminating poaching, reducing crowding in popular areas, dealing with new technologies, such as snowmobiles, hang gliders and also reducing accidents from risky activities.

译　文

加拿大人生活在一片美丽的自然风光中。卡蒂埃当年发现加拿大时，或确切地说，当他发现圣劳伦斯河的时候，他在现在的魁北克附近的一个印第安村落生活了一个冬天。部落首领带他领略了美丽的风光。首领挥手大喊Kanada（小村落），而卡蒂埃认为Kanada就是这个村落的名字。从此，卡蒂埃把圣劳伦斯河两岸的广大地区称为加拿大，所以今天我们称这个国家为加拿大。

加拿大有许多国家和省级公园。加拿大公园管理局的制度鼓励公众理解、欣赏和享受自然遗产，为"后人"保留完整的未被破坏的风景。国家公园的员工通过亲身经验或教育节目向他们家乡的人们介绍公园知识。

Unit 8　National Parks 国家公园

加拿大洛矶山脉是世界上最大的整片山区公园之一。1984年，联合国宣布了由四个相连的国家公园——班芙、杰士伯、友好、库尼——组成的总面积达20160平方公里的区域为世界文化遗产。1990年，又将邻近的阿辛尼玻因山、罗伯森山及汉伯省立公园列入世界文化遗产。

在这个地方，你可以坐在豪华的餐厅中眺望高高的山峰，观看高尔夫球掠过低头吃草的麋鹿；你可以搭乘登山缆车或滑雪缆车上到山顶眺望风景，乘游览船遨游冰湖或者坐上雪车登上冰河一游，顺着易行的小径探寻迷人的景致。或者干脆远离喧嚣的人群，深入真正的荒野去探险。这片山脉能使疲惫的身心恢复活力。

不列颠哥伦比亚省有将近400个省级公园和五个国家公园，其中有很多公园面积广阔，并且拥有美丽的森林、高山、河流与湖泊。人们到公园来远足、露营、垂钓、划船、滑雪以及划独木舟。大部分国家级和省级公园都设有露营和野餐场所，露营地通常包括野餐餐桌、点火坑和扎营的地方，人们只需花一点钱就能玩个通宵。省内还有很多私人营地，人们通常需要提前预约。

斯坦利公园是温哥华市中心的一片绿洲，那儿有不少值得欣赏的东西：花草树木、图腾柱群、水族馆、动物园和海豚表演。园内的温哥华水族馆是北美最大和最火爆的水族馆之一。

为了保护公园环境以满足游客的需求，公园的管理机构面临许多管理方面的问题。近几年公园负责人面临的问题包括维持鱼类的繁殖，防止森林火灾，禁止乱丢垃圾和故意破坏，保护游客不受到熊的攻击，禁止偷猎，减少在火爆景点人群拥挤的现象，使用新技术工具比如机动雪橇、滑翔机以及减少极限运动事故的设备。

Dialogue

You Can Say That Again

(Easter holiday is coming. Naomi and her Chinese friend Li are planning their activities.)

Naomi: Thank goodness, it's Easter tomorrow. Li, let's take advantage of the long weekend and enjoy ourselves. We've been *cooped up* in the house for the whole week. Let's get out for some fresh air.

Li: Do you have something special in mind?

Naomi: No. Not really. It doesn't have to be something exciting—something different. I need a change. I feel like *I'm in a rut*.

Li: I know that feeling. Usually I get that kind of feeling every spring. I feel I have to *get away from it all*, you know, look at the new leaves of the trees, enjoy the scenery of awakening nature after her winter's sleep.

Naomi: Sounds like the same thing to me! An English expression describes that feeling as "spring fever". What I'm talking about is a change; escape from the monotony of everyday life.

Li: I got it! Let's go to Stanley Park! I've never been there. I hear there are lots of things to see there: many trees, flowers, groups of totem poles; the Aquarium, the zoo, the dolphin performances. It's the perfect place!

Naomi: *You can say that again!* That's a wonderful idea. You'll love it, Li. Stanley Park is an oasis in the center of the city, and the Vancouver Aquarium inside the park is one of the largest and most popular aquariums in North America.

Li: How long are we going to stay at the park?

Naomi: The whole morning, I think. Then we'll have lunch in a Chinese restaurant near the park. I really want to taste that nice Peking Duck again. It's got a special taste that's quite different from Canadian barbecued food. *It's going over big* all over Canada.

Li: That's wonderful! I think I'll *fast* the whole morning tomorrow.

📖 Vocabulary and Notes

- Thank goodness! (Thank heavens! Thank God!)

  When you are very relieved about something, you say these expressions. 谢天谢地！

- Easter

  复活节，基督教会的重大节日（一般在3月22日至4月25日之间）

- take advantage of (something)

  make use of; use for one's own benefit 充分利用某事或某物；利用有利条件

- enjoy the scenery of awakening nature after her winter's sleep

  欣赏大自然冬眠后醒来的景色

- describe

  描写；描述

- spring fever | a listless, lazy feeling felt by some people during the first sudden warm weather of spring 春倦症
- monotony | 单调；千篇一律
- Stanley Park | 斯坦利公园。加拿大温哥华市最大的公园，占地约4平方公里，森林面积约1.6平方公里。公园三面环海，园内有加拿大最大的水族馆。
- aquarium | 水族馆
- dolphin performance | 海豚表演
- oasis | 绿洲
- barbecue | 烤肉；烧烤猪、牛、羊肉的野外宴会

Idioms for Everyday Use

coop up
把……禁闭（或禁锢）起来 | enclose; limit the freedom of someone or an animal; confine; lock up

- What a nice day! How would you like to be **cooped up** in the room like that? Let's go out and take some fresh air.
  多好的天呀！你怎么愿意像那样把自己关在屋子里呢？跟我一块儿到外边呼吸点新鲜空气吧。

- All last week we were **cooped up** in the house by bad weather.
  由于天气不好，上周我们在家整整闷了一星期。

- A: It's unkind to **coop** the dog **up** all day long.
  B: I'll take your advice. We'll take a walk after dinner.
  A: 把狗整天关在屋子里太不仁慈了。
  B: 听你的劝告，晚饭后我们去遛弯儿。

be in /get into a rut
照惯例过着单调乏味的生活 | be in/get into a fixed and dull way of life, and be unable to do or think anything new

- I've been doing this kind of work for ten years. I'm going to change my job. I'm **in a rut** here.
  我已经干了10年这个工作了。我打算变换一下。这儿的工作太枯燥了。

- I'm **in a real rut**. If I had enough money, I would travel abroad and see the Far East.

我的生活太单调了。如果我有足够的钱，我就到国外去旅游，去远东看看。

get away from it all
用出走的办法来摆脱繁忙（或工作责任等）；一走了之

escape from city rush, crowds, the rat race of modern life, etc.

- We bought a house in the country to **get away from it all**. I'm really tired of the city life.
  我们在乡下买了一所房子，一走了之。我对城市生活简直腻透了。
- I feel I have to **get away from it all**, you know, see green trees, enjoy the different crops, look at the cows and sheep...seek new horizons.
  我觉得我还是到郊外走走，去看看绿树、各种农作物，看看牛呀、羊呀……长长新的见识。

You can say that again! (You said it!)
对了；正是如此；你说得对！你说到点子上了！

You use this idiom when you completely agree with an opinion that someone has just expressed; You're right; I agree.

- A: We've been reading all morning. Let's go home.
  B: **You can say that again!** I'm tired.
  A: 我们看了一上午书了。让我们回家吧。
  B: 你说得对！我都累了。
- Son: Look at my shabby shoes. I need a new pair.
  Mother: **You said it!** Let's go and do some shopping.
  儿子：瞧瞧我这双又破又旧的鞋。我需要换双新的。
  母亲：你说得对！我们去买一双吧。

go over big
大受欢迎；非常成功

receive a lot of attention; be a great success

- His ideas **went over big** with the boss. Therefore, his salary was raised twice and got the promotion last week.
  他的主意很受老板的赏识。因此，他的工资涨了两次，而且上个星期又被提升了。
- A: So, you're drinking Chinese Qingdao beer.
  B: Yeah, It's great. It's got a special taste that's quite different from American beer. A lot of people are switching to it.
  A: Yeah, it's **going over big** everywhere in Canada.

A: 这么说，你在喝中国青岛啤酒。

B: 是的，真好喝。它有一种与美国啤酒完全不一样的特别味道，许多人都在喝这种啤酒。

A: 对，它在加拿大各处都大受欢迎。

A: How was the president's presentation of the new plan for next year?

B: It **went over big**. All of us thought it was a great plan.

A: 你觉得校长提出的关于明年的新计划怎么样？

B: 很受欢迎。我们都认为那是一个伟大的计划。

fast 禁食，绝食；斋戒，节食	(in this context) go without food (especially for religious reason); can be also used as a noun

A: Have you seen Susan lately?

B: No. Why?

A: Do you still remember what she looks like? You'll be surprised when you see her.

B: You mean it's her physical appearance?

A: Yes! That's it! She **fasts** a day every week, and she has lost 20 pounds.

A: 最近你见过苏珊吗？

B: 没有。怎么啦？

A: 你还记得她的长相吗？你要是见着她一定会大吃一惊。

B: 你是指她的体形吗？

A: 对了！就是她的体形！她每周禁食一天，她的体重已减了20磅。

They call it Ramadan, the ninth month of the Muslim year, when Muslims **fast** between sunrise and sunset.

他们把它叫做拉马丹月，伊斯兰教历的第九个月，这期间伊斯兰教徒在日出后到日落前斋戒。

Unit 9
Employment and Vacation
就业及休假

In Canada, if you are laid off, the employer must tell you several weeks before the job ends, or pay you extra money if you have been there for more than six months. But when a worker is fired because he is hurting the business, an employer does not have to tell him before. When you leave a full-time job, your employer must give you a "Record of Employment". You need this paper to apply for Unemployment Insurance. It may not be possible to get UI if you are fired or if you quit your job.

There are laws to protect workers from discrimination. For example, employers must hire employees on the basis of qualifications. They cannot refuse to hire you because of your religion, skin color, sex, age, marital status, and disability. Sometimes other workers discriminate against you. For example, they may treat you badly because you are a woman or call you racist names. This is against the law.

You are entitled to overtime pay after you have worked 40 hours in any one-week.

For example, if you work eight hours each day from Monday to Friday and then work eight hours on Saturday, your weekly overtime will be the eight hours. You must be paid one and one half times your regular rate of pay for the eight hours you work on the Saturday. If you work over 48 hours in one week, you must be paid two times your regular wage for every hour after the 48 hours you work.

Unit 9 Employment and Vacation 就业及休假

After you have worked at your job for one year, you must get two weeks of paid vacation. After you have worked for five years in a row with the same employer, your must get three weeks of paid vacation each year.

Your vacation must start no later than ten months after the day you started working.

Before you can get paid for General Holidays, you must have been employed for 30 days. General Holidays include: New Year's Day, January 1. Good Friday (the Friday before Easter, commemorating the Crucifixion of Christ), people have this holiday either in March or in April. Easter Monday, annual Christian festival, that occurs on a Sunday in the period of March 22 to April 25, and celebrates the resurrection of Jesus Christ after the crucifixion. Victoria Day, the birthday of Queen Victoria, has been observed in Canada since 1845, eight years after she ascended the throne. Canada Day, the national holiday commemorating the creation of the Dominion of Canada on July 1, 1867. Labor Day, the first Monday in September, has been observed in Canada since 1894. Actually the Canada Socialist International Congress had proclaimed May 21 as Labor Day in 1889 and urged workers everywhere in the world to hold a one-day strike to show up the power of the socialist world revolution. Canadians were less interested in revolution than in having a "beginning autumn holiday", so the date was moved from May to September. Thanksgiving Day, a day of thanksgiving for the harvest, has been observed since 1879, is usually celebrated on the second Monday in October. Remembrance Day, the anniversary of the armistice that ended World War I signed November 11, 1918, and is now observed in commemoration of the dead of the two world wars. Christmas Day, December 25, the biggest festival celebrated in the Christian countries of the world including Canada. Christians regard this day as the birthday of Jesus Christ, after which is the Boxing Day, but many of the celebrations are not of a religious nature. It is just like Chinese Spring Festival.

According to the Employment Standards Branch of B.C. Province, you should get vacation pay of four percent of your gross pay for the year. After you worked five years in a row with the same employer, you must get six percent of your total pay for the year.

译文

在加拿大，如果你面临下岗，老板必须提前几个星期通知你，或者如果你工作已超过了半年，老板会支付你额外的工资。但如果员工是因为损害了公司的生意被辞退，老板则不需要提前通知。当你结束一份全职工作时，你的老板必须给你出示一份"就业纪录证明"，你需要用这份证明去申请失业保险。如果是被辞退或主动辞职，就有可能得不到失业保险。

法律禁止对雇员的种族歧视，例如，雇主必须根据资格录用员工，不能因为宗教信仰、肤色、性别、年龄、婚姻状况或残疾而拒绝雇佣你。有时，其他员工会歧视你，例如他们会因为你是女性而不善待你或直呼你的种族名字。这都是违法的。

在一个星期内，如果你工作超过了40小时，就有权得到加班费。

举例来说，如果你从周一到周五每天工作8小时，而且周六加班8小时，你本周的加班时间为8小时，你应得的周六加班费是你每小时正常薪水的1.5倍。如果你一个星期工作超过48小时，超出部分的加班费必须是你每小时正常薪水的两倍。

工作满一年后，你将得到两周的带薪休假；当你跟随同一个老板连续工作满5年后，你每年会有3周的带薪休假。

休假必须在工作10个月后才能开始。

只有工作满一个月才可以享受国家带薪节假日。国家带薪节假日包括：新年，1月1日。耶稣受难日（复活节前的那个星期五，纪念耶稣被钉死在十字架上），每年的3月或4月。复活节星期一，3月22日至4月25日之间的星期日（基督教会每年的重大节日，纪念耶稣基督在十字架受刑后的复活）。维多利亚日，纪念维多利亚女王的生日（该节日在加拿大从1845年开始施行庆祝，自她登基继位8年后开始的）。加拿大国庆节，7月1日（自1867年7月1日建国时就规定为国庆节）。劳动节，9月第一个星期一（自1894年开始庆祝。实际上1889年加拿大社会主义国际交往会议宣布的是5月21日为劳动节，在这一天，号召全世界工人罢工一天，显示社会主义世界革命的力量。后来加拿大人对革命不大感兴趣，只想在初秋时节有一天假日，因此，从5月改成了9月）。感恩节，10月的第二个星期一（为感谢上帝带来的大丰收，该节日自1879年开始庆祝）。军人纪念日，11月11日（1918年第一次世界大战的停战纪念日，现在主要是纪念那些在第二次世界大战中战死的将士）。圣诞节，12月25日（包括加拿大在内的世界基督教国家庆祝的最大节日，基督教徒认为这天是耶稣基督的生日，第二天便是西方的节礼日，但许多庆祝活动不是宗教性质的，就像中国的春节一样）。

根据不列颠哥伦比亚省就业标准部门的规定，你应该得到的带薪休假相当于你全年工资总额的4%。如果你跟随同一个老板工作满5年，你得到的带薪休假就会相当于全年工资总额的6%。

He's Tight-Fisted

(Judy comes back from her work, and his Chinese friend Li is asking him about the meeting she had with her boss.)

Li: Hi, Judy! Say, how did your meeting with your boss go?

Judy: Not very well, actually. I asked him for my two weeks of paid vacation and he *turned me down.*

Li: I can't believe it! After all these years of faithful service! Man, that guy is really *tight-fisted*.

Judy: No kidding! I was very upset about it and then, to *add insult to injury*, he told me that I ask too many questions around the office, that I'm too curious about what other people are doing—in short, that I'm too *nosy*.

Li: That really is going too far. I hope you *told him off*.

Judy: You bet I did! I told him he *had a lot of nerve* talking to me like that just because he's the boss and that if he were a little more open-minded, our company would be more efficient.

LI: Good for you! How did he react to that?

Judy: He *hit the ceiling* and threw me out of his office.

Li: Wow! What's going to happen now?

Judy: Not much, I guess. I know he needs me on his staff, and he knows I need a job. So I guess things will just carry on as usual.

Li: I hope he'll let you go to take your paid vacation.

Judy: Let's keep our fingers crossed.

Li: By the way, how much vacation pay do you get each year?

Judy: According to the Employment Standards Branch of B. C. Province, I should get vacation pay of four percent of my gross pay for the year. After you worked five years in a row with the same employer, you must get six percent of your total pay for the year.

Li: When do you become eligible for General Holiday pay?

Judy: Well, you must have been employed for 30 days before you can get paid for General Holidays. This is what I all know. Sorry, I can't *fill you in on the details*.

Vocabulary and Notes

• paid vacation	带薪假期
• After all these years of faithful service!	这么多年忠心耿耿地（为他）工作！
• No kidding!	你算说对了！
• open-minded	思想开阔的；无偏见的；很虚心的
• General Holidays	法定假日

Idioms for Everyday Use

turn someone down 拒绝（某人的请求、提议等）
refuse or reject (sb., a request, an offer, etc.)

- He asked Susan to marry him but she **turned him down** because she was in love with another man.
  他向苏珊求婚，但被她拒绝了，因为她爱上了另一个男人。
- A number of unreasonable proposals were **turned down** at the plenary meeting of the committee.
  在委员会全体会议上一些不合理的提议被否决了。

tight-fisted 吝啬的（特别是在钱方面）；小气的
very ungenerous (esp. with money); not willing to spend or give money, but guard it jealously

- The children asked for some money to buy ice cream, but their **tight-fisted** father coldly refused.
  孩子们要钱买冰淇淋，但吝啬的爸爸却冷冷地拒绝了他们。
- The young man's father was quite rich, but he was so **tight-fisted** that he refused to give his son a penny to start out in business.
  这个年轻人的父亲十分富有，但很吝啬。他的儿子开办企业，他连一分钱都不给。

add insult to injury 既伤害又侮辱；进一步伤人感情（倒霉又倒霉）
hurt someone's feelings after doing him/her harm; hurt someone twice, thus making a bad situation even worse

- The boss **added insult to injury** by threatening to fire the worker after he had refused to grant him a raise.
  老板拒绝了给他涨工资，还以解雇相威胁来侮辱他。

The robbers **added insult to injury**—they called him pauper after they had robbed him.
暴徒们既伤害又侮辱——不但抢劫了他，还说他是一个穷鬼。

be nosy	be overly curious about things that are none of one's business
好打听别人事的，爱管闲事的	

She got a bad name around school for **being nosy** and spreading gossip.
因她爱打听小道消息、传播谣言，所以她在学校的名声不好。

Why don't you mind your own business, madam? Roared Stan. You're too **nosy** about my family affairs.
斯坦咆哮地说：你为什么不管自己的事呢，夫人？你对我家的事管得太多了。

tell someone off	scold someone; attack someone verbally
斥责某人，骂某人；数说某人的过错	

A: The manager finally raised Tom's salary?
B: No way! They had a heated debate. When he realized he was going to be fired, Tom **told the manager off**.
A: 经理最后给汤姆涨工资了吗？
B: 没门儿！他们俩进行了激烈的争论。当汤姆意识到他要被解雇时，他斥责了老板一通。

A: I can't imagine that. What happened then?
B: She **told me off** for about ten minutes, and then stormed off. I haven't seen her or talked to her since then.
A: 我真是想象不到。后来呢？
B: 她责备了我有10分钟，然后一甩手就走了。打那以后我一直没见到她，也没和她谈谈。

have (a lot of) nerve	be rude or impolite; not be courteous or respectful
无礼；放肆；厚颜无耻	

When he tried to find out about her private life, she told him he **had a lot of nerve**, and left the room.
当他企图打听她的私生活时，她说他太无礼了，然后离开了房间。

She started looking through the man's briefcase without asking permission, and when he came back into the room, he told her she **had a lot of nerve** and to get out.
她未经允许就翻了那个男人的皮包。当他回到房间里时，他说她太放肆了，让她滚出去。

hit the ceiling
大发脾气；暴跳如雷

become very angry; go into a rage

- When his father found out about his poor exam results, he **hit the ceiling**.
  当他父亲得知他那糟糕的考试成绩时，气得大发雷霆。
- When the workers heard that they were going to be asked to work on Christmas Day, they **hit the ceiling**.
  当工人们听说圣诞节还要工作时，气得火冒三丈。

fill someone in on the details
给某人提供详细情况

provide detailed information for someone

- A: I missed the meeting yesterday afternoon. Could you **fill me in on the details**?
  B: I'm sorry I can't. Whenever I have a meeting, I feel sleepy. I didn't even take the notes this time.
  A: 昨天下午我没去参加那个会议，你能给我说说会议的详细情况吗？
  B: 对不起，我说不了。我每次开会就想睡觉。这次甚至我都没做记录。
- On our way to the Vancouver Art Gallery, Professor Peters **filled me in on the details** of the latest developments of art in the world.
  在去温哥华美术馆的路上，彼得斯教授给我详细地介绍了有关世界艺术的最新发展。
- A: I've never seen the Chinese students perform an English play as well as this one.
  B: But I still don't understand some parts of the play.
  A: Don't worry. I know it inside out. Later I'll **fill you in on the details**.
  B: Thanks.
  A: 我从来没有看到过中国学生演过这么好的英语话剧。
  B: 可我对这个剧的一些地方还是不明白。
  A: 别急，我对这个剧一清二楚。以后我再跟你细说。
  B: 谢谢。
- I will be happy to **fill you in on the details** of our upcoming great project, so that you can better understanding the scope and objectives.
  我很乐意告诉你我们即将进行的重大项目的细节，以便你能更好地理解其范围和目标。

Unit 10
Canadian Writers
加拿大作家

    Both English Canadian Literature and French Canadian Literature reached an all-time high from the period of 1960s to 1980s. Canadian Literature had three characteristics in this period of time:

    1) The number of Canadian authors grew up rapidly.

    2) The range of the subjects of Canadian Literary works was many and varied.

    3) Critic team of Canadian Literature became mature.

    Canadian Literature forum had a small number of gifted authors that could show their brilliant talents before 1960s. However, just beginning of 1960, a new generation of writers across Canada sprang up like mushrooms. Some of them quickly became famous both in Canada and in the world. In the team of new generation of the writers include: Margaret Laurence, Alfred Earl Birney, Dorothy Livesay, Dave Godfrey, Margaret Atwood, Douglas Gordon Jones and etc., too numerous to mention. They have enjoyed great prestige among the World Literary forum.

    Margaret Laurence is one of the major contemporary Canadian writers and is very productive writer. She was born in Manitoba, Canada. From age seven, she wrote stories and from that time on she started her writing career. When she was young, her parents died and an aunt who had become her stepmother brought her up. She was educated at the University of Manitoba. After marrying an engineer, she moved with her husband to Africa and lived there for a number of years. In 1960 Margaret Laurence published her novel, *This Side of Jordan*, with a background set in Ghana. *The Stone Angel* (1964) was a landmark event for Canadian literature and the keystone of Laurence's career. Laurence's African writings introduce the themes of survival, freedom, and individual dignity that dominate her major novels. She is much beloved and has been honored in Canada and abroad, where her works are widely translated.

Dave Godfrey was born in Winnipeg, Manitoba, and he spent most of his early years in rural Ontario. He did undergraduate and graduate work in the U.S., and received M.A. from Stanford in 1961, and a Ph. D. in English from the University of Iowa in 1967. On returning to Canada from America, he taught English at Trinity College, University of Toronto and was named chairman of the creative-writing department of the University of Victoria in 1978. Dave Godfrey has been a major force in Canadian publishing. Collaboration with his colleagues, he founded some important literary publishing houses. He was also the fiction editor of the CANADIAN FORUM since 1971. He has done a great contribution to promote Canadian book publication. His representative works are: *Death Goes Better with Coca-Cola*, 1967; *The New Ancestors*, 1970, which won a Governor-General's Award; *Dark Must Yield*, 1978 and etc. The book of *The New Ancestors* has a distinct theme and it juxtaposes four different temporal perspectives of the same events to create an Einsteinian vision of relative values.

One of the most influential authors in the field of Canadian literature is Margaret Atwood. Margaret Eleanor Atwood was born in Ottawa. She graduated from Victoria College, University of Toronto, and received bachelor degree and M.A. degree from there. She then taught in a number of Canadian universities, and at the same time worked as an editor for a publishing house. Atwood's poetry includes: *The Circle Game*, 1966; *The Animals in That Country*, 1968; *Power Politics*, 1973; *You Are Happy*, 1974; *Selected Poems*, 1976; *Two-headed Poems*, 1978; *Bodily Harm*, 1981; and *Lady Oracle*, 1976. Atwood's novels include: *The Edible Woman*, 1969; *Dancing Girls*, 1977; *Murder in the Dark*, 1983; *Up in the Tree*, 1978; *Anna's Pet*, 1980; etc. She is one of the most productive literary writers in Canadian literature history.

Another famous Canadian writer that is worth mentioning is Douglas Gordon Jones. His representative works are: *Butterfly on the Rock*, 1972, which has been regarded an academic masterpiece; *Under the Thunder the Flowers Light up the Earth*, 1977, which won a Governor-General's Award in 1977.

Stephen Leacock is a famous Canadian humorist, essayist, teacher, political economist, historian, as well as an accomplished economist. He grew up on a farm in Ontario and was educated at Upper Canada College where he taught for 9 years. He studied economics and political science and received Ph. D. in 1903. He jointed McGill's Department of Economics and Political Science in 1908, and rose quickly to become department head, and remained there until retirement in 1936. His two masterpieces are *Sunshine Sketches of a Little Town* (1912) and *Arcadian Adventures with the Idle Rich* (1914).

Another exotic flower in the garden of Canadian literature is French Canadian literature. It goes without saying that the city of Montreal is the academic research center for French Canadian literature. French Canadian literature definitely has made a great contribution to the Canadian literature. Some of the French Canadian authors are also very much productive and some of their works enjoy high reputation especially in the Province of Quebec and in the country of France.

Canadian literature encyclopedia lists more than 300 authors, among them there are some famous authors originally from Europe, Africa, Asia and some other countries in the world. Their literary works have filled in the gaps in the field of Canadian literature of ethnic groups. These ethnic authors have made a special contribution to the Canadian literature.

译 文

20世纪60年代至20世纪80年代是加拿大英语文学和加拿大法语文学空前兴旺的时期。这一时期的加拿大文学具有以下三个特点：

1）加拿大作家队伍迅速扩大。
2）加拿大文学作品题材多样化。
3）加拿大文学评论家的队伍日趋成熟。

在20世纪60年代之前，加拿大文坛上只有少数才华出众的作家崭露头角。但是，从20世纪60年代初，加拿大各地涌现出许多新一代的作家。其中一些作家在加拿大和世界上很快享有很高的声誉。这些新一代的作家队伍包括：玛格丽特·劳伦斯，阿尔佛雷德·厄尔·伯尼，多萝西·利弗塞，戴夫·戈弗雷，玛格丽特·阿特伍德，道格拉斯·戈登·琼斯等，举不胜举。这些作家在世界文坛上赫赫有名。

玛格丽特·劳伦斯（Margaret Laurence）是加拿人当代著名作家之一，而且是个多产的作家。她出生于加拿大的马尼托巴省。她从七岁就写故事并由此开始了自己的写作生涯。她的父母在她很小的时候就过世了，她是被一个阿姨也就是以后的继母带大的。她在马尼托巴大学读书。与一个工程师结婚后，她随丈夫来到非洲并在那里生活了一些年。1960年玛格丽特·劳伦斯出版了她的小说《约旦河此岸》，该小说是以加纳为背景创作的。《石天使》（1964）是加拿大文学史上的里程碑，而且也是劳伦斯事业的顶峰。劳伦斯非洲作品的中心思想均与生存、自由和个人尊严有关。她很受读者欢迎并在国内外享有盛誉，她的作品被翻译成多国语言。

戴夫·戈弗雷（Dave Godfrey）出生在加拿大马尼托巴省温尼伯市。他大部分的时间是在安大略农村度过的。他是在美国获得的学士学位，而且在1961年获得斯坦福大学硕士学位。1967年，获得爱荷华大学英语博士学位。从美国回到加拿大后，他在多伦多大学三一学院教授英语。1978年被任命为维多利亚大学创意写作系主任。戴夫·戈弗雷一直是加拿大出版界的精英，和他的同事合作，共同创办了一些重要的文学出版社。自1971年，他兼任《加拿大论坛》的小说专栏编辑。他在推进加拿大文学出版方面做出了很大贡献。他的文学代表作有《有了可口可乐，死也安宁》（1967）、获得"总督奖"的《新祖先》（1970）和《黑暗总有尽头》（1978）等。《新祖先》主题鲜明，该书对同样的事件从四个不同的角度并列叙述，以说明爱因斯坦的相对价值观。

玛格丽特·阿特伍德（Margaret Atwood）是加拿大文学上最有影响力的作家之一。她出生在渥太华，毕业于多伦多大学维多利亚学院，在那里她获得了学士学位和硕士研究生学位。接着，她在一些加拿大的大学任教，并同时兼任一家出版社的编辑工作。阿特伍德的诗集有《圈圈游戏》（1966）、《国家里的动物》（1968）、《强权政治》（1973）、《你是幸福的》（1974）、《诗歌选集》（1976）、《双头诗歌》（1978）、《肉体的伤害》（1981）和《女预言家》（1976）。阿特伍德的小说包括《可食用的女人》（1969）、《跳舞的姑娘们》（1977）、《黑暗中的谋杀》（1983）、《树上》（1978）和《安娜的宠物》（1980）等。她是加拿大文学史上最多产的作家之一。

另外一个值得提及的著名加拿大作家是道格拉斯·戈登·琼斯（Douglas Gordon Jones），他的代表作有一直被认为是学术杰作的《岩石上的蝴蝶》（1972）和曾在1977年获得"总督奖"的《雷声中的花儿使大地一片明亮》（1977）。

斯蒂芬·里柯克（Stephen Leacock）是加拿大著名的幽默大师、评论家、教师、政治经济学家、历史学家和资深的经济学家。他在安大略省的一个农场长大，在当时的阿普加拿大学院接受教育，他还在那里当了九年的教师。他的专业是经济学和政治科学，1903年取得博士学位。1908年他任职于麦吉尔大学经济与政治系，并很快成为系主任，直到1936年退休。他的两部名著是《小镇艳阳录》（1912）和《阔佬的牧歌式历险》（1914）。

加拿大文苑里的另一枝奇葩是加拿大法语文学。众所周知，蒙特利尔这座城市是加拿大法语文学的学术研究中心。加拿大法语文学无疑为加拿大文学的发展做出了巨大贡献。有些法裔加拿大作家也非常多产，而且他们的一些作品也享有很高的声誉，特别是在魁北克省和法国。

加拿大文学百科全书列举了300多名作家，其中，有些著名的作家来自非洲、亚洲和其他国家，他们的文学作品填补了加拿大少数民族文学的空白。这些少数民族作家对加拿大文学做出了特殊贡献。

Dialogue

They're Selling like Hot Cakes

(A student is asleep on the sofa in the lobby. His friend comes up and tries to wake him up.)

A: Hey! Come on, you lazybones! You've been sleeping for an hour.

B: (He feels very sleepy.) What time is it? (Looks at his watch.) My gosh! It's only one o'clock. *Leave me alone*. I need my beauty sleep, you know.

A: OK, sleeping beauty. I'm sorry to disturb you, but this is really something.

B: Go fly a kite and stop *bugging me*.

A: I got three books; one for our American History course and two for our Canadian Literature course. *Shake a leg*, or you will miss the chance.

B: Listen, my friend, I share your enthusiasm. But I didn't sleep a wink last night.... Hey! Wait a minute! What did you say it was?

A: I said two books: one American History book, one Canadian Literature book. Look! They're *selling like hot cakes*.

B: That's fantastic! Why didn't you tell me?

A: I keep telling you, but you've been talking nonsense.

B: Sorry, I *was all tired out* when I finished my classes this morning. Tell me, where did you buy the book?

A: At the university bookstore. Not many left. You'd better go right away.

B: Let me have a look at the books. Ah, a new edition by Alistair Cooke.

A: This is the Short Fiction by Stephen Leacock, *Sunshine Sketches of a Little*

Town and that is *Stone Angel* by Margaret Laurence.

B: Thanks for the info. I'd better **get a more on**. Bye!

A: That's the gratitude I get from you?

Vocabulary and Notes

- lobby — entrance hall; corridor 前厅，走廊
- wake someone up — 叫醒某人
- lazybones — very lazy indeed 懒骨头
- My gosh! (My goodness!) — 天哪！哎呀！糟糕！（表示惊讶、惊奇等）
- sleeping beauty — 睡美人
- This is really something. — If you say that a situation, object, or place is really something, you mean that you are very impressed by it. Or it's very important. 这事确实很重要。
- go fly a kite — go away; leave—usually used as a command to show that you do not accept someone's ideas 走开；离开（常用于下命令，表示不接受某人的意见）
- enthusiasm — 热情；积极性
- That's fantastic! — That's wonderful! That's terrific! 太棒了！妙极了！绝了！
- new edition — 新版本
- Alistair Cooke — 阿利斯太尔·库克，美国历史学家，以对美国历史及文化所做评论生动而且深刻著称。他的《库克眼中的美国》一书畅销全美。
- Stephen Leacock — 斯蒂芬·里柯克（1869—1944），加拿大著名幽默小说家。写过三十几本轻松的随笔和短篇小说。里柯克的真正感染力在于他的幽默感。他的作品特点可以说是青春的活力和活泼的喜剧场面的创造。作为一位幽默大师，他不仅在加拿大享有很高的声誉，而且在其他英语国家也声名卓著。
- *Sunshine Sketches of a Little Town* — 《小镇艳阳录》，斯蒂芬·里柯克的主要作品，是加拿大文学中最受读者喜爱的名著之一。它以一个典型的小镇玛丽帕为背景，作者用轻松幽默的笔调描写了加拿大往昔的小镇风貌和镇上的典型人物。同时还描绘了这一资本主义上升时期旅馆老板史密斯靠开酒店和咖啡店赢利，投机取巧，后来却当选为保守党的国会议员。作者描绘这一资本主义上升时期

- Margaret Laurence

  玛格丽特·劳伦斯（1926—1987），加拿大当代知名作家。其早期作品如《约旦河此岸》《先知的驼铃》等都反映了她和丈夫在索马里和加纳的生活。后来写的许多小说以加拿大为背景，以妇女为主人公，描写坚强的妇女在男子占优势的世界中是如何为发挥自己的才干而斗争的。劳伦斯是加拿大皇家学会会员，获得过加拿大六所大学的荣誉学位，其作品曾获1967年和1974年的"加拿大总督文学奖"。

- Thanks for the info.

  (info=information) 谢谢你提供的信息。

- That's the gratitude I get from you?

  这就是你对我的感谢吗？

Idioms for Everyday Use

leave someone alone
不要打搅某人；别管他 | not disturb someone

Leave me alone! Didn't you notice I'm typing?
别打扰我！你没看见我正在打字吗？

Leave him alone. He just had a quarrel with his father.
让他在那儿别管他。他刚和他父亲吵过架。

bug someone
激怒/惹恼某人 | annoy or upset someone

Why do you let him **bug you** like this?
你为什么让他这样气你呢？

Those neighbors of us with their noisy radios and TV sets definitely **bug us**.
我们那些邻居家的收音机和电视机的嘈杂声实在把我们搅得心烦意乱。

shake a leg
赶快；办事迅速 | hurry up and do something instead of sitting about lazily

Come on, **shake a leg**! We've got a lot to do today.
快过来！我们今天有许多事要办呢。

Shake a leg! The bus won't wait.
快点过来！汽车不等人。

(something) sell like hot cakes (sell like T-shirts)
畅销；抢着购买（某物）

sell quickly; sell well, so people are very eager to buy

A: Got your tickets for Celine Dion concert yet?
B: Not yet. There's still plenty of time.
A: You'd better buy them in advance. Those tickets are always **selling like hot cakes**.
A: 买到席琳·迪翁演唱会的票了吗？
B: 还没有。时间来得及。
A: 你最好提前买票。那些票总是卖得非常快。

American Idioms Dictionary has been **selling like hot cakes**. The publisher is going to have to reprint it.
《美国成语词典》一书一直很畅销。出版商准备再版。

be tired out
精疲力竭

be exhausted

By the time we got there, we **were tired out**.
等我们到那儿的时候，都累得够呛了。

After the long journey we were **both tired out**. We didn't even take a bath before we went to bed.
长途旅行之后，我们俩都累坏了。睡觉前我们甚至都没洗澡。

get a move on (get a wiggle on)
赶快；快些

hurry up; get going

Get a move on, you two, or we'll be late.
你们两个快点儿，否则我们就要迟到了。

"Hey, **get a move on**, can't you?" His father shouted.
"嘿，你能不能快点？"他爸爸喊道。

Unit 11
CN Tower and Cable TV
加拿大国家电视塔和有线电视

The CN Tower in Toronto, Ontario is Canada's tallest building. Reaching 553.33 meters into the sky, the CN Tower has been a favorite destination and landmark for tourists since its completion in 1976. The Tower's primary function is communication, transmitting Canada's radio and television signals.

The CN Tower has a unique beauty and is a proud landmark. It was made mainly of 4,000 tons of steel, 110,000 tons of concrete and glass. Not only is it a wonder to see, but also it provides an astounding view. On a clear day, visitors can see 120 kilometers. An evening view is equally stunning, with a multitude of city lights between the blackness of Lake Ontario and the night sky.

The 360 revolving restaurant, which has a seating capacity of 425 people provides a constantly changing view of the whole city. And it revolves one round every other 65 minutes. People are overlooking different skyscrapers while enjoying the delicious meals. The wine cellar, opened in May 1997, is located in the center of the restaurant. It resembles a classic underground European-style wine cellar with climate and humidity controls and a 10,000-bottle storage capacity.

Canadian National Railway began building the Tower in 1973, and completed in 1976. All major television and radio signals in Toronto and surrounding area are pure clear since the completion of the Tower.

The CN Tower took forty months to construct and cost $63 million. A total of 2,000 courageous people built it, many of them working at dizzying heights.

Besides the giant construction cranes were used at that time, helicopters also played an important role in the construction of the Tower since it was so high. The lives of both the helicopter crew and the crane operators were at risk.

The Tower has become a major tourist attraction with 2 million people from all over the world visiting it each year. There are four high-speed transparent elevators and visitors can be taken to 346-meter Look Out Level within one minute, and then enjoy freely the most spectacular view of the whole city.

The structure of the Tower is unique. It is recognized by the western world architecture experts as "the Wonder in the History of the World Architecture". Canadians regard CN Tower as the symbol of Canada.

Television provides information and entertainment suited to the tastes and needs of a very large public. Canadian television shows many different forms: newscasts and news magazine shows or documentaries, talk shows, children's programs, as well as a wide range of dramatic entertainment. There are three national TV networks in Canada—CBC, CTV, and Global—that broadcast nationwide through local stations. Most towns and cities have cable TV and most TV stations have local news and weather before national and international news, which is at 6 pm. Prime time is 8:00 to 12:00 pm. This is the time when most people watch TV, so the networks put their best shows on these hours.

Family members sometimes fight about which show to watch. The father wants to watch sports, the mother wants to watch a movie, the daughter wants to watch a comedy, and the son wants to watch a detective show. It is difficult to escape the influence of television. It is said by the American sociologist Robert MacNeil that "people in North American countries, by the age of 20, you will have been exposed to at least 20,000 hours of television".

However, 5,000 hours are what a typical college undergraduate spends, working on a bachelor's degree. In 10,000 hours you could have learned enough to become an astronomer or engineer. You could have learned several languages fluently. The trouble with television is that it discourages concentration.

The Canadian film industry is highly developed. The National Film Board of Canada boasts one of the World's largest government film units. Since it's founding in 1939, the Board has produced over 4000 original films. The Board has more than ten Oscar academy awards.

Believe it or not, today, although more electronic devices are used by young people, television is still an integral part of the life of many traditional North American families. Children rush home from school, plop down in front of the TV and watch their programs while they do their homework, and parents use the TV as a source of reward and punishment: "If you mow the lawn, you can watch TV an extra hour tonight", or "No TV for you if you do not do your homework."

TV does great harm to children. Too much TV not only damages their eyes but also destroys their ability to concentrate.

But TV has made a great cultural contribution. For instance, after football tonight, there'll be an educational program, "The History of the Great Pyramid."

译文

位于安大略省多伦多市的加拿大国家电视塔是全加拿大最高的建筑物。1976年竣工以后，这座高达553.33米直冲云霄的电视塔，成为旅游者们喜爱的最佳去处。这座高塔的主要功能是通讯，即发送加拿大广播电台和电视信号。

加拿大国家电视塔具有独特的魅力，是人们骄傲的象征。它主要是由4千吨钢铁、11万吨水泥和玻璃建成的。它不但是一个奇迹，而且美丽的风景令人叹为观止。在晴朗的日子里，能见度达120公里；在黝黑的安大略湖和夜空之间，无数城市灯光的映射使得晚上的风景不逊于白天，同样迷人。

可容纳425人的360度旋转餐厅让人们享受着不断变化的全城景色。旋转餐厅每隔65分钟旋转一圈。游人可以一边品尝美味佳肴，一边欣赏着各种不同的高楼大厦。这个1997年5月开业的酒窖建在了旋转餐厅中心的显著位置。它好像是一个欧洲风格的古典地下酒窖，设有温度和湿度的调控系统，而且有容纳1万瓶酒的空间。

加拿大国家铁路局于1973年开始动工建塔，1976年落成。自从电视塔建成后，所有多伦多和周边地区的电视台和广播电台的信号纯正清晰。

电视塔的建成耗时40个月，耗资6300万加元。总共有两千多勇敢人士参与建塔，许多人是在令人眩晕的高空作业。除了使用那些庞大的建筑起重机外，在建塔时，直升机同样起到了重要作用，因为塔实在是太高了。直升机的机组人员和起重机操作人员都是在冒着生命危险建高塔。

电视塔已成为吸引游客的一道亮丽的风景线，每年有200万游客从世界各地前来欣赏。塔内装有四部高速的透明电梯，游客将会在一分钟内被送上346米高度的观景平台，尽情欣赏着全城最精彩壮观的景色。

电视塔的建筑结构是独特的。它被西方建筑行业专家认为是"世界建筑史上的奇迹"。加拿大人视国家电视塔为国家的象征。

电视为不同欣赏品位和需要的人群提供信息和娱乐。加拿大有各种形式的电视节目：新闻广播和新闻杂志秀或纪录片、脱口秀、儿童节目和各种电视剧、电影。加拿大有三家电视广播网——加拿大广播公司（CBC）、加拿大电视公司（CTV）和环球电视公司（Global）——通过当地电台全国广播。大部分乡镇和城市安装了有线电视，而且大部分电视台在下午6:00，即国内和国际新闻播出之前播放地方新闻和天气预报。晚上8:00到12:00为黄金档，这段时间人们都在看电视，所以电视台会播出最好的节目。

家里人有时候会因为节目选择发生争执，父亲愿意看体育节目，母亲想看电影，女儿喜欢看喜剧，而儿子爱看侦探片。看来想不受电视的影响是很难了。美国社会学家罗伯特·麦内尔说道："北美国家的人们20岁时至少就看了2万小时的电视节目。"

可是，一个大学生花上5千小时就能够完成学士学位，如果学习1万小时，你就足以成为一名天文学家或工程师。你也足以熟练掌握几种语言。电视的问题就在于它分散你的注意力。

加拿大电影业发展很成熟。加拿大国家电影局宣称是世界上最大的政府型电影机构之一。自从1939年成立以来，加拿大国家电影局就拍摄了超过4千部原创影片，拥有10多个奥斯卡奖项。

信不信由你，时至今日，尽管更多的电子设备被年轻人所使用，电视依然是很多北美传统家庭生活中不可或缺的一部分。孩子们放学后赶紧回家，他们坐在电视机前边做作业边看电视，而父母则把看电视作为奖惩手段："如果你现在割草，今天晚上你就能多看一个小时电视"或者"不完成作业就别看电视"。

电视对孩子的负面影响很大，看得太多不仅对视力不好，还会影响他们注意力的集中。

可是电视对文化传播做出了很大贡献，比如，今天晚上看完足球比赛后就会播出教育节目"大金字塔的历史"。

I'm in a Bind

(Li drops in on Judy, his Canadian friend, and asks Judy if she'd like to go out to see a movie.)

Judy: Hey, come on in, Li. I've just finished the sociology paper. Have some tea?

Li: Thanks. Looks like you could **use a breather**. Hey, would you like to go out tonight? I mean, we could **take in** a movie or something.

Unit 11 CN Tower and Cable TV 加拿大国家电视塔和有线电视

Judy: Oh, some of my friends are coming tonight and we'd like to watch a football game on TV. Join us?

Li: TV again? You know we've watched TV for three evenings. Seems TV is the only evening entertainment for you.

Judy: Yeah, I think you've **put your finger on** something. I've **put in** four evenings of watching TV this week. However, social scientists say the average North American watches 6 hours of TV a day, and I only watch 3 or 4 hours a day, far from that.

Li: Don't be so silly. It seems that you're already a couch potato.

Judy: You got it! You see, I try to watch TV as little as possible, but it's so hard.

Li: I didn't watch TV very much when I first got here. But TV has become tremendously popular in Canada, and now I'm also addicted to it.

Judy: So you've **jumped on the bandwagon**, eh?

Li: You'll have to **answer for** that. I learned from you.

Judy: Believe it or not, families in North America today schedule their lives around television. Children rush home from school, plop down in front of the TV and watch their programs while they do their homework, and parents use the TV as a source of reward and punishment: "If you now the lawn, you can watch TV an extra hour tonight", or "No TV for you if you do not do your homework".

Li: I think TV does great harm to children. Too much TV not only damages their eyes but also destroys their ability to concentrate.

Judy: But TV has made a great cultural contribution. For instance, after football tonight, there'll be and educational program, "The History of the Great Pyramid."

Li: So, sounds like you insist on watching TV tonight.

Judy: Stay with us, Li. My friends are coming soon. We'll have fun.

Li: I'm really *in a bind*. I've already got tickets for tonight. Is it all right if I go to the movie by myself and join you after the movie?

Judy: Let's *find a happy medium* by watching the ice hockey game tonight and going to the movie tomorrow evening, both of us. Satisfied?

Li: How about the tickets?

Judy: I'll give them to my neighbor.

Vocabulary and Notes

- sociology — the study of human societies and of the relationships, groups in these societies 社会学
- entertainment — 娱乐；乐趣；招待；款待
- a couch potato — someone who watches a lot of television and whose lifestyle is not active 电视迷
- TV has become tremendously popular in Canada — 电视在加拿大特别普及
- be addicted to (something) — like something or doing something very much 沉溺于……，热衷于……；使……成瘾
- schedule their lives around television — 他们的生活围着电视转
- punishment — 惩罚，处罚
- mow the lawn — 剪草坪
- the Great Pyramid — 大金字塔

Idioms for Everyday Use

use/take a breather
松口气休息片刻 | take a short pause for a rest

- We've been working quite a long time now—let's **take a breather**.
  我们现在已经工作好长时间了——让我们休息一会儿吧。
- A: I've just finished the book report. I've been doing this since last Monday.
  B: So now you could **use a breather**. Would you like to dine out tonight?
  A: Sounds great! It's on me this time.
  A: 我刚刚把读书报告写完。自上星期一开始，我就写这个报告了。
  B: 那么现在你可以松口气休息一会儿。今晚到外面吃晚饭，好吗？
  A: 太好了！这次我请客。

take in
观看；参观 | (in this context) go and see; visit

- The students decided to **take in** a movie while they were in town.
  当学生们在城里时，他们决定看场电影。

A: What do you plan for your trip this time?
B: Well, we plan to **take in** Niagara Falls and Yellowstone National Park, and then we'll go to Europe.
A: 这次旅行你们怎么安排？
B: 我们计划去参观尼亚加拉大瀑布和黄石公园，然后准备去欧洲。

put/lay one's finger on 准确地指出问题的所在；找出造成麻烦的原因	give exactly the right answer to the problem; find the cause of trouble

A: What's bugging Tom? He hasn't been himself lately.
B: I'm not sure, but I think He's still mad about not getting that promotion last month.
A: Yes, I think you've **put your finger on** it. I heard him complaining the other day.
A: 什么事使汤姆那么烦恼？最近他好像变了个人。
B: 我不大知道，不过我想他还是在为上个月没被提升而恼火。
A: 对，我想你分析得很有道理。那天我还听到他发牢骚来着。

I think you've **put your finger on** the problem. It seems to me that's exactly the trouble.
我认为你已指出了问题的关键。我看问题的确就在这里。

put in 花时间或花钱	(in this context) spend time or money

When he was at the university, he **put in** an hour a day listening to the Voice of America. He was very fond of the program, Words and Their Stories.
他上大学时，每天花一小时收听"美国之音"广播。他非常喜欢"词汇掌故"这个节目。

It all depends on how much time you'd like to **put in**
这完全取决于你愿意花多少时间。

jump/climb on the bandwagon 随大溜；效仿别人的做法	do something just because a lot of people are doing it; copy other people's actions

When all Mike's colleagues decided to vote for the Republican candidate, Mike **jumped on the bandwagon**
看到同事们都决定投票支持共和党的候选人，迈克也跟着投了一票。

While many stores are raising their prices, Peter thinks he will **jump on the bandwagon** and raise his prices.
在许多商店抬高物价时，彼得认为他也应该随大溜，抬高物价。

answer for
对……负责；为……的后果承担责任 | (in this context) take the responsibility or blame for (someone or something)

- You will have to **answer for** this waste since you're the director of the factory.
  既然你是厂长，那么你就应该对这种浪费现象承担责任。

- You must be careful. You'll have to **answer for** any possible damage.
  你一定要特别仔细。任何可能造成的损失都要由你负责。

in a bind
左右为难；处于困境 | in a dilemma; in a difficult situation

- A: Say, Chen Lao Shi, I'm **in a bind**. I've just been called to an urgent meeting at the chairman's, but a friend of mine is coming to see me all the way from Hong Kong.
  B: Don't worry, go ahead with your meeting. If you're not back, I'll take care of him for you.
  A: 嘿，陈老师，我正左右为难。刚刚有人叫我到主任室开个紧急会议，可我的朋友从香港专程来看我。
  B: 别急，你先去开会。如果你回不来，我替你招待他。

- Peter is **in a bind** because if he helps the blind girl find her way to the bus stop, he will be late for class; and if he doesn't, she will get lost.
  彼得左右为难，因为如果他要帮助那位盲人姑娘找到公交车站，他上学就会迟到；如果他不帮助她，她就会迷路。

find a happy medium
采取折中办法 | find a compromise

- A: As to which of our two official languages we should use for this program, I don't think we should argue about it any more.
  B: I agree. We can **find a happy medium** by allowing each person to use the language of his choice. That way everyone should be satisfied.
  A: 有关这个项目我们使用哪一种官方语言的问题，我认为我们不要再争论下去了。
  B: 我同意。我们可以采取一种折中的办法，让每个人自己选用一种语言。这样大家都满意。

- "Since you two obviously don't see eye to eye on this issue, let's try to **find a happy medium** that you can agree on." He said with a smile.
  他笑着说："既然你们俩在这个问题上有明显的分歧意见，那就让我们采取一个你们俩都同意的折中方法。"

Unit 12
The Group of Seven of Canada
加拿大七人画派

The organization of the Group of Seven in Canada was founded in 1920. They proclaimed themselves as modern artists. The members include Franklin Carmichael, Lawren Harris, Alexander Young Jackson, Franz Johnston, Arthur Lismer, James Edward Hervey Macdonald and Frederick Horsman Varley.

The Group of Seven was an early 20th-century nationalist art group whose members set out to create a distinctly Canadian art that reflected the character of the land and the people. It would be hard to find a Canadian who has not been moved by the group's works. Their paintings—displayed in galleries across the country—capture a feeling for the sublime mystery of the Canadian landscape, which is the physical and spiritual heritage of every Canadian.

The painters who would form the Group of Seven first came together in Toronto, Ontario, in the years before the World War I (1914–1918). These painters first worked as commercial artists. On weekends and vacations they painted on the outskirts of Toronto and in sparsely populated areas of Ontario. At that time, the conservative and the classical European styles frustrated them. They wanted to establish a bolder kind of painting that Canadians could call their own. Seeking new methods to interpret new material, the artists found inspiration in the nationalist romantic art of Sweden and Norway.

The Group was not exclusively landscape painters, and it was only after their first exhibition at the Art Gallery of Toronto in 1920 that they began to identify themselves as a landscape school. They were initially drawn together by a common sense of frustration with the conservative and imitative quality of most Canadian art.

Romantic, with mystical leanings, the Group and their spokesmen zealously, and sometimes contentiously, presented themselves as Canada's national school of painters. This provoked the ire of the artistic establishment, which seems to have hated their rhetoric even more than their paintings. Eric Brown, director of the National Gallery of Canada, always stood by them. He began buying their paintings for the gallery's collection several years before the Group was formally established, and in 1924 and 1925 he made sure they were well represented in the Canadian art shows that went to the prestigious Wembley exhibition in England. This enraged many members of the Royal Canadian Academy, who felt that the Group was given an unfair advantage, but British press reports were so favorable that both Brown and the Group felt vindicated.

The Group rebelled against the constraints of 19th-century naturalism and tried to establish a more equitable and independent relationship between art and nature. They shifted emphasis away from similitude—the imitation of natural effects—towards the expression of their feelings for their subjects. As they often painted together, both in the bush and in the studio, their paintings developed along somewhat similar lines. The canvases exhibited in their early shows usually have heavy impasto and bright colors, and are boldly summarized with attention drawn to surface patterning. This is as true of the portraits of Harris and Varley as of the landscapes. Following a visit to the stark north shore of Lake Superior in 1921, Harris began to radically simplify the color and layouts of his canvases. MacDonald, Carmichael and even Varley soon adopted similar methods, using thin pigment and stylized designs for many paintings. Harris went further than the others, however, and by the mid-1920s he had reduced his paintings to a few simplified and nearly monochromatic forms. Ten years later he became the only member of the Group, and one of the first Canadian artists, to turn to abstraction.

Through self-promotion and through friends at the Arts and Letters Club and the *Canadian Forum*, as well as with the support of the National Gallery, the Group's influence steadily spread during the 1920s. In 1926, after Franz Johnston's resignation, A. J. Casson was appointed a member. The Group realized they could hardly call themselves a national school of painters as long as they all lived in Toronto, so they invited other artists to join them: in 1930 Edwin Holgate from Montréal and in 1932 L. L. Fitzgerald from Winnipeg were admitted to give the organization a wider geographic base.

Harris and Jackson influenced and encouraged the next generation of Canadian artists, and Lismer, MacDonald and Varley all became distinguished and influential teachers. By the time the group disbanded in 1933, however, it had become as entrenched, and in some ways as conservative, as the art establishment it had overthrown. Its influence has therefore been a mixed blessing, and it is not surprising that it was in Montréal, which did not respond to the Group's call, that the next generation of significant Canadian painters emerged. Paintings by members of the Group of Seven can be found in most Canadian public art galleries.

The beautiful 25 stamps showing paintings by the members of the Group of Seven have been issued publicly over the years from the 1960s through 1990s.

译 文

加拿大七人画派成立于1920年。他们宣称自己是现代派艺术家。最初的成员包括弗兰克林·卡尔米歇尔、劳伦斯·哈里斯、亚历山大·扬·杰克逊、弗朗斯·约翰斯顿、阿瑟·利斯迈尔、詹姆斯·爱德华·赫维·麦克唐纳、弗雷德里克·霍斯曼·瓦利。

七人画派是起始于20世纪早期的民族主义艺术画派，其成员旨在通过描绘加拿大的风土人情，创造出一种独具特色的加拿大本土艺术。几乎每一个加拿大人都深受其作品的影响。他们的作品遍布每个艺术展厅，捕捉加拿大山水所蕴含的庄严的神秘感，为加拿大人创造了珍贵的物质和精神财富。

早在第一次世界大战爆发的前几年（1914—1918），七人画派的几个创始人就云集在安大略省多伦多市。他们起初是商业画家，周末和节假日的时候在多伦多郊区或者人烟稀少的安大略地区作画。那时，欧洲的保守派和古典派使他们深受困扰。所以他们试图创立一种加拿大人自己的、画风大胆的作画风格。他们从瑞典和挪威的民族浪漫主义画家身上发掘灵感，试图寻求全新的艺术表现手法来诠释新的素材。

起初，并不是所有的成员都是风景派画家。直到1920年他们在多伦多美术馆里举办了首次画展之后，才将自己定性为风景画派。他们最初聚拢在一起，是因为大多数加拿大艺术中保守和模仿的特点让他们有着同样的挫败感。

画派所推崇的浪漫主义带有神秘色彩，各成员和代表人物时而热情洋溢，时而又喋喋不休，宣称自己为加拿大国画派。这就激怒了那些风雅的组织，比起其作品他们更厌恶七人画派的花言巧语。加拿大国家美术馆的馆长埃里克·布朗总是站出来支持他们。早在七人画派正式创立之前，他就一直购买其作品作为美术馆的收藏。在1924年和1925年，他极力促成七人画派的作品列入加拿大艺术展，并参加了享有盛誉的英国温布利艺术展。此举激怒了许多加拿大皇家学院的成员，他们认为七人画派受到了优先照顾，但是，英国媒体的报道却给予其极高的评价，这让布朗和画派成员都感觉受到了维护。

画派成员奋力反抗19世纪自然主义的束缚，试图在艺术与自然之间建立一种更平等、独立的关系。他们不再强调相似性，即对自然现象的模仿，转为强调自己主观感情的流露。无论是在灌木丛还是在画室，他们总在一起绘画，所以他们创作的思路不约而同地相似。在他们早期的画展中，油布画通常颜料厚重，颜色亮眼，利用大胆的着色吸引人们的眼球。哈里斯与瓦利的人物肖像画同风景画一样真实。1921年，在游览了荒凉的苏比利尔湖北部之后，哈里斯突然简化了油布画的颜色和线条。继而，麦克唐纳、卡尔米歇尔，甚至连瓦利都采用相似的方式，在作品中运用薄薄的颜料和风格化的设计。与他人相比，哈里斯的作品更加精湛，然而，到了20世纪20年代中期，他画作的颜色变得更单一，几乎趋向于单色调。10年后，他是七人画派中唯一一位向抽象派转型的画家，同时也在加拿大首批转型艺术家之列。

七人画派在20世纪20年代声名远播，这多亏了来自文学艺术俱乐部和《加拿大论坛》的一些朋友的帮助，还有国家美术馆的大力支持，当然也离不开他们的自我宣传。在1926年，弗朗斯·约翰斯顿退出画派，卡逊成为画派中的一员。画派意识到如果他们所有的人仍然都聚集在多伦多，他们就无法自称为国派，所以他们邀请了其他画家加入画派：1903年蒙特利尔的霍尔盖特的加入，还有1932年来自温尼伯湖的菲茨杰拉德的加入，无疑给画派创造了一个更广阔的地域性的发展空间。

哈里斯和杰克逊都给加拿大下一代画家带来了深厚的影响，并鼓励其成长；利斯迈尔、麦克唐纳、瓦利也都成了著名的、极其有影响力的导师。然而，到七人画派1933年解散时，它和它所颠覆的艺术流派一样保守顽固。因此，它的影响是双刃剑，在蒙特利尔，无须七人画派的号召而涌现出新一代重量级的加拿大画家，也就不足为奇了。现如今，七人画派的作品仍在加拿大大多数的公共美术馆展出。

美丽精致的25张以七人画派绘出的风景画印制的邮票从20世纪60年代到90年代连续公开发行。

This Idiom Baffles Me

(Lawrence is asking his Chinese friend Li about his TESL course.)

Lawrence: How is your TESL class going these days?

Li: Great! I've never had a course like this before. It really ***turns me on***. I've learned some new methods of teaching English as a second language. I'm starting to make friends. Some of the guys asked me if I wanted to go out with them tonight. They said they were going to do some painting. As you know I'm not artistically-minded. I don't know anything about painting.

Lawrence: Painting? Tonight?

Li: Yeah, painting something red. That's what they told me.

Lawrence: Ah! I see! You misunderstood them. "***Painting the town red***" is an idiom; it means going out to drink and have a good time.

Li: Is that so? I feel so bad that I politely refused their invitation. You see, that kind of idiom really ***baffles me***. I do have trouble with idioms sometimes. They are ***over my head***. I studied English for many years in China, but people here just don't talk the way I was taught. Maybe, I should throw out my grammar books and ***start from scratch.***

Lawrence: You're kidding. I wouldn't go that far. I just think you have to listen to people talking as well as study from books. Don't worry. You'll soon ***catch on to*** what they're saying.

Li: One of these years. I think it takes time to master the idioms, since new idioms come up very often.

Lawrence: Anyway, idioms are important in English study, and idioms add life and vitality to the English language. Without idioms the English language would be rather dull. So Li, try to use idioms in your daily speech. That would ***serve your turn.***

Li: I'm trying to use idioms, but it's really hard to use them in my speech. When I speak, the idioms disappear from my mind, especially when I speak *off the cuff*.

Lawrence: Then you need practice. Practice makes perfect. Try to learn and use essential idioms. The idioms chosen for study should be well within your grasp and of practical value.

Li: *You've never said a truer word*. I'll *buy it*. Well, could you tell me the difference between American English and Canadian English?

Lawrence: Well, Canadian English is very close to American English in pronunciation and idioms. Some Canadians' spelling reflects British usage. They have kept "-our" spellings in words such as "honor" and "color".

Li: Nice talking with you. I learned a lot from you. Many thanks.

Lawrence: My pleasure.

Vocabulary and Notes

• TESL (Teaching English as a Second or Foreign Language)	英语作为第二种语言的教学
• I'm not artistically-minded.	我没有艺术细胞。
• You misunderstood them.	你误解了他们。
• I politely refused their invitation.	我婉言拒绝了他们的邀请。
• throw out	扔掉
• one of these years	it will take a long time; it will seem like forever 猴年马月；不一定什么时候
• vitality	生命力
• essential idioms	基础成语
• pronunciation	发音
• Some Canadians' spelling reflects British usage.	一些加拿大人的拼写受英式英语的影响。

Idioms for Everyday Use

turn someone on
使某人感兴趣；使某人兴奋、激动

stimulate one's interest; excite someone

- A: Do you like the Rolling Stones' music?
  B: I'll say! Any kind of rock music really **turns me on**.
  A: 你喜欢滚石乐队吗？
  B: 当然喜欢！任何摇滚乐队我都喜欢。
  [注：the Rolling Stones滚石乐队（英国继the Beatles乐队后风靡一时的摇滚乐队）]

- Actually, I don't want to watch the movie tonight. I just want to see Rachel McAdams. I think she's fantastic. She really **turns me on**.
  实际上我今晚不想看电影。我只想欣赏一下瑞秋·麦克亚当斯。我认为她太迷人了，她真让我感到兴奋。

- A: Did you read the article in the paper? Something about the scandal of Epstein?
  B: This kind of article **turns** people off rather than **on**.
  A: 你读报纸上的那篇文章了吗？就是那篇有关爱泼斯坦的丑闻。
  B: 读了。这种文章不是使人越读越想读，而是使人感到讨厌。

paint the town red
狂欢，痛饮作乐

go out and have a good time in a lively way, especially by drinking a lot, often to celebrate something

- Whenever the Spring Festival comes, we get together and **paint the town red**.
  一到春节，我们就聚在一起，开怀畅饮。

- The soccer players are **painting the town red** in celebration of their success at the Olympics.
  足球运动员为庆祝他们在奥林匹克运动会上所取得的胜利而狂欢痛饮。

baffle someone (or be baffled)
使人迷惑；不能理解或解释某事

confuse someone; cannot understand or explain something

- I know Canadian English is closer to American English in pronunciation and idioms. But the spelling **baffles me**.
  我知道加拿大英语在语音和成语方面接近美式英语，但拼写使我不解。

- I **was baffled** by his refusal.
  他的拒绝把我搞糊涂了。

over / above one's head
太难以至超出某人的理解力

too difficult for someone to understand

A: How's your computer course going?

B: Well, I understand the manuals, but I don't understand half of what the professor talks about. He uses too many technical words in class. I'm afraid his lectures are **over my head**. Maybe I should have taken the introductory course.

A: 你的计算机课进展如何？

B: 课本我还懂，但是教授所讲的，我连一半都听不懂。他在课上使用大量的专业术语。我想他的课程对我太难。没准儿我应该先选学入门课程。

A: Didn't you notice that he also laughed when we were listening to the funny story given by Chris?

B: He laughed just to be polite, but the joke Chris told him was really **over his head**.

A: 你没有注意到？当我们听克里斯的笑话时，他也笑了。

B: 仅仅出于礼貌，他笑了，实际上，他根本就没听懂克里斯给他讲的笑话。

start from scratch
从头做起；白手起家

start from beginning

When the factory was destroyed in that big fire, the firm had to **start from scratch**.

工厂被那场大火烧毁后，这个公司只好从头开始建立企业。

Let's sell our restaurant and get away from this city and **start again from scratch**.

让我们卖掉这个饭馆，离开这个城市，一切从头做起。

catch on to something
理解某人的意思，特别是理解笑话的含义

understand what someone has said, particularly to grasp the meaning of a joke

Since she doesn't understand English well, she did not **catch on to** any of the jokes we told.

由于她不太懂英语，所以她不懂我们讲的笑话。

To me it was a very funny story, but when I told it, nobody seemed to **catch on**.

在我看来，这是一个非常有趣的故事，可当我讲这个故事时，貌似没人能懂。

serve one's turn / purpose
适合某人需要；对某人有用

suit one's purpose; be useful

A: Have you found the screwdriver yet?

B: No, I haven't. I only found a knife. I think the knife will **serve your turn**.

A: 你找到螺丝刀了吗？

B: 没找到。我只找到了一把刀子。我想这把刀子会管用的。
A: Did he make any good suggestions?
B: I don't think so. His proposal didn't *serve my turn*.
A: 他有什么好的建议吗?
B: 我看没有。他的建议对我无用。

off the cuff
无准备地，即席，当场 | without preparation

A: The speaker can't come today. Could you fill in for him?
B: Please find somebody else. You know I'm no good at making speeches even when I have time to prepare them. I'm even worse when I have to speak *off the cuff*.
A: 演讲人今天不能来了。你能代替他做讲座吗?
B: 请找别人代替吧。你知道即使有时间准备我都做不好报告。让我即席演讲就更糟糕了。
A: I was surprised that nobody stood up and answered the questions. The speaker looked very much embarrassed.
B: This is not the kind of question that one can answer *off the cuff*.
A: 我感到很奇怪，竟然没有人站起来回答问题，讲话人看上去十分尴尬。
B: 这可不是那种可以当场答复的问题。

You've never said a truer word.
你说得真好/真对。 | What you said is absolutely correct.

A: What you need right now is to guild a solid foundation, not to move on too fast to advanced courses.
B: *You've never said a truer word.*
A: 现在你所需要的是打一个坚实的基础。不要着急去学那些程度很高的课程。
B: 你说得太对了。
A: World War II was a turning point in American History.
B: *You've never said a truer word.*
A: 第二次世界大战在美国历史上是个转折点。
B: 你说得对。

buy it/that
接受或赞成某观点或意见 | accept or approve of an idea, offer, or suggestion

- A: I suggest that we offer a prize to the best salesman in our office.
- B: I'll **buy that**.
- A: 我建议我们应该奖励办公室里最好的销售员。
- B: 我赞成。

- If you offer Mr. Tim Segger more money than he is getting from the Computer Center, I'm sure all of us will **buy it**.

  如果你给蒂姆·西格先生的钱比他在计算机中心挣得多，我相信我们大伙儿会同意的。

- A: Upon further consideration, I find myself in complete agreement with your proposal. Therefore, I will **buy that idea** wholeheartedly.
- B: Thank you indeed for your enthusiastic support.
- A: 经过进一步考虑，我完全同意你的提议。因此，我将全心全意接受这个想法。
- B: 特别感谢你的热情支持。

Unit 13
Women and Children
妇女和儿童

In Canada, the new status that women have developed for themselves has transformed family life. Children are raised differently. They spend more time with adults who are not their parents—baby sitters, day-care center personnel, relatives, or neighbors. And many child psychologists point out that children kept in day-care centers, kindergartens everyday are brighter than those raised at home. In order to help their children grow up healthy and sound, mothers employ child psychologists, counselors, and social workers to help children with problems at school or in the family. Many books on how to raise children have become best-sellers.

Wife assault is a crime. When a man beats up a woman in Canada, it is called assault. That means he breaks the law and commits a crime. The police can arrest the man. He may have to go to court and to be questioned. The judge may tell the husband to stay away from his wife or he may get a fine or go to jail.

If a woman is a permanent resident of Canada, she will not be deported if she leaves an abusive husband. A transition house gives safe, free, emergency care to abused women and their children, and food, shelter, and medical help will be provided.

The Institute for Prevention of Wife Abuse in Toronto has made an investigation lately into the problems of wife abuse. The result indicates that wife abuse is still one of the major social problems in Canada. They made an urgent appeal for the protection of abused women.

What is child abuse? The term "child abuse" refers to the violence, mistreatment or neglect that a child or adolescent may experience while in the care of someone they either trust or depend on, such as a parent, sibling, other relative, caregiver or guardian. Abuse may take place anywhere and may occur, for example, within the child's home.

Sometimes parents don't take proper care of their children. They may hit them or leave young children at home alone. There are laws to protect children in these situations. The local government sometimes sends the social worker to check on a child. If a social worker thinks the child is in danger, he or she can take the child out of the home to a safe place.

译文

在加拿大，妇女为自己逐步获得的新的地位改变了今天的家庭生活。抚养孩子的方式起了变化。孩子们更多的时间是与那些不是父母的成年人待在一起——临时保姆、日托中心工作人员、亲戚或邻居。许多儿童心理专家指出，天天放在日托中心的孩子比经常在家里长大的孩子要聪明得多。为了使孩子从精神上和身体上健康成长，妈妈们雇用儿童心理学家、学生辅导员和社会工作者来帮助那些在学校或家庭中有问题的孩子。很多关于如何抚养孩子的书成了畅销书。

打老婆犯法。在加拿大，男人打女人被称为暴力行为，这属于违法犯罪。警察可以逮捕这个男人。他可能会被告去法院并接受问话。法官可以不让这个男人接近他的妻子，或对他进行罚款，或判他入狱。

如果一个女人是加拿大永久居民，那么她与虐待她的丈夫离婚是不会被驱逐的。被虐待的妻子和孩子可以暂时在庇护所里生活，那里为他们提供安全、自由和应付紧急情况的服务，并提供食物、住处和药品。

多伦多受虐妇女保护协会最近进行了关于虐待妻子问题的调查，结果显示虐待妻子仍然是加拿大重大社会问题之一。他们紧急呼吁保护受虐女性。

什么是虐童问题？"虐童"是指儿童或青少年可能承受的来自于他们依赖或信赖的父母、兄弟姐妹、亲属、看护人或监护人的暴行、虐待或冷漠。虐童随处可能发生，包括发生在孩子自己家里。

有时候，家长没有好好照顾孩子，他们可能打孩子或把小孩子独自留在家里。孩子在这样的情况下是受法律保护的。地方政府有时候会派遣社会工作者去检查。如果社会工作者认为孩子身处危险，他/她就可以把孩子从家里带走到安全的地方。

 **Dialogue**

The Pot Calling the Kettle Black

(A couple and Chinese guest are going to concert.)

Susan: Are you ready, guys? Twenty minutes to go.

Li: I'm ready.

Susan: Good. Steve, are you ready? What on earth are you doing? Don't you know the curtain *goes up* at exactly seven?

Steve: My zipper's stuck. My shirt's caught in the zipper. Could you give me a hand?

Susan: You always boast that you're good at everything. But in fact, you're all thumbs.

Steve: *Give me a break*, will you?

Susan: OK, OK, but have you seen our tickets? I know I put them on the table and now they've gone.

Steve: Aha, so it's *the pot calling the kettle black*. You're always saying you're a careful person. As a matter of fact you're absentminded. I told you a thousand times to put the tickets in a safe place.

Susan: And I told you a billion times not to exaggerate!

Li: *Keep your shirt on*, Susan, and let's try to find our tickets. To tell you the truth, I saw our tickets somewhere this morning, but I can't think of it *right off the bat*. Hey! I remember, on the TV set.

Steve: Look! Here they are, on the TV set.

Susan: Give them to me! I'll put them in my purse! (She snatches the tickets from Steve.)

Steve: That's gratitude for you!

Susan: You're wasting your breath! How's your zipper?

Steve: Well, I worked it out *little by little* and finally I got the zipper clear without tearing anything.

Susan: Yes. I know my husband's a man of great ability, and very good at ...

Steve: No, no, that's enough. Don't flatter me. Well, Susan, let's give up arguing from now on. You know Alice and Ralph fought about small things all the time. See, they're getting divorced.

Susan: You're kidding! When? I'll never believe that.

Steve: Well, I don't really know the details. I **heard it through the grapevine** that Ralph slapped Alice in the face and they've been separated for two months already. It is said that it's hard for Alice to keep **on speaking terms** with Ralph.

Susan: That's really surprising—I always thought that they were so well suited to each other, such similar personalities... I just can't believe it. Alice and Ralph! They're the perfect couple.

Steve: So, it just shows how little you know about what goes on in people's lives, doesn't it?

Susan: Oh, it's only ten minutes to go. Let's hurry up, or we'll be late.

Steve: Could you tell me again the name of the play tonight?

Susan: It's called *At My Heart's Core* and this play has won Governor General Literary Awards.

Steve: It rings a bell. The author of the play is Robertson Davies.

Susan: That's right. Let's go to the concert.

Vocabulary and Notes

on earth	（用于疑问句、否定词或最高级后加强语气）究竟；到底
be stuck	被卡住；被阻塞
zipper	拉锁
boast	talk too proudly 吹牛；说大话
absent-minded	心不在焉的
billion	10亿
exaggerate	say more than the truth about (something) 夸张；夸大；对……言过其实
tell you the truth	说真的；说实话
purse	（女用）钱包；小手提包
snatch something from someone	take (something or someone) suddenly away from (someone or something) 从某人手中抢走或夺走什么东西

Unit 13　Women and Children 妇女和儿童

- That's gratitude for you! 这就是你的感谢呀!
- tear 撕裂，扯破
- be suited to be fitted; have the right qualities 适合于；有资格
  be suited to each other 俩人很相配
- *At My Heart's Core* 《在我心灵深处》是为1950年的彼得伯勒市建市百年纪念写的，于1950年8月28日在该市夏季剧院首演。作者亲自执导，他的妻子扮演女主角之一。该剧讽刺了所谓的标准和价值观念。
- Governor General Literary Awards 加拿大总督文学奖。凡是加拿大作家上一年出版的小说、诗歌、儿童文学、翻译、非小说、戏剧等六类作品都可以申报此奖项，每年评选一次。由评审从上千件的英语、法语作品中评选出入围作品与得主，分别颁发上述六大奖项。开始时授予获奖者一枚铜质奖章，1942年改成一枚银质奖章，1951年开始由加拿大杂志出版商捐助，给每位获奖者增加了奖金。从1981年开始将戏剧作品单列奖项进行评奖。
- Robertson Davies 罗伯逊·戴维斯(1913—1995)，誉满全球文坛的加拿大小说家、剧作家和批评家，当过演员和导演。他的作品对加拿大的乡土观念和循规蹈矩做了细致的描述。戴维斯的小说和剧作奠定了他在加拿大文坛上举足轻重的地位，为他赢得了国际声誉。他从1960年开始在多伦多执教，直到1981年退休。曾任梅西学院第一任院长。在他和另一位教授的主持下，多伦多大学于1966年创建了戏剧研究中心。1961年被授予洛恩·皮尔斯奖奖章，以表彰他对加拿大文学做出的杰出贡献。1972年被授予加拿大勋章。1980年荣获美国文学艺术院荣誉院士，他是获得此项殊荣的第一位加拿大人，也是第一个使加拿大戏剧艺术富有职业特征的剧作家。

Idioms for Everyday Use

go up | (in this context) the curtain in a theater "goes up" means the curtain is raised and the performance starts
幕布升起，演出开始

What time does the curtain **go up**?

什么时候开演?

There was a burst of applause as the curtain went up.
当帷幕拉开时,一片掌声响起。

| give someone a break
再给某人提供一次机会 | give someone an opportunity; offer someone another chance |

A: I'm going to fire that clerk. He's been here for two months now, but his speed hasn't improved at all. I've warned him many times. This time I've had it with him. He's out.

B: Keep your cool, Bob. Give him a break. He promised to work harder.

A: 我准备解雇那个职员。目前他到这儿已有两个月了,可他的工作效率一点儿没改进。我警告他很多次了。这回我可受够了。让他走吧。

B: 冷静点儿,鲍勃。再给他一次机会吧。他答应要更加努力工作。

"Give me just a little break," begged the driver after the police had stopped him for speeding.
开车超速被警察逮住后,驾驶员乞求道:"就原谅我这一次吧。"

| the pot calling the kettle black
批评他人者实际上自己也有同样的毛病;
黑锅笑话茶壶黑 | one person is criticizing another person for faults which in fact they both have |

Lawrence said Mike was cheating at a game but Mike replied that the pot was calling the kettle black.
劳伦斯说迈克在游戏中搞鬼,迈克说彼此彼此,谁也别说谁。

Wife: Peter, you've been sitting there doing nothing for about half an hour.
Husband: Really? And how much work have you been doing during that half an hour? Just watching TV and eating cookies. Talk about the pot calling the kettle black.
妻子:彼得,你什么都不干,在那里坐了约半个小时啦。
丈夫:是吗?你在这半个小时里做了些什么呢?就是看电视、吃饼干。咱俩谁也别说谁。

| keep one's shirt on
冷静;保持镇静,不发脾气 | calm down; don't lose your temper (usually used as a command) |

All right, keep your shirt on! Nobody's blaming you.
行啦,冷静些!没人怪你。

John said to Jim, "Keep your shirt on. Don't get excited."
约翰对吉姆说:"冷静些,别那么激动。"

right off the bat
马上；一下子；不能马上记起某事

without delay; right away; cannot remember something immediately

- A: How's your new boss?
  B: I don't think she's going to be very popular.
  A: What makes you say that?
  B: Well, the first day she introduced herself and then, **right off the bat**, she told us that we'd all better start working harder or we'd be looking for other jobs.
  A: 你们的新老板怎么样啊？
  B: 我看人们不喜欢她。
  A: 你怎么这样说呢？
  B: 嗯，第一天她做了自我介绍，然后她马上就告诉我们都要努力工作，不然就辞退我们。

- I can't think of his name **right off the bat**.
  我一时想不起他的名字。

little by little
逐渐地；一点儿一点儿地

gradually; slowly by degrees

- If you keep reading those books regularly each day, **little by little** your vocabulary of English words will increase.
  如果你每天坚持有规律地看那些书，渐渐地你的英语词汇量就会加大。

- His health seems to be improving **little by little**.
  他的身体看起来逐渐地好起来了。

hear something through the grapevine
从亲戚、朋友或同事那儿听到的小道消息；非官方的

hear a piece of news or rumor from one's friends or acquaintances, not from official sources

- A: Hey, have you heard the latest? Our Chairman is leaving.
  B: You must be joking. Who told you?
  A: I **heard it through the grapevine**.
  B: You know you shouldn't believe all those rumors. I'll believe it when I see it.
  A: 嘿，你听到最新消息了吗？我们主任要调走。
  B: 别开玩笑了。谁告诉你的？
  A: 听大伙儿说的。
  B: 你不应该相信这些小道消息。等我看到了我才相信呢。

A: Who told you Tim's getting the Director's job?
B: I **heard it through the grapevine**. I don't remember who said it.
A: 谁告诉你蒂姆要做主任工作的？
B: 听同事说的。我记不得谁说的了。

on speaking terms
关系好，彼此友好（特别是吵架后）

willing to talk and be polite to another, esp. after a quarrel

It is difficult to keep **on speaking terms** with such a person. He is always unhappy and has a very hot temper.

和这种人处好关系是困难的。他总是不高兴，而且脾气还很大。

A: What's wrong? You look upset.
B: I had a quarrel with my girl friend a few days ago. Since our quarrel we haven't been **on speaking terms**. To tell the truth, I'm really ticked off at her.
A: Oh, come on. Let bygones be bygones. Why don't you get in touch with her and talk things over quietly? I'm sure you'll be able to work things out.
A: 怎么了？你看上去好像心事重重。
B: 几天前我和女朋友吵架了。从那以后我们关系一直不好。说实话，对她这种人我简直受不了。
A: 噢，不要这样。过去的事儿就让它过去吧。你应该找找她，和她心平气和地谈谈。我相信你能解决好这个问题。

A: I'm not really **on speaking terms** with my neighbor anymore after that argument we had.
B: What a pity!
A: 自打上次吵架后，我真的不再和邻居说话了。
B: 太遗憾了！

Despite their differences, they have managed to stay **on speaking terms** with each other.

尽管他们有不同见解，他们彼此还是在保持着友好关系。

Unit 14
Leisure Activities
休闲活动

　　Canadians have more time for leisure than our Chinese. Most workers receive two weeks of paid leave each year. The mini-vacation is very popular. People head out of town for a long weekend of four or five days so as to burn up all their holiday time at once.

　　Canada offers vast holiday resources. The average family modus operandi for holidays is to pack the children and a huge amount of luggage into a car or RV (recreational vehicle—a motorized small house with all the comforts of home) and drive thousands of miles.

　　Favorite activities include camping, fishing, and visiting Canadian National Museums and sights. They cross thousands of miles of interprovince while going on their holiday. This kind of traveling is a real exciting time for children. When Canadians go on holiday, they look very much leisure than usual, wearing crazy-patterned shorts, white running shoes, and T-shirts with colorful slogans. They often listen to light music or hum melodious country songs while driving smoothly.

　　Traveling is one of the leisure activities in Canada. Canada is vast and there is enormous variety within its boundaries. Canadians also find it easier and cheaper to travel outside the country, especially to the United States. During the winter, thousands of Canadians flock to warmer climates for vacations. Florida, California, Hawaii and Mexico are popular winter vacation areas.

Each province in Canada has many places for people to enjoy cultural activities. You can visit museums, art galleries, and historical sites. You can also go to plays, musical concerts, operas, and ballets. Some communities have their own special events such as festivals and fairs. Many cities and towns have community centers. They usually have swimming pools, ice rinks, tennis courts, and play grounds. Community centers also have classes in arts and crafts, dancing, physical fitness, and computers.

Most communities have public libraries. You can borrow books, magazines and videotapes. Many libraries have special services for people with disabilities. For example, a library may have the books for blind people. Borrowing books at these public libraries is free. You only need a library card and you can apply for a card at any library.

People in Vancouver, for example, have enjoyed a variety of cultural activities. In honor of the 1958 B. C. centennial, the city built the Maritime Museum.

People, both domestic and foreign visitors, appreciate the historical relics on displays. The Queen Elizabeth Theatre, a civic auditorium, opened in 1959 and many professional theatrical companies mushroomed in the 1960s and 1970s. Vancouver has become a regular stop for touring concert artists and theatrical companies.

Mall shopping has become Canada's biggest leisure activity. This not only includes shopping in physical stores, but also encompasses people's spending on dining and entertainment in malls. More and more Canadians are becoming enthusiastic about the integrated shopping experience, which involves online shopping followed by offline pickup and entertainment at malls.

There're lots of bookshops, restaurants and stores downtown. You may also consider exploring Chinatown, where many of the buildings have undergone consistent renovations in recent years. The community has taken pride in refurbishing the area. The area consists of many restaurants, and retail stores. At night the area comes to life, and no matter what time of year there is always something to do.

译 文

和我们中国人相比,加拿大人有更多的闲暇时间。大多数上班职员每年有两个星期的带薪假期,短期度假非常普及。人们会在周末离开所在城市四五天,这样就不会把假期一次用尽。

加拿大有丰富的假日资源,一般家庭的度假方法是把孩子和鼓鼓的行囊塞进汽车或者房车(一种活动的小房子,里面有各种家庭日用品),开上几千英里。

加拿大人最喜欢的活动包括野营、钓鱼、参观国家博物馆和风景名胜。要进行这些活动就得穿越几千英里的省际公路,这种旅游对于孩子们很是刺激。每当他们要出去旅游,加拿大人看上去可像那么回事,穿上花色奇异的短裤、白色的旅游鞋、带有五颜六色口号的T恤衫。他们潇洒地开着车,播放着美妙的音乐或哼哼着乡村歌曲。

旅行是加拿大人的休闲活动之一。加拿大幅员辽阔,景色各种各样。加拿大人还认为出国旅行既容易且经济,特别是前往美国。在冬季,成千上万的加拿大人都聚集到温暖的地方度假。佛罗里达、加利福尼亚、夏威夷和墨西哥都是冬季度假的好去处。

加拿大每个省份都有许多地方供人们参与文化活动。你可以参观博物馆、画廊和历史遗迹,还可以看戏剧,听音乐会、歌剧和欣赏芭蕾。有些社区有自己专门的活动,比如节日庆典和交易会。许多城镇都有社区中心,设有游泳池、溜冰场、网球场和运动场。社区中心还有涉及工艺、舞蹈、健身和电脑方面的课程。

大部分社区建有公共图书馆,人们可以借阅书籍、杂志和录影带。许多图书馆还为残疾人提供专门服务,例如提供盲文书籍。在公共图书馆借书是免费的。在任何一个图书馆借书,你只需办理一张借书证就可以了。

举例来说,生活在温哥华的人们就参与了各种各样的文化活动。为了庆祝1958年不列颠哥伦比亚省成立一百周年,温哥华建立了海洋博物馆。

国人和外宾都可以欣赏历史遗迹。1959年开放的伊丽莎白女王剧院是一个大众剧场。在20世纪60年代和70年代,许多专业戏剧公司如雨后春笋般地涌现。旅行音乐家和戏剧公司已经是温哥华的常客了。

商场购物已经成为加拿大人最大的休闲活动。这不仅包括在实体店购物,也包括人们在商场餐饮和娱乐上的花费。越来越多的加拿大人开始热衷于复合式购物体验,即通过互联网购物后到线下商场取货和娱乐。

市中心有很多书店、饭馆和商场,你可能还有兴趣看看中国城。现在在唐人街看到的许多建筑都是近年来不断翻新的。当地的人们为整修这些地区倍感自豪。这里有很多饭馆和零售店。到了晚上这里更是生机焕发,不论在哪个季节来到这里,都会有休闲活动等着你参加。

Dialogue

They Were Absolutely Breathtaking

(After a day's tour of Vancouver City, Naomi and her Chinese friend Li are in the car going back home.)

Li: Great day! There is just so much to see and so little time.

Naomi: Well, you know what they say— "Time files when you're having fun." We did have fun today, didn't we?

Li: Oh, it was fascinating. Vancouver is so beautiful. I like the styles of the buildings, both contemporary and historic. I enjoyed the natural beauty of the city. And the peaceful forests, those mountain views—they *were* absolutely *breathtaking*.

Naomi: Well, sightseeing can be such a *hit-or-miss* thing. Next time I'd like to take you to some specific places, not just wander around aimlessly. By the way, did you enjoy the SeaBus and Skytrain today?

Li: Oh, yes! Out of this world. That was my first time to take the SeaBus.

Naomi: And I noticed that you sat inside the SeaBus like a *seasoned traveler*, taking pictures, making some notes, and all the usual touristy things.

Li: I did take some pictures of the scenery. By the way, Naomi, could you drop me downtown? I'll get those pictures developed. I also want to take a look at the night life of the city.

Naomi: OK, no problem. I'll drop you near the Vancouver Art Gallery and then you could *do some browsing* on your own. There're lots of bookshops, restaurants and stores downtown. You may also want to take a look at Chinatown located near Gastown. Many of the structures now seen in Chinatown were built in recent years. The community has taken pride in refurbishing the area. The area consists of many restaurants, and retail stores. At night the area comes to life, and no matter what time of year there is always something to do.

Li: Sounds interesting. I'll browse in Chinatown, anyway.

Naomi: I'm going to my mom's. I'll *pick you up* at 7:00 in front of the Kentucky Fried Chicken restaurant, and then we'll go to the movies.

Li: Got the tickets yet?
Naomi: Not yet. There's still plenty of time.
Li: You'd better buy them right now or we'll *miss the boat.*
Naomi: Never mind. I'm sure we'll be able to get the tickets.

Vocabulary and Notes

- contemporary — modern 当代的
- absolutely — definitely 一定，肯定地
- aimlessly — without any purpose; lacking intention 无目标地；无目的地
- SeaBus — a passenger ferry between Vancouver and North Vancouver 水上汽车
- Skytrain — 空中列车
- touristy — (a slang) adjective form of "tourist" （俚）tourist的形容词：吸引很多游客的
- get pictures developed — 扩印照片
- Vancouver Art Gallery — 温哥华美术馆
- Kentucky Fried Chicken restaurant — Most of the KFC in North America are small, some without even tables. They provide with take-out service primarily. 肯德基炸鸡店

Idioms for Everyday Use

be breathtaking — be exciting or wonderful
大为惊讶的，令人激动的

A: It is a great pity that you didn't have the opportunity to travel Huangshan Mountain. The beauty of the sunrise **is** really **breathtaking**.
B: I'm planning on going there in the summer vacation after finishing my paper.
A: 你没有机会去游览黄山，真是太可惜了。日出的美真是令人心旷神怡。
B: 我计划写完论文以后暑假去。

We were traveling at **breathtaking** speed on the highway.

我们在高速公路上飞速疾驰。

hit-or-miss (adj. & adv.) (hit or miss)
随便的/地；马虎的/地；漫无目的的/地 | haphazard; careless; aimless

David didn't know which cassette had the songs by Michael Jackson, so he began playing the record anyway, trying the cassette **hit-or-miss**.

大卫不知道迈克尔·杰克逊唱的歌在哪盘唱片上，因此他就无目的地听着找。

A: Shall we go and visit the antique shop near the Cultural Street?

B: I don't like the **hit-or-miss** traveling. Let's stay here for a while.

A: 我们去参观文化街附近的古玩店好吗？

B: 我不喜欢漫无目的地游逛。我们就在这儿待一会儿吧。

seasoned traveler
有经验的旅游者 | experienced traveler

By the look of his traveling bag, he must be a **seasoned traveler**.

瞧瞧他的旅行包，便知他是个旅游老手。

It could turn your vacation into a tragedy if you're not a **seasoned traveler**.

如果你对旅行毫不在行，那么你的假期就可能过得不愉快。

do some browsing (browse v.)
浏览，随便翻阅 | look around without a specific purpose; wander in a casual unhurried way

A: Do you have a map of the city? I'd like to **do some browsing** on my own.

B: Sorry, I don't have a map, but I have a tourist brochure.

A: 你有这个城市的地图吗？我想亲自浏览一下。

B: 对不起，我没有这个城市的地图，但我有一本旅游手册。

She **browses** a while, and then picks up a sports magazine.

她随便翻阅了一会儿，然后便拿起一份体育杂志。

pick someone up
（车辆等）中途搭人，开车接某人 | stop driving and take someone when he wants to go

A: We can take the bus home when the yoga class is over.

B: No, I told my brother to come and **pick me up**.

A: 瑜伽学习班结束后我们可以坐公共汽车回家。

B: 不，我告诉我哥哥了，让他来接我。

I'll **pick you up** in front of the English Department Building.

我开车到英语系楼门前接你。

miss the boat
错过机会

miss the chance

A: Hi, Paul's still house-hunting?

B: Yes, but not very successfully. I guess he really **missed the boat** when he didn't buy that house in Ottawa.

A: 嗨,保尔还在为房子奔波吗?

B: 是的,但不是十分顺利。我想他没买下在渥太华的那所房子,真是错过了好机会。

A: I hear you want to take some coffee to China. Now coffee is on sale. Three jars for the price of one! Hurry up! Don't **miss the boat**!

B: Terrific! Thanks for the info and I'm going right away.

A: 我听说你想带些咖啡回中国。现在正促销咖啡,花一瓶的钱买三瓶!赶快去!不要错过这个机会!

B: 太棒了!谢谢你的消息,我马上就去。

A: Hello my friend! You look unhappy today. What's up?

B: Well, I'm very stupid that I have **missed the boat** this time. I forgot to buy the ticket yesterday and I cannot enjoy the concert tonight. I feel like I'm always a step behind.

A: Take it easy. There must be some other chances. Be ready to seize the opportunity when it comes.

A: 嘿,老朋友!你看上去不高兴啊,有什么心事吗?

B: 嗨,我真傻啊,我错过了机会。我忘记了昨天买票,今天晚上我享受不了音乐会了。总觉得我比别人慢半拍。

A: 别着急。还会有机会的。时刻准备着,只要机会再来,你准能抓住。

Unit 15
Looking for a Job
找工作

In Canada, almost everyone looks for a job at some time. Finding a job can be difficult and it can take time. If you want a job, you can begin by looking in the newspaper. You can also find companies in the yellow pages of the telephone book and phone them to see if they have openings. If you find an opening, you will have to go for a job interview. At an interview, it is important to be prepared and to make a good impression. The most important document a person needs when looking for work in Canada is a social insurance card, which shows the person's Social Insurance Number. Employers are required by law to ask for this number.

Canadians feel that what they do for a living is extremely important. A job often determines social standing in the community, and the amount of money earned often defines lifestyle.

Canadian people do not have registrations of residency, personal records or files. On what basis does the government or private company hire applications for positions? How would one know anything about the job applicant's history without such a file? The employees tend to rely on personal resume and personal interviews. In general, the new employer does not survey the applicant's entire record of previous performance item by item. Sometimes, a telephone inquiry suffices. And if a person has changed jobs or places several times, the employer won't take the time to investigate all of them. The key to getting and keeping a job is ability. It makes no difference if you fabricate your resume. When you apply for a job, the employees value your ability and your outstanding achievements highly. Your "bright history" won't help you at all if you do not have the ability to do the job well.

If you want to have a job in important government departments—such as the Ministry of Defense; the Ministry of Foreign Affairs or the Judicial Department—you have to undergo a background investigation. However, the job applicant must sign a trust deed document which authorizes the check, declaring that as a part of the application process and the employee gives the employer the right to investigate. Without the declaration, even the Prime Minister of Canada has no right to run a background check on a Canadian citizen.

If a person who once violated the law wants a job but is refused because of his record, he has the right to sue the employer. According to Canadian legal principles, once a person is released from prison, he or she should have the same rights as others since he has paid for his criminal behavior by serving his prison term. In Canada, if someone wants to start a new life and does not want others to know about his or her past, it is a good idea for the person to move to another place to look for a job.

Besides earning a living and having social standing, Canadians generally want to get ahead and be successful in their chosen fields. Such is the "work ethic" prevalent in Canadian society. This traditional attitude in Canada still holds for many people. They believe if they work hard, they can find success for themselves and their families.

Traditionally, sons followed in their fathers' footsteps when choosing an occupation and daughters became housewives and mothers. But today, Canadians have many career choices available to them and many change careers often in a lifetime. A job may become obsolete because of changing technology, for example, and a person then has to be retrained. In the changing society no job is secure.

Although Canada is the land of liberty in which each individual has rights, the mere availability of those rights does not guarantee an easy life. Each individual must struggle for a good education. Each must struggle for financial freedom, and each must struggle for a good job. There are course to teach you how to look for a job. There are also job-training courses. In many of these programs, you are paid while you learn new skills. Many credentials from other countries are acceptable in Canada. To get a job or more education, your certificates may have to be translated and evaluated.

译文

在加拿大，几乎总是有人在找工作。找到一份工作可能很困难并且需要时间。如果你需要一份工作，可以先从报纸上寻找，也可以在电话簿的黄页上寻找公司的信息，然后给他们打电话，看看是否有空缺职位。如果有，你要参加面试。面试的准备工作很重要，以便给对方留下好印象。在加拿大，一个人在找工作的过程中最重要的文件就是社会保险卡，上面显示有此人的社保号码。按法律要求，雇主要确认这个号码。

加拿大人认为，找到什么样的工作是非常重要的，工作通常决定社会地位，薪水通常决定生活方式。

加拿大人没有档案。那么，政府机关和公司老板根据什么来雇用求职者呢？没有档案怎么了解某人过去的履历呢？加拿大公司老板主要看个人简历和面试。一般说来，老板并不去原单位一项一项地调查之前的整个工作表现，至多打个电话问问。如果一个人换了好几个单位，老板根本不会长时间调查的。一个人能否保得住职务，关键看能力。在求职中伪造了履历无所谓，雇主更看重的是你的能力和光辉业绩。如果没本事，"光辉的历史"一点也帮不了忙，照样会被解雇。

如果想在国防部、外交部或司法部这类国家重要机关求职，那就要接受调查。但只有在求职者写一份可以调查自己的授权书，声明是为了求职，该部门才能有权去调查某人的背景。如果没有本人的授权书，国家总理也无权随便调查某人的背景。

如果有"前科"的人想求职，却被老板以"前科"为由拒之门外，他便有权起诉老板。按照法律，一个刑满释放分子已经为罪行付出了服刑的代价，那么出狱后在找工作方面便应享受与别人相同的权利。在加拿大，如果一个人想开始新的生活，又不想让别人知道自己的历史，换个地方去找工作往往奏效。

除了挣钱和拥有社会地位以外，加拿大人一般都希望他们可以在自己的领域里领先和成功，这就是加拿大社会盛行的职业道德标准。这种传统观念仍然束缚着许多人，他们相信只要工作努力就可以为自己和家庭带来成功。

从前在选择职业时，儿子通常要步父亲的后尘，而女儿则成为家庭主妇和母亲。而如今，加拿大人有许多职业可供选择，而且很多加拿大人一生当中还会更换很多职业。比如，一份工作可能因为技术变革而过时，这个人就必须接受再次培训。在这个不断变化的社会中，是不存在"铁饭碗"的。

虽然加拿大是个自由国度，每个人都有权利，但这些权利并不能保证舒适的生活。每个人都要特别努力争取得到良好教育、经济自主和一份不错的工作。加拿大有专门讲授如何找工作的课程，还有如何找工作的培训课程。在许多这样的项目中，你在学习技能的同时还可以获得报酬。加拿大认可其他国家的很多证书。如果你求职或求学，你的各种证书可能需要翻译和评估。

This Job Gets Me Down

(Kelly is back from her work. She looks unhappy.)

Li: Did you have a good time today?

Kelly: Oh, no, Li, my job is really starting to **get me down**. I just don't feel inspired about it anymore. I'm tired out after the long hours of work all day.

Li: I thought you liked working in that computer center.

Kelly: I did. I thought it was a decent job as a technician. But now with the long hours of typing work, it's starting to **get to me**. Our vice manager is so demanding. Almost every day he asks me to type the reports or memos. I suddenly realized that I'm working as a typist.

Li: You told me you would talk to him over lunch today.

Kelly: No way. He talked so much. **I couldn't get a word in edgewise**.

Li: Then you should try to talk to your manager.

Kelly: I don't see the manager very often. He is always **on the road**.

Li: Well, there is no sense in just **griping about** it. You should try to find another job. I'm sure there are lots of jobs you'd be good at.

Kelly: Thanks, Li. I'll see if I can find out about other jobs. I've always enjoyed working with people and I **have a good head for** mathematics and statistics.

Li: Then why don't you apply for a job as a clerk in a bank?

Kelly: I actually went to Royal Bank of Canada and also CIBC, but unfortunately, the bank is in the process of **laying off** people.

Li: Why don't you *look into* counselling services? They must have a position that would utilize your computer skills.

Kelly: You're probably right. I'll go there tomorrow.

Li: Cheer up, Kelly. Don't lose heart.

Kelly: I feel much better now. Thank you for your comfort. You know, Li, a well-paying job for these currently in the work force is getting harder to find. Those who have not been exposed to computers and other new methods of communication are even harder to find jobs.

Li: Well, try, try, never say die. I feel confident that you can find a good job.

Vocabulary and Notes

feel inspired about (something)	对……产生希望或信心
be tired out	completely exhausted 精疲力竭
computer center	计算机中心
decent job	体面的工作，令人满意的工作
Our vice manager is so demanding.	我们的副经理要求过高。
memo (= memorandum)	备忘录
mathematics	数学
statistics	统计学
Royal Bank of Canada	加拿大皇家银行，是加拿大的商业银行，总行在蒙特利尔。1869年成立，原名哈利法克斯商人银行，1901年取现名。1903~1981年间，除了创建伦敦加拿大皇家银行外，曾有过多次兼并与联合。20世纪初收购了几家古巴的银行。国外有附属银行和联号。
CIBC (Canadian Imperial Bank of Commerce)	加拿大帝国商业银行，是加拿大主要的商业银行，办理国内外业务，总行在多伦多。1858年成立的时候叫加拿大银行，1867年改组为加拿大商业银行。1961年加拿大商业银行和加拿大帝国银行（1875年建立）合并后改为现名。后来陆续吸收了许多小银行，并在外国的许多投资公司中持有股份。
in (the) process of	正在……之中；在进行中

- counseling service 咨询服务处
- utilize / utilise　　make use of; find a use for 使有用；可利用

Idioms for Everyday Use

| **get someone down** 使沮丧；使情绪低落；使某人不高兴 | depress or discourage someone; make someone unhappy |

- It isn't just the work that **gets her down**.
  并不仅仅是工作才使她情绪低落。
- Don't let the low marks **get you down**. Try again next time.
  不必为低分沮丧，下次再争取。

| **get to someone** 对某人产生影响或令人厌烦 | affect or bother someone |

- A: How do you like the concert?
  B: Marvelous! This music really **got to me**.
  A: 音乐会怎么样啊？
  B: 太棒了！这音乐确实使我激动。
- The daily work of the eight to five routine is starting to **get to me**.
  我对每天上午八点到下午五点的工作开始感到厌烦。
- A: The only music I like is rock'n'roll.
  B: What? You must be joking. That's terrible music. It really **gets to me**.
  A: 我唯一喜欢的音乐就是摇滚乐。
  B: 什么？你一定在开玩笑。那种音乐糟透了，实在令人讨厌。

| **can't get a word in edgewise** 没有说话的机会 | don't have a chance to say anything because someone else is talking so much |

- A: Then why didn't you tell Tom that you couldn't go to the cottage with him this summer?
  B: Jim talked all evening to Tom without stopping. I **couldn't get a word in edgewise**!
  A: 那么你为什么不告诉汤姆今年你不能跟他一起去别墅呢？
  B: 吉姆和汤姆整个晚上不停地说。我插不上话！
- A: Well, did the boss approve your request?
  B: Oh, no, he was busy talking to the secretary—he went on and on for at least half an hour.

I tried to interrupt a couple of times but I **couldn't get a word in edgewise**. After a while I just stood up and left.

A: 老板答应你的请求了吗?

B: 噢,没有。他一直忙着和秘书谈话——至少不停地说了半小时。我几次试图打断他们,可我根本插不上嘴。过了一会儿,我只好起身离去。

A: Did you explain your new idea to the manager over dinner?

B: No way. He talked so much I **couldn't get a word in edgewise**.

A: 吃饭的时候你向经理解释你的新想法了吗?

B: 根本不可能。他滔滔不绝,都没有我讲话的机会。

on the road
在旅行中(尤指经商) | traveling, usually for business

I was stiff after seven hours **on the road**.
长途旅行七小时后,我的腿脚不灵活了。

He's been **on the road** and seldom stays with his family.
他一直在出差推销商品,很少和家人团聚。

gripe about
抱怨 | keep on complaining about something

Don't pay any attention to him; he's always **griping about** something or other.
别管他,他总是抱怨这抱怨那的。

Students get together sometimes to **gripe about** the food in their cafeteria.
学生有时聚在一起抱怨自助食堂的伙食。

have a head for
擅长;有天分(一般指在数学上或算术上) | be good at or talented in (usually used with mathematics or arithmetic)

That boy **has a good head for** mathematics. He won the championship in the national mathematics competition.
那个男孩是个数学尖子生。他在全国数学竞赛中获得了冠军。

A: Could you help me with this cubic equation?

B: You asked the wrong person. I don't **have a head for** mathematics.

A: 你能帮我解出这道三次方程题吗?

B: 你问错人了。我没有数学头脑。

lay off (someone)
解雇（尤指短暂地）

dismiss or put out of work temporarily (generally because of lack of work)

- A: Was William serious when he said the company's going to **lay off** a couple of hundred men?
  B: Don't believe everything William tells you. You should take what he says with a grain of salt.
  A: 威廉说的公司准备暂时解雇200人是真的吗？
  B: 不要事事听威廉的话。他说的不可全信。
- During this season of the year they often **lay off** many workers at that plant.
  每年的这个季节里，那个工厂常常解雇许多工人。

look into
到某处做短暂访问；到某处去一会儿

(in this context) make a brief call to try to find information in (something); enter (a house, etc.)

- I'll **look into** the library on the way home to find out more information about Canadian literature.
  回家路上，我要去一趟图书馆，以便找出更多的有关加拿大文学的资料。
- Yesterday we **looked into** Tianjin University of Technology, and the students taking the joint program Business Administration are all burying themselves in their study.
  昨天我们顺便走访了天津理工大学，那些注册合作办学的工商管理专业学生都在埋头读书。

Unit 16
Friendliness
友善

Canadian people have a lively disposition, intelligent, hardworking, reasonable open-minded, usually spontaneous, friendly open, and enjoy meeting new people. Foreign people once lived in Canada are especially impressed by the Canadian witty remarks and humorous jokes.

Canadians are willing to help strangers. They will be most happy to lead you a hand if you have difficulties. If you have English language obstacles in study, Canadian students may give you English coach free of charge. When I studied English in Canada, Canadian students organized the tutoring team and gave us English coaching twice a week, and they never concerned about the pay.

Canadians have strong feelings about proximity, responsibilities, and obligations associated with being a neighbor. Neighbors should be friendly, helpful and agreeable; cut their lawns, look after their plants while the neighbors go away.

However, they are not expected to interact with each other socially unless they have a real desire to do so. On the whole, they do not pry into the others' private affairs.

Canadians are also modest and modesty makes it easier for them to get along well with the people in the world. In the world family of nations, Canadians have friendly and harmonious relations with most developing countries. That is an illustration that Canadians do not have the arrogance, which characterizes those from a superpower.

Most Canadians appreciate your honesty. Therefore if you have a problem with your work, either with the long hours, the unsatisfactory working conditions or with other employees, you should discuss the situation privately with your supervisor as soon as possible. This is the Canadian way to address such problems directly.

If you have a poor relationship with a fellow worker, it is the best way to approach him or her first and try to settle the problem independently. Do not discuss the problems with the boss unless you cannot solve them.

It is very important for you to get along with your colleagues. If you want to make your point and you really do not want to hurt your colleagues, you should listen to what they are saying. Try to find out if there are things you can both agree on, particularly important things rather than details. Admit clearly and readily when you are wrong. Express through your behavior as well as your words that you respect them even if you don't agree with them.

In Canada, there are lots of warm-hearted volunteers. They work for no pay and served voluntarily. These volunteers are from all walks of life, but most of them are retired people. Volunteers provide various services—providing necessary information to "International Visitors", directing the streets traffic lights in the countryside, guiding visitors under the burning sun, being narrators in various museums and galleries.

The communities in which, volunteers serve are recorded in a registration book in each city and locality. If someone needs help, he or she and the volunteer can be matched by this sort of "bridge". If a blind person cannot read a letter, a high school student may read for him or her after school; if an elderly lady's house is run-down, someone might come to do some painting over the weekend.

The reason that the volunteers like to do these sorts of good deeds is that they get happiness from it. It is said that happiness is the reward of them in soul. Besides the pleasure, other benefits are realized. Elderly persons no longer feel lonely and young people acquire life experiences.

In Canada, there is a sufficient network of non-governmental volunteers. Their presence and activity make people, especially foreigners and new immigrants feel a certain warmth for and closeness to each other. If people have the opportunities to go to Canada or you do not know anyone there, you can write to the local volunteer organization. The organization will arrange to meet you in the airport, take you to the hotel, help you contact with the places in which you are interested. On the whole, Canadian people are friendly, hospitable, selfless, and truthful and give disinterested assistance permeated.

译文

加拿大人生性活泼、聪明、勤奋、善于接受新思想，通常自然、坦诚而且愿意结交新朋友。尤其是在加拿大居住过的人，一般都对加拿大人有较好的印象，加拿大人说话的风趣幽默让你捧腹大笑。

加拿大人乐于帮助陌生人。如果你有困难，他们都非常愿意拉你一把。假如你在学习中遇到英语语言方面的困难，加拿大的学生可能会为你免费辅导英语。我在加拿大学习英语期间，加拿大学生自愿组织成"辅导队伍"，给我们进行每周两次的英语辅导，而且他们从来不计报酬。

加拿大人有强烈的亲切感、责任感和职责意识。邻居们和睦相处，互相帮助，而且感情融洽。邻居外出时，他们会帮忙除草，照看种植的花草。

然而，加拿大人不会在社交方面互相干涉，除非他们真想那么做。总的来说，他们不会探察别人的隐私。

加拿大人还很谦虚，这使得他们与世界各地的人们都能融洽相处。在全世界范围内，加拿大人与大多数发展中国家关系和睦，这说明加拿大人并不以大国自居而傲慢不逊。

加拿大人多数崇尚诚实的品格。因此，如果你在工作上有问题，不管是工作时间过长、工作环境不尽人意还是与同事关系不好，你自己应该尽快私下与你的主管沟通。这是加拿大人处理此类问题最直接的方法。

如果你与某个同事关系不是很好，首先要同他/她接触，然后想办法自己解决与同事的关系，这是最好的办法。除非你自己解决不了，才需要和老板谈这个问题。

与同事融洽相处是非常重要的。如果你想表明自己的观点但又不想伤害他人，你必须听取他们的意见，试着找出你们的共识，尤其是重点而不是细节问题。当你出了差错时，要主动地、坦诚地承认。即使你和他人意见不统一，也要通过言语和行动表示对他们的尊重。

在加拿大，你能接触到许多热心肠的志愿者。他们工作不计报酬，纯属义务。这些志愿者来自各个阶层，但以退休的老人居多。这些志愿者服务的内容多种多样：给国际友人提供必要信息；在乡村指挥交通；顶着烈日给友人引路；在许多不同的博物馆、美术馆做义务讲解员。

每个城市和地区的社区志愿者的登记册中，记录了每个人乐于提供的服务项目。一旦有需求者，工作人员便为他们搭桥。如果一个盲人读不了信，一个高中生放学后便去他家代读；一位孤寡老人的房子破旧了，周末时候便会有人到他家将房子粉刷一新。

志愿者们如此地喜欢做好事的动机是他们能从中得到快乐。他们常说，快乐便是他们精神上的所得。除此还有别的所得，那就是老年人不再孤独，年轻人也可以从中获得人生经验。

在加拿大，有一个高效的发自民间的志愿者网。他们的存在和活动使得人与人之间增添了温馨，特别是对外国人和新移民。如果人们有机会去加拿大旅游，又无亲无故，便可以写信给该地的志愿者组织。他们会到机场接你，带你联系旅馆，按你的兴趣联系要参观的场所。总的来说，加拿大人和善友好，热情好客，无私奉献，诚实可靠，总是伸出援助之手。

Dialogue

We're on the Same Wave-length

(Kelly comes home from his work. His Chinese friend, Li, is talking to him.)

Li: How are you getting along with your new supervisor?

Kelly: Just great! We cooperate well with each other. He's got some really modern ideas about how to organize the work. What impresses me most is that he manages to *cut through the red tape* and get things done very fast.

Li: Sounds like you two are *on the same wave-length*.

Kelly: Right! He is a knowledgeable person and had lots of experience on computers. We are going to do a research program together. *I'm high on* this work because this is the way life is going to be in the future.

Li: I'm glad to hear that. It sounds like the new supervisor has a different working style from the former one.

Kelly: Definitely. The former supervisor lacked sincerity. He sometimes only *paid lip service to* some work. But the new one does what he says. In fact, he's doing all the things I always said we should be doing. He's set an example for our staff, and we're *following suit*. He *takes great pains* with everything he does.

Li: Do you have to work overtime as you did in that computer center before?

Kelly: Not at all. The supervisor takes care of the unfinished work. He always stays behind at the end of the day. I don't have to rush, rush, and rush all the time as I did before. It's a nice change from *the rat race*.

Li: I wish you success. Remember we'll dine out this weekend after you get your bonus.

Kelly: I won't forget. How about McDonald's?

Li: Great! I've never been there.

Vocabulary and Notes

- supervisor — someone who directs or watches over the work; boss 管理人员，上司；老板
- cooperate — work or act together in order to bring about a result 合作；相配合
- What impresses me most is that ... — 给我印象最深的是……
- knowledgeable — well informed; knowing a great deal 有见识的；知识渊博的
- research program — 科研项目
- be different from ... — 与……不同
- sincerity — truthfulness, honesty 真诚，诚意
- staff — （全体）工作人员；（全体）职员
- computer center — 计算机中心
- stay behind — remain behind; remain at a place after others have left; keep behind 留下来；别人离开后仍留在原地
- bonus — payment in addition to what is usual 奖金

Idioms for Everyday Use

cut through the red tape
摆脱烦琐的、浪费时间的手续或公文；简化拖拉的公事

avoid bureaucracy; refuse to use official methods which waste time and effort; shorten official procedures

He managed to **cut through the red tape** and get me a new passport in a matter of hours

instead of the usual two weeks.
他设法摆脱了烦琐的手续，只用了几小时而不是通常要用的两周时间就为我拿到了护照。

- We don't have time to go through the proper procedure; let's **cut through the red tape** and take your request right to the director.
我们没时间例行公事，让我们摒弃官僚作风，把你的要求直接反映给主任。

on the same wave-length (on the different wave-length)
两人趣味（不）相投；观点（不）一致；互相非常（不）了解；（没）有共同语言

two people have the same sort of ideas and share the same interests and understand each other very well

- A: I hear Peter is also working in your company. Getting along well with him?
  B: Well, Peter and I have been working **on the same wave-length**.
  A: 我听说彼得和你在同一个公司工作。你们俩相处得怎么样啊？
  B: 哦，我们俩工作上很协调。

- Nowadays, many young people and their parents are not **on the same wave-length**.
眼下，许多年轻人和他们的父母格格不入。

be high on
对……极感兴趣；热衷于；非常喜欢某物/某人

be enthusiastic about something; like something or someone very much

- I'**m high on** my new job.
我对新工作非常感兴趣。

- She'**s high on** you. Don't you know that?
她非常喜欢你。你难道不知道吗？

pay lip service to
只是口头上表示赞成或支持

show support by words only and not by actions

- I agree with your opinion, but it's not enough to **pay lip service to** that project. They've got to do something about it.
我赞同你的观点，但只是口头上支持那个项目是不够的。他们应该拿出些行动来。

- He only **pays lip service to** our research program. He didn't even give us permission to use the lab.
他对我们的科研项目只是口头上支持。他甚至不允许我们使用实验室。

follow suit
效仿某人；以某人为榜样，跟着做 | do as someone else has done; follow someone's example

- If you're going there on foot, I think I'll **follow suit**.
  如果你步行去那儿，我想我也步行去吧。
- When the foreign guest came into the classroom, the professor stood up, and all the students immediately **followed suit**.
  外国客人走进教室时，教授站了起来，所有的学生也都马上跟着起立。

take pains/trouble
费心，费力；下功夫做某事 | make a great effort to do something; work carefully and conscientiously

- She **took great pains** making the garment because it was to be her wedding dress.
  她不辞辛苦地做成了那件衣服，因为那是她的结婚礼服。
- We're very grateful to you for **taking so much trouble** to make us comfortable here.
  您如此费心地为我们在这儿做了舒适的安排，我们非常感谢。

the rat race
为获得成功而进行的疯狂竞争；激烈竞争的地方 | the way of life of people competing fiercely with each other to be successful; busy and competitive work place

- He got so tired of **the rat race** that he left his job and came to China to teach.
  他对社会上的你争我夺非常烦恼，因而放弃了他的工作来到中国教学。
- We're all living in **the rat race**.
  我们都生活在激烈的竞争中。
- A: You had a nice job at the university. I just don't understand why you've joined **the rat race** and got involved in the money market.
  B: I think that's very exciting. I enjoy working with the business people.
  A: 你在大学里的工作轻松而体面。我不明白你为什么要下海从商，卷入到你争我夺的竞争中去。
  B: 我认为这样做很刺激。我喜欢和商人打交道。
- A: I haven't seen Manager Sun lately. Do you have any ideas where he is now?
  B: Well, he got tired of **the rat race** in the city and went to the countryside to start his new business.
  A: 我最近没有见到孙经理。你知道他现在在哪儿吗？
  B: 呃，他厌倦了城里的激烈竞争，到乡下开拓新事业去了。

Unit 17
Fitness Craze
健身热

Over the past twenty years or so, health and fitness have become increasingly popular in Canada. Everyone wants to live a longer and healthier life. There has been a lot of research about how to eat healthier and exercise better. There are lots of TV shows, magazines, health food stories and gyms, all associated with health and fitness.

Eating healthy food and getting exercise is very popular with people in their forties and fifties. People that are this age want to protect themselves from heart attacks, cancer, and other diseases. They want to wake up each day with more energy and live a longer life.

In the Canadian culture, there is a lot of emphasis on body image. Young men want to look very strong with hard abs, a big chest, abroad shoulders, and a slim waist. To achieve this look, many young men go to the gym and lift weights, eat a low-fat diet with lots of protein, and play sports or go running. Young girls want to have a "Britney Spears Look". This look involves small waists, tight legs, and thin arms. Like young men, many girls participate in some physical clubs and do as much sports as possible to lose fat.

Canadians, like all people, enjoy participating in, and watching a variety of athletic activities. Some of the sports include running, swimming, golf, tennis, skiing, boating, hiking, fishing and mountain climbing and so on.

Golf is an expensive sport. You need special shoes, golf clubs and golf balls.

The green fee for playing each time can be easily 30-40 per person. With a free golf course in some apartment complexes you can learn how to play golf easily.

Canadians have become very health-conscious. Most cities and towns have community centers. They usually have swimming pools, ice rinks, tennis courts and playground. Many community centers also have classes in arts and crafts, dancing and physical fitness. With the fitness craze, sports and fitness clubs have also become popular and many join them not only for exercise, but also to meet people. The government is also encouraging the fitness craze, continuing a program started in the 1970s that had the slogan: "Participation."

Canadians are learning that a healthier lifestyle leads to fewer medical problems. Heart disease and cancer are only two of the major diseases that have been linked to diet and lack of exercise. In addition to a renewed interest in health, Canadians enjoy the benefit of a national health care plan. As a result, the quality of health care in Canada is often considered to be among the best in the world.

According to the Survey (2021), 20.1 million Canadians (62% of those aged 12 and over) are physically active in their leisure time; walking is a favorite activity, followed by bicycling, swimming, jogging and gardening.

Active Canadians are more likely to be young. Males in Canada are fitter than females and the young are generally fitter than the old. Concern for becoming and staying fit is increasingly important to Canadians. Interest is reflected in all age groups, but involvement in physical activity by people 60 years of age and over has increased 3 times faster than that of younger generation over the past few years.

Canada's national health-insurance program (also called Medicare) is designed to ensure that every resident of Canada receives medical care and hospital treatment, the cost of which is paid through general taxes or through compulsory heath-insurance premiums.

译 文

在过去的大约20年时间里，加拿大人越来越重视保健和健身。每个人都想生活得更加健康长寿。他们一直在研究怎样饮食更健康、怎样锻炼更好。许多电视节目、杂志、健康饮食新闻报道和体育课，都是关于健康和健身的。

Unit 17　Fitness Craze 健身热

40岁和50岁年龄段的人们非常讲究健康饮食和适当锻炼，以预防心脏病、癌症和其他一些疾病。他们希望的是每天醒来精力充沛，并且可以长寿。

在加拿大文化里，他们很重视身体塑形。年轻的小伙子希望有结实的腹肌、发达的胸肌、宽阔的肩膀和窄细的腰身，使他们看起来非常强壮。为了使自己有这种外形，许多年轻小伙子去体育馆进行举重锻炼，吃高蛋白低脂肪的食物，坚持跑步并做其他一些运动。年轻的女孩们也希望自己拥有健美的身条，比如说，纤细的腰、修长的腿和细瘦的胳膊。像那些小伙子一样，这些女孩子也参加一些健身俱乐部，尽可能多地运动以减少脂肪。

加拿大人，和所有人一样，热衷于参与和观看各种体育活动，包括跑步、游泳、高尔夫、网球、滑雪、划船、远足、钓鱼和登山等等。

打高尔夫球是一项高消费的运动。你要有特殊的鞋、球杆和球。场地费每人每次要30~40加元。有的公寓园内有免费的高尔夫球场，在那里你很容易学会打高尔夫球。

加拿大人非常注重身体健康，许多城市和乡镇都有社区中心，设有游泳池、溜冰场、网球场和操场。许多社区中心还有涉及艺术与工艺、舞蹈和健身的课程。随着健身热的到来，健身俱乐部也越来越受欢迎，很多人加入健身俱乐部不仅是为了锻炼，还为了结交朋友。政府也支持健身热，从20世纪70年代开始一直进行一个名为"重在参与"的项目。

加拿大人懂得，健康的生活方式可以减少得病的概率。心脏病和癌症是两种与饮食和缺乏运动相关的主要疾病。除了他们自己在保健方面产生新的兴趣外，加拿大人还受益于国家卫生保健计划。因此，加拿大的保健质量经常被认为是世界上最好的。

统计数字（2021）显示，2010万加拿大人（占12岁及以上人口的62%）在业余时间喜欢运动，其中散步是最受欢迎的活动，其后依次是骑单车、游泳、慢跑和做园艺。

活跃的加拿大人更喜欢活得年轻。男性通常比女性健康，年轻人比老年人健康。如何关注健康和怎样保持健康对加拿大人来说是越来越重要了。不同年龄层的人都有侧重，但是这几年来，60及60岁以上参与运动的人的增长速度是年轻人的三倍。

加拿大国家健康保险项目（也被称为医疗保险）的设立是为了确保加拿大每个居民都可以得到医疗保障和治疗，相关费用通过税收或义务健康保险保费支付。

I've Got Two Left Feet

(Diana comes home from her work. She's talking to Li, her guest from China.)

Diana: Thank goodness it's Friday. I've been looking forward to the weekend since Monday.

Li: I thought you enjoyed your work.

Diana: Oh, I do. I mean, it's not that bad. But I'm not a workaholic or anything. I really appreciate my time off. Saturday I have my fitness class, though.

Li: Fitness class! How do you find the energy? After a week's working, I just don't *feel up to* anything but a good dinner and some TV.

Diana: But I find that the fitness class actually makes me feel more energetic. You should try it.

Li: What kind of class is it? Tell me something more.

Diana: Aerobics—it's fun, a lot of dance-type steps.

Li: Dance? You're kidding me. *I've got two left feet*—I can't dance. I'm no Fred Astaire myself.

Diana: Don't worry about it, Li. I'm no Ginger Rogers, either. When I first started aerobics I *felt pretty self-conscious*, but everybody's too busy huffing and puffing to notice anyone else. Actually the lively music immediately puts you *at ease*.

Li: Sounds like a popular thing to do. Many people there?

Diana: Sure. A lot of people are into it—especially we baby boomers. Since the fitness craze, sports and fitness clubs have become popular. In Canada, many people get into them not only for exercise, but also to meet people.

Li: It seems to me that Canadians are very health-conscious.

Diana: Yes, a healthier lifestyle leads to fewer medical problems. So everyone's getting into the fitness craze nowadays.

Li: I suppose I might as well join the fitness class, as you say. But it'll probably kill me.

Diana: *No sweat*. You can *take a back seat* the first time. Now the only *stumbling block* is where you can get a good pair of runners.

Li: Oh, I brought runners with me when I left China.

Diana: That's perfect. We can go to the class together.

Vocabulary and Notes

- Thank goodness it's Friday.   谢天谢地，可盼到星期五了。

Unit 17　Fitness Craze 健身热

- workaholic | non-stop worker; someone addicted to working 不停顿地工作者；沉醉于工作中的人，工作过分的人
- fitness class | 健身班
- The fitness class actually makes me feel more energetic. | 参加健身班实际上使我感到精力更加旺盛。
- aerobics | a form of exercise which increases the amount of oxygen in your blood, and strengthens your heart and lungs 有氧健身术（一种以促进人的机体使用氧气为本的健身法）
- You're kidding me. | You are telling someone that you do not believe what he or she is saying. 你一定是在跟我开玩笑。
- I'm no Fred Astaire myself. | 我可不是个舞蹈家。（弗雷德·阿斯泰尔是美国著名的舞台和电影舞蹈家。他的歌舞表演极为轰动，由于和金格·罗杰斯合演喜剧影片而驰名于世。）
- I'm no Ginger Rogers, either. | 我也不是罗杰斯；我也不是跳舞的。（金格·罗杰斯是美国著名的舞台及银幕上的舞蹈家和女演员。她与弗雷德·阿斯泰尔合作演出了10部歌舞片，享有国际声誉。）
- buffing and puffing | breathing hard 气喘吁吁；喘不上气来
- baby boomers | the large number of people born during the baby boom in Canada (1946–1962) and the United States 加拿大和美国（1946~1962年）生育高峰时期出生的人
- fitness craze | 健身热
- health-conscious | 有健康意识的
- But it'll probably kill me. | 那简直是太可笑了。

Idioms for Everyday Use

feel up/equal to | feel capable of; feel well enough to
觉得能够担当、能够胜任某事；感到有力气去做某事

  A:　I can help you with the suitcase.
  B:　No, thank you. I **feel quite up to** it.
  A:　我来帮你提这个箱子。

B: 不用，谢谢。我能提得动。

He didn't **feel up to** going such a long way after his recent illness.
他病刚好，觉得没有力气走这么长的路。

get two left feet
极其笨拙；笨手笨脚，不能跳舞 | be clumsy; unable to dance

A: How was the ballet last night?
B: Well, generally it was good. But one of the lady dancers really **had two left feet**.
A: 昨晚的芭蕾怎么样啊？
B: 总的来讲，还不错。可其中有一位女演员简直太笨拙了。

A: Shall we go to the club and have a dance?
B: Sorry, I can't dance. I've **got two left feet**.
A: 咱们去俱乐部跳舞吧？
B: 对不起，我不会跳舞，我笨手笨脚的。

feel/be self-conscious
害羞的；不自然的；感到别人都在注视自己 | (in this context) be shy and easily embarrassed, and feel that everyone is looking at them

At first I **was self-conscious** about being a movie star.
起初，我很不好意思当电影明星。

I could never be an actor: I'm too **self-conscious**.
我永远也当不了演员，我太害羞。

at ease (at one's ease)
无拘无束；舒适；自由自在地和别人交谈 | feel confident and comfortable; be able to talk to people without feeling worried

She's different from her brothers and sisters, as she is always **at ease** with strangers.
她与她的兄弟姐妹不一样，她与生人相处总是无拘无束的。

He is an easy-going person, and Peter felt **at ease** with him at once.
他这个人很好相处，彼得很快就感到和他在一起没有什么拘束了。

no sweat (slang)
没问题；容易极了；不费力气地 | no problem; something can be done easily without causing problems or effort

A: Can we finish the job on time?
B: Sure—**no sweat!**
A: 我们能按时完成这项工作吗？

Unit 17 · Fitness Craze 健身热

B: 当然了——没问题!

Don't boast about yourself. Anybody can do it. **No sweat**.
别自吹自擂了。任何人都能做,那有什么难的。

take a back seat
处于次要或等级低的位置;和别人相比逊色 | accept a poorer or lower position; be second to someone else

A: Hey, did you hear? John Redmond's been appointed head of the marketing department.
B: Well, well, Sam isn't going to like that.
A: You can say that again. He's been the acting head for so long that he isn't going to like having to **take back seat** to somebody else.
A: 嘿,听说了没有?约翰·雷蒙德被任命为市场部的负责人了。
B: 噢,噢,山姆可该不愿意了。
A: 你说对了。他当负责人的时间那么长,不可能愿意在别人手下做事。

She doesn't have to **take a back seat** to any singer alive.
她不亚于当今的任何一位歌手。

stumbling block
问题的焦点;绊脚石;障碍 | problem point; difficulty

A: That's a surprise. The last time I heard everything was going well. What was it you couldn't reach agreement on?
B: The **stumbling block** was the four-day work week.
A: 真奇怪,上次我还听说一切进展顺利呢。又出什么问题了,以至不能达成协议?
B: 问题就出在每周四天工作日这件事上。

Perhaps the biggest **stumbling block** to disarmament is the deterrent theory.
或许裁军的最大障碍是威慑理论。

Unit 18
Food and Drink
饮食

Bread is a basic food in Canada. Many Canadians eat bread two or three times a day. They have toast for breakfast, a sandwich for lunch, and bread and butter with their supper.

Breakfast has an honored place in the Canadian diet. Restaurants post signs advertising Breakfast Served until 11:00 am or in the case of all-night dinners, Breakfast 24 hours a day.

Breakfast food, which can be highly regional, and there are lots of varieties, including cold cereal with milk, bacon, coffee, oatmeal, sausage, ham, eggs (boiled or scrambled), scrapple, boiled potatoes, maple syrup (made from the sap of maple trees), waffles, pancakes and so on.

Different countries use different grains to make bread. For example, in Mexico, corn is used to make some kinds of bread. Most of the bread they eat is made from wheat, but other grains, such as oats and rye, are used to make bread too.

Many different kinds of bread are available. White sliced bread is good for toast or sandwiches. Bagels are popular for breakfast. Rolls are good to eat with lunch, and French bread is often served in restaurants.

In many restaurants in Canada, sandwiches are made in front of you. You need to tell the server what kind of bread you want. You need to choose what kind of meat or ham you want on the sandwiches. You will also need to choose the kind of cheese, usually American, Canada or Swiss. You need to select the vegetables you want on the sandwiches, usually lettuce, tomato and onion. Onion is good for the health, and it is Canadian's favorite. In some restaurants in Canada, bread sometimes is free of charge, and water costs nothing. But soft drinks, generally speaking, are relatively expensive, and actually they are bad to your health.

People like to put different toppings on bread. You can spread butter, margarine, jam, or peanut butter on bread or toast, and cream cheese is a popular topping for a bagel. People often put mustard or ketchup on rolls or buns when they make sandwiches. But you don't have to put anything on bread at all. It's delicious by itself, especially when it is hot and fresh.

Sweet doughnuts are the Canadian people's favorite. They are served in almost all the coffee shops across Canada. They can be brown with cinnamon, white with powdered sugar, pink with icing, round, long, or twisted. They are dunked, licked, munched and sometimes twirled on a finger. But no matter what shape or flavor they are or how they're eaten they have a long history of the Canadian people's favorite breakfast treat.

You can find coffee shops on almost every corner of large cities in Canada. Many people like coffee in the morning because it helps them wake up. Coffee has caffeine in it. Caffeine gives people more energy.

Coffee drinking is very much welcomed by the people from all walks of life and it is a multi-million dollar a year industry in Canada. There is a restaurant chain called Tim Hortons. They are famous for their fresh coffee. Starbucks is a popular American coffee shop that has many chain stores throughout North America, including Canada.

Many doctors in Canada warn people that a little coffee is OK, but too much can be a health problem. It causes heart attack. Most parents in Canada do not allow young children to drink coffee. Usually, people start to drink coffee in high schools or universities. If a person is very tired in the morning but must wake up for school or for work, drinking a cup of coffee will help them feel more awake.

Like in America, Coca-Cola is the best-selling (non-alcoholic) drink in Canada, and Pepsi Cola is a well-known rival and has its devotees, for it is not as sweet as Coke. Cola drinks contain caffeine extracted from cola nuts and are soft drinks, which are stimulating as well as refreshing.

Each country has its own way of drinking coffee. In Canada, people add cream and sugar. In France, people put hot milk in their coffee. Europeans drink strong black coffee and Italians like to add cinnamon or chocolate. Irish coffee is the strongest coffee. It has whisky in it!

The average Canadian eats about 100 pounds of beef each year, another 40 pounds of pork, and about 60 pounds of chicken—or a total of some 200 pounds of meat each year. *The Globe and Mail* reported. That's a very high proportion as compared with the amount of meat eaten in China.

译　文

面包是加拿大最基本的食物。许多加拿大人一天要吃两三顿面包。早餐吃烤面包片，午餐是三明治，晚餐是面包配黄油。

在加拿大的日常饮食中，早餐的地位是崇高的。餐馆会贴出早餐供应到11点的广告，或者考虑到为那些在夜里就餐的人提供方便，有些餐馆还24小时供应早餐。

早餐非常有地方特色，而且丰富多彩，品种很多，其中包括加牛奶的凉麦片粥、咸肉条、咖啡、燕麦粥、香肠、火腿、鸡蛋（煮鸡蛋或炒鸡蛋）、玉米肉饼、煮土豆、枫树糖浆（由枫树树液制成）、华夫饼干、烙饼等等。

不同的国家采用不同的粮食来制作面包。比如在墨西哥，人们用玉米制作某些面包。大部分面包是由小麦制成的，其他粮食比如燕麦和黑麦也用来制作面包。

面包的种类很多，烤面包片和三明治经常用白切片面包。面包圈属于大众早餐。面包卷适合午餐时吃，在饭店则通常可以吃到法式面包。

加拿大许多餐馆当着顾客的面制作三明治。你首先要告诉服务员要什么样的面包，也要选择什么样的肉或火腿肉放在面包上。还要选择奶酪，通常有美国式、加拿大式或瑞士式。蔬菜的选择通常是生菜、西红柿和洋葱。洋葱对健康有利，几乎所有的加拿大人都爱吃。在加拿大的餐厅里，面包有时是免费的，水也是免费的。饮料一般都比较贵，实际上对健康也不利。

人们喜欢在面包上抹上各种调味酱。面包或面包片上经常抹黄油、人造奶油、果酱或花生酱，而面包圈上经常抹乳脂干酪。做三明治时人们经常给面包卷或小圆面包抹些芥末酱或番茄酱。不过你也可以什么都不抹。面包本身就很好吃，尤其是新鲜出炉的那种。

香甜的油炸圈饼是加拿大人的最爱，它们在遍及加拿大的咖啡店里随处都有。它们或是洒着肉桂的红棕色的，或是裹着白色糖粉的，或者粘着粉红的糖霜，有圆圆的、长长的或是扭花的。人们可以泡着吃，舔着吃，可以大嚼大咽，也可以缠绕在手指上。但是不管它们什么形状、什么味道，它们一直被认为是加拿大人最喜爱的早餐。

在加拿大的大城市，咖啡店几乎随处可见。很多人喜欢早上喝咖啡，因为它可以帮助人们消除困意。咖啡中含有咖啡因，咖啡因使人们更加精力充沛。

在加拿大，各行各业的人们都喜欢喝咖啡，咖啡饮用是一项年盈利数百万加元的饮料产业。其中有一家连锁店叫做提姆-荷顿，以其新鲜的咖啡著名。星巴克是一家非常受欢迎的美国咖啡连锁店，遍布包括加拿大在内的整个北美地区。

加拿大的许多医生提醒人们，适量的咖啡是可以的，但是太多的咖啡可能导致心脏病等健康问题。许多父母是不允许年轻的孩子喝咖啡的。人们往往从高中或者大学开始饮用咖啡。当你早上醒来觉得困倦但又不得不上学或者工作时，一杯咖啡则可以让你精神很多。

可口可乐，就像在美国一样，是加拿大最畅销的不含酒精的饮料，而百事可乐是知名的竞争对手，同样有自己的拥护者，因为它的味道没有可口可乐那么甜。可乐类饮料含有从柯拉果提取的咖啡因，是既提神又清爽的软性饮料。

每个国家都有自己喝咖啡的方式。在加拿大，人们在咖啡中加入乳脂和食糖。在法国，人们把热牛奶加入到咖啡中。欧洲人喝的浓咖啡什么都不放，而意大利人喜欢加入肉桂粉或巧克力。爱尔兰人喝的是最浓烈的咖啡，因为里面加了威士忌酒！

《环球邮报》曾报道说，一个普通的加拿大人每年要吃掉大约100磅牛肉、40磅猪肉和60磅鸡肉，也就是说每年要吃大约200磅肉。与中国的肉类食用量相比，这可真是非常高的比例。

I Can't Tell Them Apart

(Diana and her Chinese friend Li are talking about the dinner party they're going to give tomorrow.)

Diana: Breakfast is ready. You will have brown bread or white one?

Li: Bread again this morning? You Canadian people are addicted to bread, aren't you?

Diana: That's right. But we will certainly try something new tomorrow.

Li: By the way, we'd better get our shopping list together for the dinner party after breakfast.

Diana: You're right, but we don't have to *dish up* as much food as we did last time. Remember we ate the leftovers for two days. We've already got enough stuff for tomorrow's party. I've already taken the meat out of the freezer. Do you like roast beef or fried steak? They're both easy to cook.

Li: To me, they're about the same. I can't **tell them apart**. But I'll tell you something, I can't handle rare steak. I think it'll take me a long time to **get into** eating rare meat.

Diana: Oh, I see, forget the rare steak. I'll try some medium or well-done this time. Li, how about chicken? I can cook very good chicken dishes.

Li: Now I understand why they say Canadians are heavy meat eaters. You eat too much meat.

Diana: That's probably right! *The Globe and Mail* reports that the average Canadian eats about 100 pounds of beef each year another 40 pounds of pork, and about 60 pounds of chicken—or a total of some 200 pounds of meat each year.

Li: Wow! That's a very high proportion as compared with the amount of meat eaten in China. Well, let's get down to our dishes for the party tomorrow.

Diana: Li, why don't you cook some Chinese food? **Every now and then** I get hungry for Chinese food.

Li: Hey! I got it! Let's make Chinese dumplings instead of cooking all the meat dishes. I could make three different fillings for the dumplings, **to say the least**.

Diana: That's great! But Li, between your friends and my friends there will be ten of us altogether. I think we've **got our work cut out** for us.

Li: Oh, don't be such a worrywart. Everything will turn out all right. Let's see—we need some shrimp, eggs, celery, cabbage, pork, chives... I've got a bottle of Chinese strong liquor. Do you think the people in the party will enjoy it?

Diana: I think they will love to try it, since we are not temperance people.

Vocabulary and Notes

- shopping list 采购单
- leftovers the food that remains uneaten after a meal 剩饭；吃剩的食物

roast beef	烤牛肉
fried steak	炸牛排
rare	(of meat) undone so that the red color and juices are retained （肉类）未煮熟的，半熟的
rare steak	半生不熟的牛排
medium	（肉类）不老不嫩的
well done	烧透的
The Globe and Mail	《环球邮报》（加拿大全国发行的报纸），1844年在多伦多创刊，是加拿大的纪录报，致力于报道国际和国内事务，发表政府官员的正式讲话和其他文件原文。该报有驻外记者队伍，具有国际风格。
proportion	比率，比重
(as) compared with	与……比较
get down to (something)	deal seriously with (something) 认真对付某事；专心做某事
I get hungry for Chinese food.	我想吃中餐。
instead of	代替
three different fillings	三种不同的饺子馅
worrywart	someone who worries too much 过分担心的人；忧虑重重的人
shrimp	虾
celery	芹菜
cabbage	卷心菜
chives	韭菜
sesame oil	香油
ginger	姜
temperance people	主张节制饮酒或绝对禁酒的人。戒酒运动于19世纪起源于美国，后发展到欧洲，成为国际性运动。加拿大的戒酒运动始于19世纪20年代，当时人们认为酗酒不但违背教会的教义，还阻碍社会经济的发展。联邦和地方政府纷纷立法限制酒类的生产和销售。1909年世界戒酒大会在伦敦举行，决定成立国际戒酒联合会。

Idioms for Everyday Use

dish up
上菜；把饭菜盛到盘子里端上桌 | put the food into dishes, and then serve

- A: I'll be ready to **dish up** in a few minutes; is the family all at table?
- B: Yes, we're all here, except our little brother.
- A: 几分钟后我就给你们上菜，家里人都到齐了吗？
- B: 是的，除了小弟弟，我们都到齐了。

- A: How was the party last night?
- B: Fascinating! The host **dished up** a lot of food and then we danced far into the night.
- A: 昨天晚上的晚会怎么样？
- B: 太棒了！主人准备了许多饭菜，饭后我们跳舞，一直跳到深夜。

tell (two things) apart
区别；区分 | distinguish between two things or persons

- A: Can you see any difference between this nylon shirt and the silk one?
- B: No, I can't **tell them apart**.
- A: 你能看出这件尼龙衬衫与那件丝绸衬衫有什么不同吗？
- B: 不能，我无法区分它们。

Actually there were two pairs of shoes that John liked. One pair cost ten dollars more than the other, but to John they looked the same. It was almost impossible to **tell them apart**.
其实约翰看中了两双鞋。一双比另一双贵10美元，但在约翰看来，这两双鞋一模一样。他几乎无法将它们区分开来。

get into
染上（习惯）；习惯于 | (in this context) cause to start (a habit)

- A: Don't you think he smokes?
- B: Thirty years ago, he **got into** the habit of smoking, but because of his heart attack, he quit it just last year.
- A: 你不认为他抽烟吗？
- B: 30年前他染上了抽烟的习惯，但由于心脏病的原因，他去年刚刚戒烟。

- A: What are you reading now?
- B: A biography of Saddam Hussein.
- A: Well, I can't **get into** it.

A: 你看什么书呢?
B: 萨达姆·侯赛因传记。
A: 噢，我对这书不感兴趣。

Some children in Canada **got into** the bad habit of switching on the television as soon as they got home.
加拿大的一些孩子养成了一种坏习惯，一回到家就打开电视机。

(every) now and then
有时；偶尔

from time to time; occasionally

A: I hear you've given up skiing.
B: Not completely. I still go **every now and then**, but I'm much more interested in skating.
A: 听说你已放弃滑雪了。
B: 没完全放弃。我有时还去，但我对滑冰更感兴趣。

A: Do you often hear from him?
B: No, he doesn't write us often, but we do get letters from him **now and then**.
A: 你经常收到他的信吗?
B: 不，他不常给我们写信，但我们偶尔也收到几封。

to say the least (of it)
就最小限度而言；至少可以这样说

comment as little as possible about something

A: Did you see the movie on Channel 8 last night? That was boring one, **to say the least**.
B: You can say that again!
A: 昨晚你看了八频道播放的电影了吗? 至少可以说那是一部枯燥乏味的片子。
B: 你说得太对了!

Some students call him crazy; he is sometimes a little strange, **to say the least**.
一些学生说他疯癫；至少可以说，他有时有点儿不正常。

get/have one's work cut out
工作量很大；某人面临困难任务

have a lot of work to do; it's very difficult for someone to do it

Sounds like we've **got our work cut out** for us—let's get a paper and list all the problems.
听起来我们的困难还不小——找一张纸，把这些问题列出来。

If he wants to withdraw his troops from the Persian Gulf, he **has his work cut out** for him.
如果他想把他的部队从波斯湾撤出来，他要面临很大的困难。

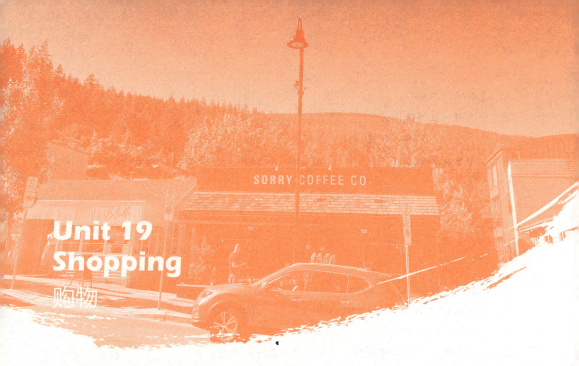

Unit 19
Shopping
购物

Canadian consumers are constantly bombarded by various kinds of advertisements—in newspapers and magazines, on radio and television. There are many ways for Canadian consumers to save money, however.

Newspapers often contain advertisements for special sales and many businesses offer coupons and special deals. Second-hand stores can also be a source of less expensive items.

In general, higher price means better quality, but it is not always so. The best way to shop is to compare prices. You could see all kinds of catalogs in almost all stores, so it is easy to compare. Take a little time to read the catalogs and you can save a lot of money. Items at a Flea Market can be inexpensive, and most of them are new, ranging from jewelry to clothes, from furniture to household necessities. Garage Sales, Yard Sales and Moving Sales are other ways to save money. The items on sale are mostly used. In Canada, once something is used, its values decrease a lot. It is a good place for furniture, toys, or something you just need temporarily.

Stores in Canada have sales a few times a year; usually have sales at the end of the season. They reduce the prices at the end of the season to make room for new merchandise. For example, in January, all the winter clothes go on sale. You can buy a winter coat for much less money than it would cost in October or November.

Although there are federal and provincial laws to protect the consumer from false advertising, high-pressure selling, and below standard products, it is still up to the careful consumer to avoid impulse buying and poor budgeting.

If you were not happy with something you bought in a department store, you could return it and get your money back. Be sure to return them as soon as possible, within a week, and always bring the receipt. You will have to show the receipt to the store that you paid for the item.

If the store does not have another item like the one you want, the clerk may offer you something similar. He will probably offer you a more expensive item and you will have to pay the difference. However, if you do not want it, you simply get your money back. You are not obligated to keep something you do not want.

In checking prices in Canada, you should be aware that the price on the label is not the price you pay. You will have to pay tax also.

Many people in Canada pay for something with credit cards. The credit card company sends you a monthly statement that shows the purchases you made. If you write a personal check, you will have to pay the bank a high service charge on it. Many stores that sell expensive items—home appliances like washing machines, refrigerators and computers for example—allow their customers to pay for them on the installment plan. Customers make a down payment of 10% or more on the purchase price and pay the rest in monthly installments. They have to pay interest.

译 文

加拿大的消费者经常不断地受到报纸、杂志、收音机和电视上各种广告的冲击和诱惑。尽管如此，他们在购物上还是有许多省钱的方法。

报纸经常刊登那些特价商品的广告，许多商家会提供赠券或搞特卖活动。二手店也是购买便宜货的地方。

一般来说，价钱高质量好，但这也不是绝对的，最好是货比三家。在加拿大，你随时都能在几乎所有商店看到各种各样的广告，所以很容易做比较。花点时间，会省很多钱。跳蚤市场的物品比较便宜，并且多数是新的，从首饰到衣服，从家具到日用品，应有尽有。车库里的拍卖、院子里的拍卖和搬家前的拍卖也是让人们可以省钱的好去处。这里的东西大多数是用过的。在加拿大，东西用过了就不值钱了。去这些地方买家具、玩具和一些临时要用的东西也不错。

加拿大的商店一年当中经常有减价活动，通常是在季末。减价活动是为了给新品留出摆放空间。比如，在1月所有的冬装打折，这时买冬装的价格要比在10月或11月便宜多了。

虽然消费者受到联邦政府和省级法律的保护，使之免受虚伪广告、强买强卖或伪劣商品的影响，但是要避免冲动或盲目购物仍然要靠消费者自身的细心。

如果你对在某个商场买的东西不满意，你可以退货并索回钱款。要在一个星期内尽快退货，并且要带上收据。你必须向商店出示你所买物品的收据。

如果这家商场没有你要的那种商品，售货员可能会推荐类似商品。他可能会推荐一个价钱更高的商品，那你就需要补足差价了。不过如果你还是不想要，你只需要拿回钱就行了。你没必要保留自己不喜欢的东西。

在加拿大购物查看价格时，你应该知道标签上的价格并非你实际要支付的价格。你还需要额外付商品税。

加拿大人多用信用卡来付账。信用卡公司每月为你寄去账单，上面有你上月购物的支出情况。如果你签发个人支票，你必须支付银行高额的手续费。许多经营贵重物品的商店，比如洗衣机、电冰箱和电脑这些家用电器，商店允许顾客分期付款。顾客可以先付10%或更多的定金，剩下的余额就每个月来分期付款。这当然要附加利息。

I Finally Picked out a Good One

(Mary bumps into his Chinese friend Li on his way shopping.)

Li: Hi Mary, how are you doing?

Mary: Just fine, Li. How about yourself?

Li: Fine, thanks. Where are you headed on this fine sunny day?

Mary: Well, I'm **hard up for** a pair of pants and some pens and papers. And fortunately, some of the stores have sales.

Li: That's neat! Where were you thinking of going?

Mary: Hudson's Bay. Did you read today's paper and advertising flyers? Lots of things there on sales, you know. I need a bicycle.

Li: Do you mind if I **tag along**?

Mary: Not at all, but I'll probably be going for at least an hours, because I plan to do a lot of window shopping, too.

Li: I see. Well, to be honest, I think shopping is **a pain in the neck**. I actually bought a second-hand bike two months ago, but it doesn't work well, so I decided to buy a new ten-speed bicycle.

Mary: I just bought a brand new bike last week at the Department Store of Sears. There are many bicycles to choose from. I *went over some of them with a fine-tooth comb*, and I finally picked out a good one. I'm very happy with it because it works wonderfully. How about *going out for a spin* with me if you find the bike with ten speeds today?

Li: That sounds like a good idea. How much did your bike *run* you?

Mary: A little bit expensive—it was $220. But you can buy it today with 20% off since many goods are on sales.

Li: I'm very curious about these sales. Could you tell me when the stores usually have sales?

Mary: Stores in Canada have sales a few times a year; they usually have sales at the end of the season. They reduce the prices at the end of the season to make room for new merchandise. For example, in January, all the winter clothes go on sale. You can buy a winter coat for much less money than it would cost in October or November.

Li: My opinion is that when you buy on sale you have to be careful. Be sure to check it carefully. Before you buy it, ask yourself why it is on sale. Perhaps it is damaged or out of style.

Mary: You've never said a truer word. Here comes the bus now. Let's go.

Vocabulary and Notes

- bump into
- Where are you headed on this fine sunny day?
- some of the stores now have sales
- That's neat!
- Hudson's Bay

偶然遇见，碰见

大晴天儿的到哪儿去啊？

一些商店正在减价出售商品

That's wonderful! 太棒了！

哈德逊湾公司。The Hudson's Bay Company，是北美最早的商业股份公司，也是全世界最早的公司之一。曾经控制了几个世纪大部分英占北美地区的皮毛贸易，后来在皮毛生意衰退后，进入了商品市场，成了全加拿大最著名的百货公司之一。

advertising flyer	广告传单
on sales	减价出售；削价出售
Do you mind if I tag along?	我可以跟你去吗？
window shopping	不进商店，只是浏览商店橱窗
a ten-speed bicycle	一辆十速的自行车
I went over some of them with a fine tooth comb, ...	我把一些（自行车）仔细地挨个都挑了一遍，……
merchandise	商品（货物的总称）
out of style	out of fashion 不合时尚，过时

Idioms for Everyday Use

hard up for
急需；奇缺

in want of; need (something) badly

A: He was **hard up for** cash, so I lent him 5000 yuan RMB.

B: That is very kind of you. His mother is going to have an operation soon and he also borrowed some money from me.

A: 他急需现金，因此我借给他5千元人民币。

B: 你真是太好了。他的母亲不久要做手术，他从我这里也借了一些钱。

I'm **hard up for** a new bicycle. My old one is broken.

我急需一辆新自行车。那辆旧的坏了。

A: We are **hard up for** a pair of pingpong paddles, because we are competing with a team tomorrow morning.

B: Let's go together.

A: 我们急需一副乒乓球拍，因为明天早上我们要与一个队比赛。

B: 让我们一起去。

tag along
跟随；跟在后面

go along; follow in the rear

Two or three small boys **tagged along** behind the band.

两三个小孩儿紧紧跟在乐队的后面。

I'll just **tag along** and watch you guys play, OK?

Unit 19　Shopping 购物

我跟在你们后面看你们玩，好吗？

a pain in the neck
极其棘手的事，使人讨厌（惹人生气）的人或事 | a very troublesome or irritating thing or person

- I've always hated studying mathematics. It's such **a pain in the neck**.
  我一直讨厌学习数学。这门课让我头疼。
- Nobody likes to work with him, for he's a big **pain in the neck**.
  没有人愿意和他一起工作，因为他使人讨厌。

go over/through something with a fine-tooth comb
仔细搜查或彻底调查某事 | inspect or examine something very carefully and thoroughly

- They police **went over the scene of the crime with a fine-tooth comb**, hoping to find some clues.
  警察对犯罪现场进行了仔细的搜查，希望能找到一些线索。
- I just don't understand it—I've **gone over this desk with a fine-tooth comb**, and I still can't find my pen.
  我真不明白——我彻底地把课桌检查了一遍，仍然找不到我的钢笔。

go out for a spin
（乘车或骑车）出去转转 | go for a short ride (by car or bicycle)

- They **went out for a spin** before lunch.
  午饭前他们乘车出去转了一圈。
- He had just bought a new car, so he invited his girlfriend to **go out for a spin**.
  他刚刚买了一辆新车，就邀请他的女朋友出去兜了兜风。

run
花费 | (in this context) cost

- How much does it **run** you to have milk delivered to your house every day?
  天天把牛奶为你送上门来，你需要付多少钱？
- It was **running** me $100 a week to put gas in my car, so I decided to sell it.
  每个星期我得支付100美元的加油费，因此我决定卖掉这辆小汽车。

Unit 20
Maple Syrup Festival
枫糖节

Maple syrup is a unique Canadian food product, and it is a pure, natural sweetener. Maple syrup has an abundance of trace minerals that are essential to good nutrition: potassium, magnesium, phosphorus, manganese, iron, zinc, copper and tin, as well as calcium in concentrations 15 times higher than honey.

The sweet sap of the maple tree was known and valued by the native peoples of eastern North America long before the arrival of European settlers. French settlers probably learned from the native Indians how to tap trees to obtain sap and how to boil it to reduce it to sweet syrup or sugar slabs to be stored for later use. Many of the tapped trees are well over 100 years old.

It is said that "Indian Maple Syrup" existed right in the eastern part of Canada 1,600 years ago. It was Canadian Aboriginals—Indians that discovered the sweet and refreshing sap in the sugar maples. Winter season in the eastern part of Canada was extremely cold and long, and all the crops and vegetables could not be grown there at that time. The only means of subsistence for the Indians was to hunt and the meat was the only food for them. Therefore, lots of people died of vitamin-deficiency and mineral-deficiency. Later on, the Indians discovered the sweet sap in the sugar maples and gradually they learned how to tap the sap and how to make it edible. Because the maple syrup provided rich nutrient, the Indians who suffered from the lack of vitamin were saved, and their health were guaranteed.

Unit 20 Maple Syrup Festival 枫糖节

There are various sap-gathering methods. Traditional bucket collection involves making a hole in a tree, hanging a pail or a bucket, and putting a little trough into the tree. Then the sap flows into the pail. When the pail's full, they put the sap into a big pot and boil it. You may stir it with a very big spoon. Soon, the sap becomes thicker and thicker. Then you use a stick, a little piece of wood, to take some of the syrup and put it into the snow. This time the sugar becomes very hard, tough. Then you eat it.

Traditional bucket collection, although still used throughout the Maple Belt, is being replaced by a vacuum-tubing system that reduces labor and creates a more sanitary environment for collection. Once the maple sap is collected, it is evaporated into syrup.

Canadian people, especially children, are looking forward to the middle of March which is the time for collecting sugar maple sap, and making the syrup by boiling. From mid March to mid April, up to 10,000 maple syrup farms in the provinces of Ontario and Quebec are colorfully decorated for the Maple Syrup Festival. People from all directions come to the farms and enjoy this spectacular scene and taste the natural sweet and refreshing syrup.

The most common way of eating syrup is to drip the syrup liquid on top of the soft pancakes. Another way is to be called "Syrup on the White Snow", that means to pour the boiling syrup over a clean and tidy board which is covered with a thin layer of white snow, and then the syrup gradually is condensed. You quickly take a stick of popsicle, and then put it on the syrup and roll the cooling syrup up onto popsicle stick before it becomes solid. The stick with the syrup now turns into a solid sucker. Taste it! Very delicious!

Some watering onlookers sometimes lose their patience. They just grab at the sticks, put them into the pot, take some hot syrup out of it, and then put it into the snow, when it become hard they eat it.

The world's largest Maple Syrup Festival is the day-long Elmira Maple Syrup Festival. The town of Elmira is situated 10 kilometers in the north of the city of Waterloo, about 80 kilometers southwest of the Toronto city. In downtown of Elmira—Arthur Commercial Street, there are more than 100 vendor stands, which is closed off to cars. It is jam-packed with thousands of pedestrians on the festival day. All the stands offer visitors delicacies like pancakes, apple pies, maple candy, maple wine, and all kinds of maple syrup and many Indian handicrafts.

From mid March to mid April, the town of Elmira receives 100,000 to 200,000 visitors from both home and abroad. A special sight-seeing program there in Elmira attracts most visitors. Visitors spend three to five dollars on a cart tour through the sugar maple bush to see how maple sap is tapped from trees and then boiled into maple syrup. That is an extremely exciting maple bush tour, and it feasts your eyes on the landscape. That is out and out once in a blue moon.

There are about 20,000 maple-syrup producers in North America. It takes approximately 151.4 L of maple sap to produce 3.8 L of pure syrup. Water can be removed from sap by using various systems. During a normal crop year, some 22.7 million kg of syrup are produced worldwide. Canada would produce 15 million kg and Quebec produces nearly 12 million kg.

译 文

枫树糖浆是加拿大独特的食品，而且它是一种纯天然的甜料。枫糖含有大量的营养所必需的微量元素，有钾、镁、磷、锰、铁、锌、铜以及锡，同时，枫糖中钙的含量要比蜂蜜高15倍。

远在欧洲移民来到加拿大之前，北美东部的本土人就已经了解并懂得珍视这枫树中甜甜的树液。法国移民可能就是从当地的印第安人那里学到了如何在树干上划痕并取得树液，以及如何熬煮那些树液，使之变为糖浆或枫糖块，以备后用。许多被采集树液的枫树都有超过100年的树龄。

据说，在大约1600年前加拿大东部就已经有了"印第安糖浆"。加拿大土著居民——印第安人在甜枫树里首先发现了甘甜的树液。加拿大东部的冬天又冷又长，因此，在这期间根本没有农作物和蔬菜可以生长，人们只能打猎吃肉，很多人因为缺乏维生素和矿物质等营养而死去。后来，他们发现了枫树里的糖液，并逐渐学会了制作和食用枫树糖浆。由于枫树糖浆提供了丰富的营养素，缺乏维生素的状况得到改善，他们的健康才有了保障。

采集树液的方法有很多种。传统的吊桶收集法是在树上挖一个洞，挂上一个桶，然后往树洞里插一个细长的金属槽形工具，于是树液就顺着它流进桶里。等到桶流满了之后，再把树液倒入一个大罐子里熬煮。你可以用一个大勺进行搅动，很快树液就变得越来越浓稠。接下来你可以用一根小木棍儿,取一些糖浆放到雪中,糖浆会变得坚硬,你就可以吃了。

传统的吊桶收集法虽然仍然在枫树区使用,但是正在被一种既节能又能创造一个更卫生的环境的真空管道系统所取代。一旦收集到枫树液,它就被脱去水分变成枫树糖浆。

每年春天,加拿大人,特别是孩子们,都盼望着3月中旬的到来,这是采集枫汁、熬制枫液糖浆的季节。3月中旬到4月中旬,加拿大魁北克省和安大略省上万个生产枫糖浆的农场纷纷披上枫糖节节日的盛装。人们从四面八方前来参加这盛大的场面,同时品尝大自然赋予的甜蜜食品。

枫糖浆的最普通的吃法是直接淋在松软的烤饼上吃。另一种吃法是被称为"白雪上的枫糖浆",即在一块干净的木板上铺上一层干净的白雪,把煮沸的枫糖浆直接淋在雪上面,枫糖浆会慢慢凝固。在枫糖浆还没成固体前,人们迅速地用一根小木棒把冷却后的枫糖浆慢慢卷起来,制成枫糖棒棒糖。吃在嘴里,甜在心里,回味无穷!

也有一些游客耐不住饥馋,于是他们干脆直接用小棍从大锅沾一些糖浆,然后迅速放到雪里,等糖浆变硬,拿起便可享受。

"世界最大枫糖节"是艾美热"一日枫糖节"。艾美热小镇位于滑铁卢市区以北10多公里处,距多伦多市西南方向80公里。从3月中旬直到4月中旬,在镇中的商业街——阿瑟大街,有一百多个摊点,整条大街车辆禁行。在枫糖节这一天,成千上万的行人把该镇的阿瑟大街围得水泄不通。所有的摊位向游客出售着各种小吃,有松饼、苹果派、枫糖浆糖块、枫糖酒和各种各样的枫树糖浆以及其他枫糖食品,还有许多印第安工艺品。

艾美热镇每年3~4月要接待国内外10万~20万游客。艾美热地区的一项特殊的旅游观光项目吸引着许多游客,这就是游客花上3~5加元,坐上农用的马车到郊外的枫树林中现场观光,目睹树液提取和枫糖浆制作的全过程。那是令人激动的枫林行,让你大饱眼福!这绝对是一次千载难逢的好机会!

北美有大约两万家枫糖制造厂。大约151.4升的树液可以生产3.8升纯枫糖。树液中的水分可以用各种设备去除。一般说来,全球每个农业年度的枫糖产量达2270万公斤,其中加拿大的枫糖产量为1500万公斤,而这其中将近1200万公斤的枫糖产自魁北克省。

Dialogue

You Couldn't Beat That Deal with a Stick

(Helen, Li's friend, has just come back from a farm, and meets Li at the students' cafeteria.)

Li: Hey, Helen. Where were you today? I searched for you everywhere. I thought we could study together for tomorrow's quiz.

Helen: I went to the countryside and enjoyed sugaring off. I decided to go there *on the spur of the moment*. I forgot we would have the history quiz tomorrow. In fact, my trips to the countryside are *few and far between*.

Li: What's sugaring off by the way? You ate some sugar? Give me an idea. What are you talking about?

Helen: Well, generally speaking, people get together in early spring in some country villages and taste maple sugar. In other words, city people go to the farms to eat maple sugar before the snow melts. I mean snow still covers the ground. So, it's called sugaring off.

Li: But, how do you get maple sugar? Don't keep me in the dark. Tell me *straight from the shoulder*.

Helen: OK. I'll give you an account of it from the very beginning. First of all, the maple sap is collected. There're various sap-gathering methods. Traditional bucket collection involves making a hole in a tree, hanging a pail or a bucket, and putting a little rough into the tree. Then the sap flows into the pail. When the pail's full, they put the sap into a big pot and boil it. I *tried my hand at* stirring it with a very big spoon today. Soon, the sap becomes thicker and thicker. Then you use a stick, a little piece of wood, to take some of the syrup and put it into the snow. This time the sugar becomes very hard, tough. Then you eat it. I tried it many times today. Later on, all the visitors joined in the country dance with the local people, very well organized. We really had a good time. You *couldn't beat that deal with a stick*!

Li: That sounds fascinating! I wish I could have gone with you.

Helen: I don't think you could have gone and enjoyed yourself knowing the quiz is *in store for* you. You seem very serious about exams, quizzes and marks.

Li: You're probably right. I'm the person that *sets the greatest store on* taking exams.

Helen: Anyway, it's high time for me to review the lessons for the quiz tomorrow. See you.

Unit 20 Maple Syrup Festival 枫糖节

Vocabulary and Notes

- sugaring off — 把枫树汁熬成糖；熬糖会（熬糖时节的点心招待会）
- Give me an idea. — 告诉我是怎么回事。
- in other words — 换句话说
- melt — cause (a solid) to become liquid 融化，熔化
- keep someone in the dark — 把某人蒙在鼓里，瞒着某人
- give someone an account of something — 给某人描述某事
- sap — liquid in a plant 树液
- There're various sap-gathering methods. — 有多种采集树液的方法。
- bucket — a pail or other container to hold or carry water, milk, etc. 盛水或牛奶的桶，提桶
- trough — 槽；饮水槽；饲料槽
- It's high time for me to review the lessons... — 我早该复习（明天要考试的）课程了……

Idioms for Everyday Use

on the spur of the moment
心血来潮；脑子一热；凭一时高兴
on a sudden impulse; at that moment; without previous thought or plan

A: Would you like a ticket to the soccer game on Saturday? I bought it **on the spur of the moment**, forgetting I'd be away this weekend.

B: Thanks a lot. I haven't been to any games this year.

A: 星期六你想去看足球赛吗？这里有张票。我当时脑子一热买的票，忘记了我这个周末要外出。

B: 非常感谢。今年我还没有去看任何比赛。

A: Would you like a ticket to the concert tonight? I bought it **on the spur of the moment**. I forgot I would visit my professor to discuss my paper.

B: Thanks. I'd like to go. I haven't been to any concerts this month.

A: 我有一张今晚的音乐会票，你想要吗？这张票是我随意买的。当时我忘了我还得去教授那儿讨论我的论文。

B: 谢谢，我愿意去。这个月我还没听过音乐会呢。

A: Is Alice going to participate in the sports meet?

B: No, she's left for Chicago **on the spur of the moment**.

A: 艾丽丝准备参加运动会吗？
B: 不，她一时心血来潮，去芝加哥了。

few and far between
不经常；稀少；相隔很长时间才发生 | infrequent; rare; not happening often

- Such a snowfall is **few and far between** in our city.
  下这么大的雪在我们这个城市是少见的。

- Mary and I were very close friends when we were at school, but then she moved to another town. I do hear from her, but her letters are **few and far between**.
  上学时，我和玛丽是亲密无间的朋友，但后来她迁居到另一个城市了。她倒是给我来信，但隔很长时间才写一封。

- A: Do you often go abroad?
  B: Oh, no. My trips to foreign countries are **few and far between**.
  A: 你经常出国吗？
  B: 噢，不，我难得有机会出国旅游。

straight from the shoulder
坦率地；直截了当地；一针见血地 | frankly

- A: Didn't you know that? Oh, I thought you knew about her...
  B: No, what happened? Come on. Tell me **straight from the shoulder**.
  A: 难道你不知道那事？噢，我以为你知道她的……
  B: 我什么都不知道，发生什么事了？快说，直截了当告诉我吧。

- I prefer a person who speaks **straight from the shoulder**, because then I know exactly what he means.
  我喜欢说话爽快的人，这样我可以确切地理解他的意思。

try one's hand at (something)
试着做某事；尝试（一般指以前从未做过的事） | make an attempt at something to see if one is able to do it (usually something that one has not tried before)

- A: Are you brave enough to **try your hand at** things you've never attempted before?
  B: That all depends. Generally speaking I don't want to risk my life.
  A: 你敢不敢冒险试一试你以前从来没尝试过的事情？
  B: 那得看情况而定。总的讲，我不想拿生命去冒险。

- I've never driven a truck before, but I'm willing to **try my hand at** it.
  尽管我以前从未开过卡车，但我想试着开一次。

- A: This is a clarinet. Have you ever played this instrument?

B: Well, I've never played this instrument but I'm always willing to **try my hand at** learning anything new.

A: 这是黑管。你吹奏过这种乐器吗？

B: 哦，从来没玩过，但是我见到新玩意儿就总是跃跃欲试。

can't beat something with a stick
最佳的安排，十全十美 | can't find a better arrangement anywhere

A: Hey there, globe-trotter. How was your trip?

B: Really great! We went to London, Paris, Bonn and Moscow. We stayed at a 4-Star Hotel—great food, great rooms, great service. You **couldn't beat that deal with a stick**!

A: 嘿，天涯游客归来了。这趟旅行怎么样？

B: 太棒了！我们去了伦敦、巴黎、波恩，还有莫斯科。我们住的是四星级饭店——伙食好，住得舒服，服务周到。无可挑剔！

A: Dan's new job is wonderful! He earns a good salary, travels a lot and meets lots of interesting people.

B: That sounds great! You **can't beat that with a stick**.

A: 丹新找的工作太好了！他能挣高工资，到处旅游，还能接触许多有趣的人。

B: 听起来很棒！哪儿也找不到这么好的工作了。

in store for (someone)
即将发生，马上到来 | about to happen, coming to

It was evening now. And a new trouble **was in store for** Pompeii. The earth trembled and quaked!
现在已是傍晚了。一场新的灾难即将降临庞培城。大地在颤抖、晃动！

Who knows what the future has **in store for** us.
谁知道我们将来的前途会如何。

set (great) store on
对某事特别重视(通常可以在store前加一些形容词，如great/ much 特别重视、not不重视、not much不太重视等) | someone thinks that it is extremely important and cares a great deal about it

A: I'm a bit embarrassed to ask her.

B: Well, if you really **set great store on** knowing it, I think I should ask her point blank.

A: 我有点儿不好意思问她。

B: 如果你真的认为了解这件事很重要，我可以直截了当地问她。

He put forward some suggestions at the meeting, but they **set little store on** his opinions.
他在会上提出了一些建议，可他们根本不重视他的意见。

Unit 21
College Life
大学生活

Over the past four decades Canadian higher education has changed dramatically. This is most evident with respect to the growth in numbers of students, faculty and new institutions. At the same time, qualitative changes have happened, for example, an emphasis on applied research, internationalization and commercialization.

It is said that there are more than 150,000 international students who come to Canada every year to study and more than 9,000 are from China. In addition, many more come to Canada to learn English or French. International students bring a rich culture to the classrooms. Your knowledge and skills are welcome in the schools.

Tuition fees for international students in Canada, and the cost of living, are among the lowest in the world. Eligible students can gain valuable Canadian work experience through off campus employment.

Universities in Canada have their respective advantages. Some universities may be well known for some of their faculties, while other universities may be famous for a particular college. University of Toronto, for example, has been regarded as one of the leading universities. Dozens of faculties and departments are famous in the world and some of which have distinguished themselves in scientific technological achievements. McGill University is known for its humanities departments and medical college.

Universities and colleges in Canada offer four seasons of recreational opportunities, cultural activities and year-round sports in world-class facilities. Sports teams are popular at the universities. Some of these include hockey, baseball, basketball, soccer, golf, tennis, badminton, squash, swimming and so on. The students in the teams are very much active in the various competitive events. A healthy balance between studying and social life can be achieved. In fact, your social life might actually make you a more successful student by making you feel more at home in Canada. Almost all the students love their own university and they are proud of becoming part of the college community. The successful students are those actively involved in some school social activities besides study.

Studying in university demands more reading and thinking, less memorization than in high school. Most professors are very willing to give help to those who do not understand the courses. Students naturally organize study groups in which they meet regularly with a few classmates to discuss course materials and review the lectures they had. If you are in the first semester, you should focus on adjusting to the new academic demands. Better try to find an upperclassman who can be of a mentor. It is common knowledge that older students on campus can offer advice on courses plus social activities to join.

University students often find a romantic love on campus. It is common to see two lovers hand in hand as they walk down the street. Parents in Canada usually do not mind if their child has found a romantic love. And also universities do not mind if students date.

In the first year of university, students usually live in residence where they meet classmates easily. Most residence rooms are double rooms where two students share one room.

Canadian students join different clubs where they can do photograph, art, drama, or many other things. Some students may not like to participate in the extra-curriculum activities that are offered by the school. However, they go to the other clubs to drink alcohol and dance. Some students both girls and boys like to drink beer or drink alcohol as well. After a hard week at school, the weekend is usually the time that people go to their clubs. To get into the clubs in Canada, you must be at least 19 years old. The reason for this is that this is the legal drinking age in Canada.

Smoking marijuana is becoming more and more common. Recently in Canada, a new law was made to decriminalize possession of small amounts of marijuana. This means that you do not get charged as a criminal by the law. However, marijuana is still illegal. You can still be charged as breaking a law and fined money if you are caught with marijuana, but you will not go to jail. It has been decriminalized, but not legalized.

Almost all the campuses in all the universities in Canada are green meadow and fresh flowers, green trees and grasses everywhere. The students enjoy the beautiful public lawns. A stroll through a grassy area on a campus is a favorite way of enjoying fresh air and sunshine. If the day is warm and the grass green and lush, some students will walk bare foot on the grass. On sunny warm days on any Canadian university campus you will find students sitting or lying on the grass, breathing the fragrant smell of the grass or reading, talking with friends, or just resting. Access to and use of open space and parks is a part of the culture of Canada.

译 文

加拿大高等教育在过去的40年里急剧变化，主要表现为高等院校学生、教师及院校数量的显著增加。其质变主要表现为越来越强调应用研究、国际化和商业化。

据报道，每年有多于15万的国际学生来加拿大学习，其中9千多学生来自中国。除此以外，还有更多的人来到加拿大学习英语或法语。国际学生为加拿大课堂带来了丰富多彩的文化。加拿大学校欢迎你带来的知识和技能。

加拿大国际学生的学费以及生活费用相对于世界水平较低。符合条件的学生还可以通过校外工作获得宝贵的加拿大工作经验。

加拿大的大学各有各的优势。有些可能以科系闻名，而其他的可能以某个学院著称。以多伦多大学为例，这是公认的顶尖大学之一。它的几十个学院和科系在世界上都很出名，其中有些在科学技术发展方面成绩卓著。麦吉尔大学以人文学科和医学院而著名。

加拿大的大学和学院在一年四季里为娱乐活动、文化活动和年度运动会提供世界一流的设施。各种体育队在学校也十分流行，包括冰球、棒球、篮球、足球、高尔夫球、网球、羽毛球、壁球和游泳等等。体育队的学生们都积极参与各种竞技比赛。这里的学习生活和社会生活之间可以达到很好的平衡。事实上，在你适应了加拿大的生活后，你的社会生活可能会使你成为一个更出色的学生。几乎所有的大学生都热爱自己的大学，而且他们都为自己是该大学的一员而骄傲。成功的学生是那些除了好好学习还参加一些社会活动的学生。

在大学里学习，不像中学那样死记硬背，要求多读书和多思考。大多数教授们都自愿给那些课上没听懂的学生辅导。大学生很主动地组织一些学习小组，几个同学一起定期见面来讨论和复习所学课程的内容。如果你刚进入第一学期，你应该把重点放在熟悉新课程的要求上。你最好尽可能找一位高年级的学长作为你的辅导老师。大家都知道，学长能在课程和参加社会活动方面给你指导。

大学生往往在大学校园有一段浪漫的爱情故事。我们会经常看到一对情侣手牵手漫步在街头。通常情况下，在加拿大，家长不介意他们的孩子是不是谈恋爱，校方也不约束同学约会。

读大一的时候，学生们一般都住在公寓宿舍里，这样他们比较容易见到自己的同学。大多数宿舍都是两人间的。

加拿大学生加入不同的俱乐部，在那里，他们可以学习摄影、艺术、戏剧或参加其他一些活动。也有一些学生可能不喜欢参加学校组织的课外活动，于是他们去其他俱乐部喝酒跳舞。有一些男生和女生都喜欢喝啤酒和白酒。在一周紧张的学校生活后，他们往往利用周末的时间去他们的俱乐部。在加拿大，要是想加入俱乐部，你就至少得19岁，因为那个年龄才是他们的法定喝酒年龄。

吸食大麻毒品的大学生越来越多。最近，加拿大制定了一条新法律，根据这条新法律，少量吸食大麻毒品的人不被指控为罪犯。但吸食大麻还是不合法的。如果你被发现吸食大麻，你还是会被定名为触犯法律以及被罚款，但是你不会坐牢。尽管吸食大麻已经被非刑事化了，但是还没有得到法律的认可。

几乎所有的加拿大大学的校园都是绿荫成片，到处是鲜花、绿树和青草。学生们尽情地享受着这些美丽的绿色公共草坪。在校园的草坪上散步是学生喜爱的享受新鲜空气和阳光的方式。如果天气温暖，草坪碧绿而茂盛，学生们会赤脚在草坪上行走。在那些阳光灿烂的日子里，加拿大大学校园里会有很多人坐在或躺在草坪上呼吸着青草的香味，或看书，或跟朋友聊天，或休息。进入和享用开放空间和公园是加拿大文化的一部分。

I'm on Top of the World

(Li's just finished his exam and meets his American friend Lucy on campus.)

Lucy: Hello there, Li. You're *looking a bit run-down*. What have you been doing?

Li: I've been overworking myself, with all my exams and all my other work. I just finished my history exam and I made a terrible mistake. There was a fill-in-the-blank exercise. I tried very hard to think of the name of a history book, but I kept *drawing a blank*. Well, I'm behind in my sleep and I think I'm *coming down with* something.

Lucy: What you need now is some rest. Everyone in my dormitory talked about you. You were cooped up in the dorm for several days. Why don't you go out and take some fresh air?

Li: That's a good idea. But I'm *running a temperature*, and I've got a sore throat. I'm going to follow your advice and I'll catch up on my sleep this weekend. What about you, Lucy? How are you feeling? You look like you're *in great shape*.

Lucy: I feel good. I don't take as many courses as you do. I'm on the university hockey team. I have a healthy diet, and I get enough sleep. Tell you the truth, I feel like I'm *on top of the world*.

Li: Well, as soon as I get better, I'm going to start doing some exercises every day. I'm sure physical exercise *does wonders for* a person's health and sense of well-being.

Lucy: I'd like to take you to the city gym if you get better. That's an ideal place for us to do physical exercise. It has some equipments such as bars, mats and rings.

Li: Good idea. Thanks, Lucy. I will have to *brush up on* my yoga lesson for tomorrow's exam. I'll try to call you next week.

Vocabulary and Notes

• with all my exams and all my other work	一方面是由于我的考试，一方面是由于其他的工作
• fill-in-the-blank exercise	填空练习
• behind in one's sleep	睡眠不足，缺觉
• catch up on one's sleep	补一觉

- sore throat 嗓子疼
- the university hockey team 大学冰球队。加拿大人创造了现代冰球运动，人们把冰球誉为加拿大的"国球"。冰球流行于全加拿大，进而发展到美国和欧洲。1908年国际冰球联合会（the International Ice Hockey Federation）在法国巴黎创立。自1920年冰球运动在第七届奥运会上被列为比赛项目以来，直到1958年，加拿大冰球在世界上常处于领先地位，多次赢得世界冠军。冰球比赛每场60分钟，分3局进行，每局实际比赛时间为20分钟，中间休息15分钟。比赛时每队6人，前锋3人，后卫2人，守门1人。比赛过程中可以随时替换队员和守门员。运动员穿着冰鞋在冰上滑行，用球杆把球击入对方球门为胜。
- well-being　general health and happiness　健康；幸福
- bars (parallel bars)　双杠
- mat　（体操或角斗用的）垫子
- rings　吊环

Idioms for Everyday Use

look/feel/get run-down
由于疾病、过度工作、紧张而显得疲劳、虚弱　　look/be tired and weak due to illness, overwork, tension, etc.

- The last time I saw him, he **looked run-down**—he'd been working 70 hours a week.
  上次我看见他满脸倦容——他当时一周工作70个小时。
- If you don't get more rest and relax a little, you're going to **get run-down**.
  如果你不多休息放松一下，你会累垮的。

draw a blank
记不起某事；白费力气，一无所得；不成功　　be unable to remember something; obtain nothing in return for an effort made; be unsuccessful

- I'm trying to think of his name but I keep **drawing a blank**.
  我使劲在想他叫什么名字，可就是想不起来。
- A: Did you find that book I asked you to get for me?

B: No, I'm afraid not. I tried the university library, the bookstore and some other libraries in the city but I **drew a blank**.

A: I'm sorry, maybe I gave the wrong title. Let me check.

A: 你找到我让你买的书了吗？

B: 我恐怕没找到。我到过大学的图书馆、城里的书店和其他图书馆，结果一无所获。

A: 对不起，或许我给你写错了书名，让我来核对一下。

come down with (an illness) 得病，患病	catch an illness/disease (usually a minor illness)

- She coughed a lot last night. She probably **came down with** pneumonia.
  她昨晚咳嗽得很厉害，可能得了肺炎。
- Last month Steve **came down with** the flu and was in bed for 3 days.
  上个月史蒂夫得了流感，卧床休息了三天。

run a temperature 发烧	run/have a fever

- The baby looks pale, but he isn't **running a temperature**, so we aren't too worried.
  这孩子脸色苍白，但他没有发烧，所以我们不太担心。
- Bob's **running a temperature** of 39 Celsius—you'd better call the doctor.
  鲍勃发烧39度，你最好请医生来。

be in good/bad/great/terrible shape 健康状况良好/不佳/特别好/特别糟糕	be in good/bad/great/terrible health

- After spending two weeks in the healthy mountain air, she **was in great shape**.
  在有益健康的山区里生活了两周后，她的身体很结实。
- He never gets any exercise—**he's in terrible shape**.
  他从不进行锻炼——身体状况很糟糕。

feel/be on top of the world 对情况或生活感到非常满意和自信；幸福到了极点，对一切都感到满意	feel extremely happy and confident about one's situation or life

- First he got a great job, then he got married—he was **feeling on top of the world**.
  他先是得到一份不错的工作，然后结了婚——他感到幸福极了。
- Having won first prize in the recitation contest, he **is on top of the world**.
  他在演讲比赛中得了一等奖，高兴得要命。

Unit 21　College Life 大学生活

do/work wonders for
有益于；使某人或某物受到积极的影响

be very beneficial to; be/exert a positive influence on someone or something

▍ Try this medicine. It **did wonders for** my cold. I'm sure it will help you too!
　试试这种药，它对治疗我的感冒有疗效。我相信对你也会起作用的！

▍ Being married to Barbara has **done wonders for** John. His pessimistic attitude has almost completely disappeared.
　与芭芭拉结婚使约翰受益匪浅。他的悲观情绪几乎看不到了。

brush up on something
重温，复习

refresh one's memory of; renew one's skill in or knowledge of

▍ I have been asked to repeat my speech on William Shakespeare. It's been over a year since I lectured on this topic. Therefore, I will have to **brush up on** my notes.
　我被邀请去再做一次有关莎士比亚的报告。我已经一年多没做这个报告了，所以我得重温我的讲稿。

▍ I can't go with you. The delegation from Germany is coming tomorrow. I'll **brush up on** my German this evening.
　我不能和你去了。德国代表团明天到，今天晚上我要温习我的德语。

▍ If you are going to Mexico, you should **brush up on** your Spanish.
　如果你去墨西哥，你应该重新温习一下你的西班牙语。

▍ A: Would you like to come to the countryside to enjoy the beautiful autumn landscape this weekend?
　B: I'm sorry. I cannot. I'm planning to **brush up on** my cooking skills by taking a few online courses this weekend.
　A: Oh, I see. Good luck.
　A: 这个周末想跟我一起去乡村玩吗？享受一下秋天的美景。
　B: 对不起，我去不成。这个周末我计划在网上温习烹饪技巧的几门课程。
　A: 噢，我知道了。祝你好运。

Unit 22
Gatherings
聚会

Canadians often have large social gatherings. They may be called "coffee hours" or "open houses". On many occasions, when groups of friends or colleagues at work get together for dinner or for a social evening, almost all the guests offer to contribute something to eat or drink. These gatherings are called potluck dinners; they usually consist of a salad or vegetable and several more substantial dishes such as chicken, meatballs, lasagna, or special ethnic delicacies.

Another common gathering is the backyard barbecue. Nowadays, the backyard barbecue has become a mainstream of the suburban lifestyle. It is not only a culinary event, but a social activity as well, where people get together to celebrate national holidays, birthdays, and other social occasions. You may be asked to bring a dish of food. It is common to arrive ten or fifteen minutes late and leave half an hour before it is scheduled to end. This depends upon the occasion degree of familiarity with the people there.

Canadian people take family gatherings seriously. Thanksgiving is time for far-flung families to join around a common table. Grown children brave the busiest travel season of the year to return to their ancestral nest, where they eat too much, drink too much, and pick up year-old arguments as though they had never left home. The traditional meal centers around a roast turkey supplemented by mashed potatoes with gravy, baked potatoes, baked winter squash, mashed winter squash, jellied salad, green salad, stewed tomatoes, canned green beans, creamed onions, cabbage, cornbread, dinner rolls, celery, olives, pumpkin pie, apple pie, mince pie, Indian pudding, and ice cream. The goal is to eat so much that nobody can move, and then watch football on television or some other TV programs. On this day it is traditional to bow one's head and give thanks for many blessings in life.

When people in North America participate in the gatherings for the first time, they talk about subjects of general interest. They talk about the weather, movies or entertainment, school, work, or local events. These are topics that you can talk about freely if you don't know the other person well. On these occasions you should talk for a few minutes to one person, and then move on to talk to another one.

People in Canada do not talk about things that are personal when they first meet. Some subjects are private and it is impolite to ask people about their individual matters. For example, they don't talk about why they aren't married or why they don't have children. People often talk about their jobs, but they don't make inquires about their salaries. Topics to avoid are politics, sex, and religion.

When there is a gathering in public, Canadians do not ask questions about why the other person is there or what the other person is doing. You are certainly seen as nosey if you are doing so.

As contact between the countries increases, more and more Canadians will approach Chinese in an attempt to learn about China. It is good to have appropriate topics in mind for these short encounters, which will give you practice in talking with Canadians.

译 文

加拿大人经常举办大型社交聚会,可称为"茶话会"或"家庭招待会"。在很多场合,当朋友们或同事们聚在一起吃晚饭或参加社交晚会时,几乎所有的客人都会自带一些食物和饮料。这些聚会叫做聚餐会。客人们自带的食物通常包括沙拉或者蔬菜,以及其他几种更加丰盛的菜肴,比如鸡肉、肉丸子、意大利式卤汁面条或者是具有异国特色风味的佳肴。

另外一种常见的聚会是后院烧烤。现在这已成为加拿大郊区生活方式的主流。烧烤不仅是一种烹饪方式,而且成了一种聚会社交活动。人们聚在一起烧烤,庆祝国家法定假日、生日和其他一些特殊的社交活动。他们可能会要求你带一道菜过来。通常你来的时候应该晚到10或15分钟,走的时候应该提前半小时离去。这要视情况而定,要看你与在场的人的熟悉程度。

加拿大人特别重视家庭聚会。感恩节是分散在各处的家人团聚在一起同桌就餐的日子。长大成人的孩子在一年当中客运最繁忙的时候勇敢地返回他们的鸟巢。他们一边大吃大喝,一边拾起一年前争论的旧话题,就好像他们从未离开过家。传统的饭菜是以烤火鸡为中心,除此还有肉汁土豆泥、烤土豆、烤南瓜、南瓜泥、果冻沙拉、蔬菜沙拉、焖西红柿、青豆罐头、奶油洋葱、卷心菜、玉米面包、小圆面包、芹菜、橄榄、南瓜馅饼、苹果馅饼、肉馅饼、印度布丁和冰淇淋。目标是让人吃得都动弹不了,然后就看电视转播的橄榄球比赛和其他电视节目。就是在这一天,人们会按传统习惯垂首感谢生活中许多幸事。

在北美,人们初次见面时都会谈论大家普遍感兴趣的事情。他们谈论天气、电影或娱乐活动、学校、工作或当地的一些事情。在你还不太了解他人时,这些都是可以自由谈论的话题。在这种场合,你应该在与一个人谈上几分钟后再找其他人聊聊。

加拿大人在初次见面时不会谈论私人话题。有些话题涉及隐私,而且询问个人问题是很不礼貌的。比如,他们不去谈论谁为什么没有结婚或谁为什么没有小孩。他们经常谈论工作,但他们不谈自己的薪水。还要避免提及有关政治、性和宗教信仰方面的话题。

当有公众集会时,加拿大人不会询问某某人为什么出现在那里或他/她正在做什么的问题。如果你这么做,就会被认为是爱管闲事的人。

随着各国间的联系增多,越来越多的加拿大人开始接近中国人,他们想知道关于中国的事情。你最好在脑子里准备好一些适当的交谈话题,这也会带给你与加拿大人交谈的锻炼机会。

 Dialogue

She Drew Me out of My Shell

(Li and his Canadian friend May are talking about the party they had last night.)

Li: The party last night was certainly an interesting one, wasn't it?

May: You enjoyed it, then?

Li: Immensely. I don't think I've ever been with such a stimulating group of people. I'm so lucky to have had a chance to talk to those people. The conversations we had last night *covered a lot of ground.* Most of them are

Unit 22　Gatherings 聚会

	not of English descent, are they?
May:	Oh, no. As you know, Canada is a multicultural society. We've many Italians, many Ukrainians, Finns, Japanese, Chinese, Greek…it's a mixture of many different nationalities. The term "Multiculturalism" is used to describe the different ethnic groups in Canada. It's worth remembering that the population in Canada is enriched by immigrants, and the descendants of immigrants, from every part of globe. Around the year of 1880, for example, thousands of Chinese arrived to work on the Canadian Pacific Railway. Today, more than 500,000 Chinese live in British Columbia.
Li:	I see. Since Canadians are from different parts of the world, I think their manners are not strictly according to British etiquette. For instance, that group of people last night behaved casually. People just came up to me, introduced themselves and then started conversation. It *threw me* at first.
May:	Well, that was an informal party. It's quite proper and permissible for you to introduce yourself. There's nothing wrong with making your own introduction at that kind of party.
Li:	I struggled to *cope with* the situation at the beginning. Take Helen for example. She came up to me and made her own introduction, but I just stood there speechless. It seemed that I was shying compared to her.
May:	You ought to know how to start a conversation. If someone, for instance, tells you that he's from another place, then you say: "Oh, I'd like to travel to that place. What's it like over there?" Don't just stand there, and wait for them to speak.
Li:	Well, Helen was very talkative. She talked a lot about good manners in Canada and in the United States. She told me about table manners, greeting manners, and how to address different people—she really *got to the bottom of* good manners in North America. She also *drew me out of my shell*. I told her about lots of good manners in China. I found that there are many things different *as far as* manners go.
May:	I think so. In our country, for example, we never ask a stranger "how much money do you make?" That's considered *prying into* their personal affairs. It's nosy.

Li: She did tell me that. Besides, she told me about some table manners. She mentioned that people here never slurp or suck noodles noisily.

May: That's right. It would be rude to slurp noodles in the presence of people. I, personally, approve of many things the Chinese people do so far as manners go, but I *take a dim view of* the way some Chinese people slurp noodles. I think it's impolite.

Li: That's just what I was going to say. You *took the words out of my mouth.*

📖 Vocabulary and Notes

- immensely — very much 非常（喜爱）；好极了
- English descent — 英国后裔（子孙）
- multicultural society — 多元文化的社会
- Italian — 意大利人；意大利的
- Finn — 芬兰人
- mixture of many different nationalities — 许多不同民族的混合体
- multiculturalism — 多元文化学说（主义）
- the Canadian Pacific Railway — 加拿大太平洋铁路，是加拿大第一条横跨大陆的铁路线。2023年4月，加拿大太平洋铁路与堪萨斯城南方铁路公司整合为加拿大太平洋堪萨斯城铁路公司，成为第一家连接加拿大、美国和墨西哥三国的一级铁路运营商。
- English etiquette — 英国礼节
- pry into — 探听
- permissible — allowed 允许的
- stand there speechless — 站在那里一言不发
- timid — fearful; lacking courage 胆小的；胆怯的
- slurp noodles — 吸溜面条
- approve of — consider good, right, wise, etc. 赞成

Unit 22 Gatherings 聚会

📖 Idioms for Everyday Use

cover a lot of/much ground
涉及，包括很多

be extensive; discuss several matters

- In his first lecture on Galileo, our philosophy teacher **covered a lot of ground**.
  我们哲学老师关于伽利略的第一次讲座，涉及的内容很广泛。
- The committee's report on our urban problems **covers much new ground**.
  委员会有关贫民区的报告涉及了许多新问题。

throw someone
由于事情的意外或奇怪而不解

it means that something makes someone feel confused because it is unexpected or strange

- A: How come the new dish-washer isn't working?
  B: Don't know. It really **threw me**. The repairman just left fifteen minutes ago and said it was working fine.
  A: 新的洗碗机怎么坏了呢？
  B: 不知道。我真纳闷，修理工刚走了15分钟，而且他说这机器挺好用。
- It was the fact that she was married that **threw me**.
  她结婚的事实把我搞糊涂了。

cope with
对付；应付；妥善处理（一般指棘手的或困难的事情）

find a way to deal with something or someone (often troublesome or difficult)

- A: I haven't seen much of you lately. What have you been up to?
  B: Oh, no. I'm tired out. It seems that I can't **cope with** looking after my family and doing a full-time job at the same time.
  A: 最近很少看见你。你在忙什么？
  B: 噢，别提了。我累垮了。看来我应付不了在做全日制工作的同时还要照顾家庭。
- The police in Belgrade were scarcely able to **cope with** the noisy crowd.
  贝尔格莱德的警察几乎对付不了吵闹的人群。
- We can certainly **cope with** these enemy forces, and even with larger ones.
  我们当然对付得了这些敌军，甚至更多些也没问题。

get/go to the bottom of
弄清……的基本事实；了解……的底细

discover the basic facts of something

- The professor talked with several students to **get to the bottom of** the dispute between them.
  为了弄清他们之间的这场纠纷的真正原因，教授找好几个学生进行了谈话。
- By studying all the clues carefully, the detective **got to the bottom of** the case and soon found out who the murderer was.
  经过对全部线索的仔细研究，这位侦探弄清了这个案件的底细，并且很快查出了谁是凶手。

| **draw/bring someone out of one's shell (come out of one's shell)**
不再害羞；去掉冷淡的态度，开始愿意和别人友好交往 | make a person become bolder and less shy in the company of others; make a person become more friendly or interested in others |

- What **drew him out of his shell** was the invitation to talk about his favorite topic—the Gulf War.
  我们要请他谈谈他最喜欢的话题——海湾战争，他就会谈笑风生了。
- Dee Thompson was a taciturn mountain boy hard to talk to. He didn't **come out of his shell** until I mentioned King Solomon (a ball) the other day.
  迪·汤普森是个不爱讲话的山里孩子，不易接近。那天我提起所罗门王（一条鲈鱼）后，他才开始愿意和我交谈。

| **as/so far as**
就……而言；从……来看 | with reference to; as for |

- A: Did John work hard yesterday?
  B: Well, he did a good job **as far as** he went, but he didn't finish it.
  A: 约翰昨天工作卖劲儿吗？
  B: 就他所做的工作来看，做得很好，但他没有全部做完。
- What you've done is pretty good **as far as** it goes; but you should still remain modest.
  就你目前已做的工作来说，还是不错的；不过仍要保持谦虚谨慎的态度。

| **pry into**
过于好奇地打听；探问（别人的事情、秘密等） | inquire with too much interest into (other people's affairs, a secret, etc.) |

- She's always **prying into** other people's affairs. I don't want her to know our plan, so keep it quiet.
  她总是爱打听别人的私事。我不想让她知道我们的计划，你要保密。
- Look! There's the village scandalmonger **prying into** people's business.
  看！村里这位造谣生事专家又在四处打听别人的事了。

A: Richard is really upset about something.
B: Don't you know that? He was very angry at Helen. He accused Helen of **prying into** everything about his private life.
A: 理查德一定在为什么事情烦恼。
B: 难道你不知道吗？他对海伦非常恼火。他责怪海伦对他的私生活样样都问。

take a dim view of something 对……持不赞成态度	disapprove of; have a negative opinion of something

A: How did the meeting go yesterday?
B: Well, the members of the club took turns making suggestions. Most of the members thought the variety show was a wonderful idea. Only one or tow **took a dim view of** it.
A: 昨天的会议进行得怎么样？
B: 是这样的，俱乐部的成员轮流提建议。大多数人认为多种形式的节目是个好主意，只有一两个人不赞成。

▌ Most of the parents in this district **take a dim view of** the teaching methods used in our school.
这个地区的大部分家长对我们学校正在使用的教学方法持否定态度。

▌ Barbara approves of many things her sister does, but she **takes a dim view of** the way her sister Katie is raising her children.
芭芭拉对妹妹所做的许多事都认可，但对妹妹凯蒂教育孩子的方法却不赞成。

take the words out of one's mouth 讲出别人正要讲的话	say exactly what someone is going to say

A: I've just finished reading Steve's list of ways of motivating employees to work more efficiently. I really don't think his ideas are reasonable practical—they're out of touch with reality.
B: That's just what I was going to say. You **took the words out of my mouth**. Let's try to persuade the others to see things our way.
A: 我刚看完史蒂夫提出的一系列方法，是关于刺激雇员更有效地工作的。我认为他的想法不合理，或者说不实用，不符合实际。
B: 这正是我想说的，你讲出了我想讲的意见。让我们设法说服别人同意我们的方法。

▌ I was going to suggest a movie, but she **took the words out of my mouth** and said she would like to see one.
我正要建议去看电影，她却说了出来，说她想去看一场电影。

Unit 23
Concept of Equality
平等的观念

Canadians initiate each individual should have an equal chance for success. For them, equality means that everyone should have an equal chance to enter the race and win. They understand that in Canada they would not have to live among noble families and enjoy forefathers' wealth accumulated over hundreds of years. The lower social class into which many were born did not prevent them from rising to a high social position. Many found that they did have a better chance to succeed in Canada.

Because many immigrants from the other countries succeeded in all walks of life, they also come to believe in the concept of equality of opportunity. The fact of immigrants' successful cases helps them ensure that the competition for success is a fair one. In other words, a person who was born into a wealthy family does not surely win if he is not willing to compete. The pressures of competition in the life of a Canadian began in childhood and continue until retirement. Learning to compete successfully is a part of growing up in Canada. Therefore, Canadian young people are encouraged to be independent. They are inquisitive and tend to question their parents. It is not in their nature to obey blindly, and if there is a crisis and there is no one to tell them what to do, they use their own initiative.

Canadian secondary schools, junior and senior, have a good reputation. They take their responsibilities very seriously. They have guidance counselors to whom children can go privately if they have any special problems, especially about their careers. Parents are encouraged to share in the school life of their children. They sometimes go into the class and help the teachers with plays and class reading, and some schools have highly successful Parent-Teacher Associations.

Young people in Canada mature early. Most provinces in Canada allow teenagers as young as sixteen to drive provided they have completed a driver's education course at school and have passed the usual driver's test. Many youngsters earn the money by taking an evening job after school or in their vacations.

The inequality in aristocratic societies extends into the family in many countries. The father is accepted as ruler and master. The children's relations with him are very formal, and love for him is always combined with fear. In Canada, however, the democratic idea of equality destroys the father's status as ruler of the family and lessens the emotional distance between father and children. There is less formal respect for, and fear of the father. But there is more affection expressed toward him.

After children marry, their parents do not owe them a down payment on a house or money for the furniture or appliances. Their parents do not have an obligation to baby-sit or to take their grandchildren in their home when the parents are on vacation. Canadian parents respect their children's privacy and their personal belongings. That means not taking away or borrowing things without permission, not reading their diaries and mails, not looking through purses, pockets and drawers. If a mother feels that she must read her daughter's diary to know what is going on, the communication between them must be pretty bad.

译文

加拿大人倡导每个人都应该有平等的机会去获得成功。对他们来讲，平等意味着每一个人都应该有平等的机会参加激烈的竞争，以求成功。他们认为，在加拿大，你不一定非要生活在贵族家庭里，享受着父辈们几百年聚集的财富。多数人出身于下层社会，但这并不妨碍他们提升自己的社会地位。很多人发现，他们在加拿大的的确确有更多的机会获取成功。

因为许多来自其他国家的移民在各行各业取得了成功，他们也开始相信机遇公平的观念。移民们成功案例的事实促使加拿大人相信，为成功而竞争是公平的。换句话说，如果他不去竞争，即使出生在富豪家庭里，他也不会取得成功。加拿大人一生中的竞争压力是从童年开始，直到退休。在加拿大，学会成功竞争是成长的一部分。因此，加拿大的年轻人被鼓励要独立自主,他们对事物充满好奇而且经常向父母发问。他们天生就不是盲目服从的人,如果出现了问题而没有人告诉他们该怎样做的话,他们就会按自己的想法去做。

加拿大的中学教育,包括初中和高中的教育享有盛誉。学校非常负责任。学校设有指导顾问,孩子们如果有什么特殊问题,尤其是关于职业生涯方面的问题,可以单独与他们沟通。学校还鼓励家长参与孩子们的校园生活。有时他们会走进教室,帮助老师表演短剧或课堂阅读,有的学校还设有家长与教师协会,办得非常成功。

加拿大的年轻人成熟较早,大部分的省区允许16岁的孩子开车,只要他们在校完成了驾驶训练课程并通过驾驶考试就可以了。有很多的年轻人会在假期当中或放学后的晚上打工挣钱。

在很多国家,贵族社会的不平等延伸到家庭当中。父亲被认为是统治者和主人,孩子们与他的关系就变得十分正式,对他的爱也夹杂着恐惧。不过在加拿大,民主平等的观念打破了许多父亲在家庭中的主人地位,并且拉近了父亲与孩子之间的感情距离。孩子们对父亲表面上的尊敬和恐惧是少了,但对他表达的爱却多了。

孩子结婚后,父母无须资助他们买房子或家具家电。他们也没有义务为他们看孩子或在他们度假时把孙子孙女们接到家里来住。加拿大的家长尊重孩子的隐私和私人物品,就是说他们不会在未经孩子许可的前提下拿走或借用孩子的东西,不会翻看他们的日记和邮件,不会翻查钱包、口袋和抽屉。如果一位母亲认为她一定要看看女儿的日记,以便知道发生了什么事情,那她们之间的沟通一定相当糟糕。

Out of the Blue

(Rebecca meets her Chinese friend Li, and asks him whether he saw the movie on TV last night.)

Rebecca: How was your weekend, Li?

Li: I was reading a novel by Margaret Atwood, *Lady Oracle*. That's my homework.

Rebecca: Did you see the movie on Channel 8 last night?

Li: No, I missed it. My TV set went *on the blink* last night.

Rebecca: Oh, that's too bad. It was an excellent film. It was made especially for teenagers, you know.

Li: I read the preview in yesterday's paper and had hoped to watch it last night. But I turned on the TV, and it began to make a noise at first, and then it changed channels *out of the blue*. I turned it off and when I turned it on again, the picture was gone.

Rebecca: That's weird.

Li: I'll say! It was a little scary, too! Say, the name of the movie last night was *Cowboys* ...

Rebecca: Oh, *Cowboys Don't Cry* based on a book by Canadian children's novelist Marilyn Halvorson. I haven't seen such a marvelous plot and such superb acting in a long time.

Li: It describes a father-son relationship, right?

Rebecca: Well, a hot-tempered, redheaded boy, Shane, blames his father for the accident that killed his mother.

Li: The preview says that his mother was killed because of his father's *goofing off*.

Rebecca: That's right. His father was an alcoholic rodeo cowboy. The climactic scene was when the father saved his son from a charging bull at a rodeo. The boy was very grateful for his father's help when he *landed on his feet*. After that the father no longer *ran away* from his responsibilities, and Shane no longer let the past fill his present with hatred. From that day on they learned to love and accept each other. The most exciting part is that...

Li: Well, don't tell me the exciting part. I want to see that movie myself, and it's no fun if you tell me the whole story. I'd better get going before you really do *spill the beans*.

Rebecca: Hey, Li! They'll *re-run* the movie sometime next week.

Li: Great! Thanks for telling me. I should get back to my work.

Rebecca: See you later!

Li: See you.

Vocabulary and Notes

- Channel 8   八频道
- teenager   a boy or girl who is between thirteen and nineteen years old 青少年（13至19岁的少男少女）
- preview   （电影或电视）预告

- That's weird. That's very strange. 简直太奇怪了。
- I'll say! Yes indeed! (a strong form of agreement) 谁说不是呢!
- It was a little scary, too! 还真有点害怕!
- cowboy in western Canada and US, a man who tends cattle, doing his work mostly on horseback 加拿大和美国西部的骑马牧牛者; 牛仔
- marvelous plot 动人的情节
- superb acting 精彩的表演
- a hot-tempered, redheaded boy 一个长着红头发的急脾气的男孩
- an alcoholic rodeo cowboy 一个爱喝酒的驱赶牛马的牛仔
- climactic 高潮的; 顶点的
- a charging bull 一头冲过来的牛
- no longer let the past fill his present with hatred (他)不再像过去那样恨(他父亲)了
- They learned to love and accept each other. 他们懂得了互敬互爱、和睦相处。

Idioms for Everyday Use

(go/be) on the blink
(机器、仪器工具等)出了故障, 失灵了, 坏了 | out of order; broken down

A: The copy machine has broken down again.
B: Better send for the repairman.
A: That's the third time this week this machine's gone **on the blink**.
B: Maybe, we need a new one.
A: 复印机又出故障了。
B: 最好把修理工叫来。
A: 这星期这台机器可是第三次出毛病了。
B: 大概我们要买一台新的了。

A: Could you run of 20 copies of each of these documents for me, please?
B: I'm sorry. The machine's gone **on the blink**.
A: 请你把每份文件复印20份好吗?
B: 对不起, 机器坏了。

out of the blue
突如其来；蓦地，突然地

suddenly without warning; unexpectedly

- A: Did you hear that William is leaving his wife?
- B: Who told you that?
- A: He did. We were having coffee this morning and **out of the blue** he announced that he and his wife were breaking up.
- A: 你听说威廉要和他妻子分手了吗？
- B: 谁跟你说的？
- A: 他自己说的。今天早晨我们一起喝咖啡时，他突然声明他与他妻子要离婚。

- The couple started shouting and screaming at each other **out of the blue** last night.
  昨晚，夫妻俩突然间吵闹起来。

goof off
游手好闲；吊儿郎当；不认真工作

be lazy and fool around; neglect one's job

- A: I can't stand Barbara. She's really two-faced.
- B: I agree. The boss thinks she's a great worker because, whenever he's around, she really tries to impress him. But when he's not there, she **goofs off** all the time.
- A: 我受不了芭芭拉这个人，她真是个两面派。
- B: 我有同感。老板认为她是个很好的职员，因为老板一来，她就极力表现自己。但老板不在时，她总是偷懒。

- "If you **goof off** on the job too much, you'll be fired," said the boss angrily.
  "如果你工作太吊儿郎当，你将被解雇，"老板生气地说。

land/light on one's feet
幸免于难；化险为夷

recover safely from an unpleasant or dangerous situation

- A: The hijacking incident ended in Somalia last night with the death of the three kidnappers who seized the plane last Thursday.
- B: How about the passengers?
- A: Well, all the passengers and crew members **landed on their feet** finally.
- A: 昨晚劫机事件在索马里以三名劫机者的死亡而结束。他们是上星期四劫持的那架飞机。
- B: 乘客怎么样？
- A: 所有乘客和机组人员都幸免于难。

- Every time when he met with danger, he **landed on his feet**.
  他每次遇到危险，总是幸免于难。

run away (from something difficult, unpleasant)
逃避做某事；躲避

(in this context) try to avoid having to do something or having to deal with it

- It would be irresponsible of you to **run away** from difficulties. You ought to face up to them boldly.
  见了困难就躲是不负责的态度。你应该勇敢地正视困难。
- We can't **run away** from the facts: the firm is now in serious trouble.
  我们不能逃避现实：现在公司正处于困境。

spill the beans
（无意中）泄露秘密；泄露消息（尤指不想让人知道的事）

tell a secret; give away information, esp. something not intended to be made known

- A: Hey, you promised you wouldn't tell the boss we took Thursday afternoon off. You broke your word!
- B: Don't blame me. I didn't tell him. It was Kevin who **spilled the beans**.
- A: 嘿，是你许诺的不把我们星期四下午休息的事告诉老板。你说话不算数啊！
- B: 别责怪我，我没告诉他。是凯文泄露的秘密。

- A: How did you know their secret?
- B: Well, he **spilled the beans**, and I knew all about the matter.
- A: 你怎么知道他们的秘密的？
- B: 他说漏了嘴，于是我就掌握了此事的全部情况。

re-run
再次上映电影或重播电视节目

show a film or television-program again

- A: It's one of the best films I've ever seen.
- B: Oh, yes! I'd pick it as the best film of the year.
- A: I'd like to see it again if they **re-run** it.
- B: Me too.
- A: 这是我看过的电影中最好的一部。
- B: 噢，可不是嘛！我认为这是今年最受欢迎的电影。
- A: 如果再演的话，我愿意再看一遍。
- B: 我也这样想。

- A: When is the school going to **re-run** that movie?
- B: Next Friday afternoon.
- A: 学校什么时候再放映那部电影？
- B: 下星期五下午。

Unit 24
Royal Canadian Mounted Police
加拿大皇家骑警

Royal Canadian Mounted Police (RCMP)

A Red-Uniform-Clad Mountie, standing proudly beside a shining horse on the rugged frontier, is certainly an image that screams "Canada". The Royal Canadian Mounted Police are indeed a national icon and living symbol of Canadian heritage. But this vital organization is much more complex than the movies of yesterday, and the television shows of today, make it out to be.

The RCMP formed as the North-West Mounted Police (NWMP) in 1873. At that time, Canadians were struggling to settle in the western part of the country. The famous NWMP march west to ease tensions between the settlers and the Natives began the following year. A succession of duties followed, including policing the traveling labor fore of the Canadian Pacific Railway, built to join the east with the west. The Klondike Gold Rush and two world wars followed. By the 1920s the renamed RCMP established friendly relations with Native groups, controlled whiskey traders, supervised treaties between the Indian tribes and the government and generally eased the hardships of the times. The RCMP has been in most chapters and many headlines of Canadian history.

Every detail of the colorful history of the RCMP can be found at the RCMP Centennial Museum and Depot in Regina, Saskatchewan. Uniforms, replicas and stories of some of the famous exploits of the force are on display. The training facilities and barracks also can be toured. In addition to this, a drill takes place at

1 pm each weekday.

Today, the RCMP is in the information age and continues to enforce laws made by the authority of the Canadian Parliament. A computerized access system for criminal information has been in operation since 1972. The first female recruits became RCMP members in 1974 and since then, recruiting has also reflected a multicultural Canada. On top of their national security responsibilities, they still police many of the country's western and remote towns.

Mounties are not often seen fighting crime in their coats and uniform hats; however, certain members of the RCMP can be seen in full and official garb in ceremonial escort, parades and celebrations in Canada. A favorite and famous exercise of the Mounties is the RCMP Musical Ride. This combination of history, power, precision and beauty leaves a lasting impression on anyone, but especially a proud Canadian. The Musical Ride was developed out of a desire by the early members to amuse themselves while practicing and displaying their riding ability—at the same time they entertained their community. The first known riding display was given in 1876 and the first Musical Ride was performed in 1897 at the Regina barracks.

Until 1966, every member of the RCMP did recruit equitation training, but now only those who have applied and been accepted for Musical Ride duty learn how to ride in this traditional way. The Musical Ride is perfected at the RCMP Stables and Practice Ground in Ottawa. The public is always welcome to watch the practice sessions, but the greatest time to experience it is during the week leading up to Canada Day, when there is a Musical Ride, with full band, each evening in the capital.

Other Canadian Forces

Many towns and cities have established police boards. Most municipal forces are governed directly by municipal councils or their committees. Their duty is to protect the people in the community.

For example, the Metropolitan Toronto Police Committee Services has made twenty tips for Canadian people on "How available to make your life safer". Here is one of them:

If there is a fistfight, stay away from it, but call the police immediately.

If someone starts harassing you on the street, call out as soon as you feel threatened. Don't wait until you're in immediate danger.

You're more likely to attract attention and assistance by shouting "Fire!" instead of "Help!" because some people are reluctant to respond to cries of help. They just don't want to get involved. However, police will react quickly whether you shout "Fire!" or "Help!"

In most cases, the police are ready to help people because the tax money of the Canadian people pays the police. One of the most useful functions of the police is to help people when there is a danger. It is his duty for a policeman to walk you to your parking lot. Don't hesitate to ask.

译文

加拿大皇家骑警（RCMP）

在崎岖的边境线上，一位身穿红色制服的加拿大皇家骑警自豪地站在一匹油亮的骏马旁边，这幅鲜艳夺目的画面形象地告诉大家，这就是加拿大。毫无疑问，加拿大皇家骑警代表着加拿大的国家形象和历史传统。但其实这个重要组织的悠久历史远比我们在电影和电视中看到的要复杂得多。

加拿大皇家骑警的前身"西北骑警"（NWMP）成立于1873年。当时加拿大人正在奋力拼搏，力求实现在西部定居。转年，西北骑警开始了著名的西征运动，他们成功地平息了移民者和当地土著居民之间的紧张局势。随后西北骑警出色地完成了一系列任务，其中包括维持修建加拿大太平洋铁路（连接东部和西部的铁路）劳工的治安，然后是克朗代克淘金热，以及两次世界大战。在20世纪20年代被改名为皇家骑警的西北骑警已经与当地部落建立了友好的合作关系，开始管理威士忌酒贸易，监督印第安部落与政府所签署条约的实施，整体上缓和了当时的艰苦形势。因此，在加拿大历史上，皇家骑警成了浓墨重彩的一部分。

在萨斯喀彻温省里贾纳市的加拿大皇家骑警百年纪念博物馆里记录着所有加拿大皇家骑警的精彩历史。那里展出了各种制服、仿制品和部队的一些著名的丰功伟绩。训练设施和军营对游客开放。另外，每个工作日的下午一点都会举行一场队列操练。

如今，加拿大皇家骑警也步入了信息化时代，并一如既往地执行国会制定的各种法规。从1972年起，电子化的犯罪信息系统就投入了使用。1974年加拿大皇家骑警招收了第一批女骑警。从那时开始，皇家骑警的招募也呈现出了多种文化色彩。皇家骑警除了负责国家安全外，他们还负责维持许多西部和偏远城镇的治安情况。

一般来说，在加拿大，你很少能看到皇家骑警身着红色制服和帽子抓犯人，但你可以在护卫、游行和庆典等活动中看到很多身穿全套制服的皇家骑警。最受人们喜爱也是最为著名的活动就是加拿大皇家骑警的骑马舞表演。这项融合了历史、力量、精准和优美的表演会给现场每个人，特别是引以为豪的加拿大人留下长久的回忆。最初，骑马舞是由几个爱好音乐的骑警组织的，他们只是为了在训练和展示马术时自娱自乐而已，但其实他们也为整个社区带来了欢乐。据说加拿大皇家骑警的骑术表演始于1876年，在1897年骑马舞第一次在里贾纳军营上演。

直到1966年，每一位加拿大皇家骑警都接受骑马舞表演中的马术训练。但是现在只有那些提出申请并被骑马舞队接纳的骑警才会学习骑马舞中的骑术。后来，骑马舞在位于渥太华的皇家骑警马术训练场得到完善。人们非常愿意观看演出，但最棒的表演还是在国庆节前一周的骑马舞表演，那时在渥太华每天晚上都会上演有全体乐队伴奏的表演。

加拿大其他警力

许多城镇都建有自己的警察部门。市属警察通常由市委员会直接支配。他们的职责是保护该社区的民众。

举例来说：大都市多伦多警察委员会服务机构为加拿大人民制定了有关"怎样使你的生活更加安全"的20条建议。其中一则是这样的：

如果有人打架，你应该躲开，但是要立刻给警察打电话。

如果在街上有人骚扰你，你只要感觉受到了威胁就大声呼喊。不要等到危险来临时才采取措施。

要呼喊"着火了！"而不是"救命！"才能更加引起人们的注意，从而得到帮助，因为有些人不愿意理会救命的呼喊声，他们只不过是不愿卷入这些事。然而，不管你叫喊"着火了！"还是呼喊"救命！"，警察将会迅速做出反应。

通常情况下，警察会热心帮忙的，因为他们的工资是由加拿大人缴的税来支付的。警察最有用的职业功效就是危险的时候帮助人。送你到停车场去找车是他们的责任。请他们帮助不必犹豫。

Mind Your Own Business

(Ada meets Bill on the campus and is surprised to see he has a black-eye.)

Ada: Hey, Bill! What happened to you! How did you get that shiner?
Bill: Oh, don't ask. I really don't know how to explain it to you. I was walking down the street yesterday, thinking about a change, a change from the monotony of life everyday, when I saw a guy pushing a girl around. I tried

to *step in*, but he told me to *mind my own business*.

Ada: What happened then?

Bill: He started yelling at the girl again, and then pushing her around once more. I could *put two and two together*. This guy was definitely annoying that girl and I *jumped in with both feet*.

Ada: What do you mean you jumped in with both feet? What did you do?

Bill: I told the guy to quit bothering the girl and to *get lost*. "Shut up!" He barked at me, "I warned you to stay out of it." I thought I should teach him a lesson, so my right fist flashed and I *knocked him out*. Believe it or not, the girl got very angry at that, and punched me in the face. All *the lights went out*, and when I woke up, I was lying on my bed at home.

Ada: Oh, my god! Bill, maybe they're a couple.

Bill: Probably, but I'm not sure. Anyhow, my kindness came to no good. I just *couldn't make heads nor tails of them*.

Ada: I don't like to get involved in other people's affairs—especially if it's a quarrel. Do you remember that old proverb? Something about anyone who meddles in a quarrel not his own is like a guy who grabs a passing dog by the ears? My folks always taught me to mind my own business, and I think that's good advice.

Bill: Well, I don't know—what happened the other day certainly made my dull life interesting for a little while.

Ada: Yeah, but it sounds like you're too meddlesome.

Vocabulary and Notes

- Royal Canadian Mounted Police

加拿大皇家骑警(RCMP)，是加拿大联邦警察部队，也是除安大略省和魁北克省之外的其他各省的刑事警察队，负责加拿大国内安全。20世纪初，随着淘金热潮，大批探矿者涌入加拿大。当时，骑警给那些没有经验的人在荒野上生存帮了大忙。因此，1904年在骑警名称中冠上了"皇家"（Royal）二字。20世纪30年代，这支队伍增设了水上和空中分队、警犬队和刑事侦查队等。骑警的刑事侦查化验室和身份鉴定部门的全国性警务设施，可供所有经批准的警察队伍使用。

• a black-eye	a dark-colored bruise around one's eye as a result of being hit（被打得）发青的眼圈
• shiner (slang)	a black-eye, usually caused by someone hitting you 打伤的黑眼圈
• yell at (someone)	shout loudly at (someone) 向（某人）叫喊
• push around/about someone	bully someone 欺侮某人
• bark at someone	朝某人咆哮
• punch	give a sharp blow to (someone), as with the fist 用拳猛击
• ... my kindness came to no good	……好心没好报
• meddle	busy oneself in something without being asked to do so 管闲事；干预

 ## Idioms for Everyday Use

step in (to do something) 插手帮助或干预	(in this context) intervene either to help or hinder

- Seeing that I was at a loss for an answer to the police man's question, David **stepped in** to save the situation.
  大卫见我不知该怎么回答警察的问题，就插手为我解围。
- When the two groups began to fight, a policeman **stepped in** to stop it before they were hurt.
  正当两个团伙打架时，一个警察上前制止了他们相互伤害的暴力行为。
- If the local government does not meet their responsibilities, the Federal Government will definitely **step in**.
  如果地方政府不履行他们各自的职责，那么联邦政府一定会进行干预。

mind one's own business 不干涉别人的事情；管自己的事情	not be curious about other people's affairs; keep one's attention on one's own concerns or affairs

- A: Hi, Peter! How did your date with Mary go last night?
  B: **Mind you own business**!
  A: 嗨，彼得！你和玛丽昨天晚上的约会怎么样啊？
  B: 没你的事儿！

Unit 24　Royal Canadian Mounted Police　加拿大皇家骑警

I was walking down the street, **minding my own business**, when all of a sudden a guy rode up on a bicycle and threw a tomato at me!
我正在街头漫步，没招谁，也没惹谁，突然一个家伙骑到我跟前，朝我扔了一个西红柿！

put two and two together
根据所看到的或所听到的做出推断或结论

work out for oneself the real meaning of something from the things that one sees or hears

A: So you're getting the boss's job, eh?
B: No, I'm not. Who told you that?
A: Nobody told me. But, when I see a guy measuring the boss's office and moving the desk, I can **put two and two together**.
A: 看来你要当老板了，对吧？
B: 没有，不会的。谁跟你说的？
A: 没人跟我说，但是我看见有人正在老板的办公室里量尺寸，搬动办公桌，我是根据这些情况判断的。

If you **put two and two together**, there can be only one conclusion.
如果按事实推断，只能有一个结论。

jump in with both feet
热心从事；不假思索地或不顾后果地匆匆从事

be eager to do something; take action without worrying about the outcome or consequences; act urgently

When he saw the two men attacking the old lady, he didn't think about his own safety for one second—he **jumped in with both feet**.
当他见到两个男子正在欺负一位老妇人时，他一点都没考虑自己的安危——急忙去干预。

When the offer was made to him, he **jumped in with both feet**—and he has been sorry ever since.
当别人给他提出这个建议时，他没加思索就同意了——过后他一直在后悔。

get lost
走开，躲开

go away; leave someone alone

A: Can I borrow $50 until next week?
B: **Get lost**! That's the third time this month!
A: 能借给我50美元吗？下星期还你。
B: 走开！这个月你已是第三次借钱了！

He doesn't want people asking him questions now. He's already told three people to **get lost**.

他现在不愿意人们向他提问题。他已经拒绝三位了。

knock someone out
（拳击）击倒对方使其在规定的时间内不能站起；把某人击昏

(boxing) defeat an opponent by knocking him to the ground so that he can't rise within a specified time; make someone lose consciousness

- Mike **knocked his opponent out** in the first round of the contest.
  迈克在比赛的第一回合中就把对方击倒了。
- He was **knocked out** by a stone hurled at him from the other side of the road.
  从道路的另一边飞来的一块石头把他击昏在地。

the lights went out
由于眩晕或头部被击打而突然晕了过去

(in this context) describes the condition of suddenly losing consciousness, by fainting or receiving a blow to the head

- I was boxing in the gym the other day when all of a sudden **the lights went out**.
  我那天在体育馆练习拳击时，突然晕了过去。
- I can't stand the sight of blood, and when I saw them butchering a cow, all **the lights went out**.
  我晕血，当我看到屠夫杀牛时，一下便失去了知觉。

can't make head/heads nor tail/tails of (something)
弄不清或不理解某事

can't understand it

- A: Have you managed to assemble the machine yet?
- B: No, I've been studying the manual for about an hour but I **can't make head nor tail of** it.
- A: Let me have a look. Two heads are better than one.
- A: 你把机器安装好了吗？
- B: 没有，我把说明书研究了差不多一个小时，可就是搞不清楚。
- A: 让我看看。三个臭皮匠，顶个诸葛亮。

- A: I've been studying the instructions for assembling your new model airplane, son, and I **can't make heads nor tails of** them.
- B: It's easy, daddy. I'll show you.
- A: 我一直在琢磨组装你的新飞机模型，儿子，我怎么也弄不好。
- B: 这不难，爸爸。我做给你看。

- I don't understand why they don't write the contract in plain English. I just **can't make head nor tail of** it.
  我不明白他们为什么不用简单的英语起草这份合同。这份合同我一点都不理解。

Unit 25
Multiculturalism
多元文化主义

Canada is a multinational country. For hundreds of years, citizens from many countries have come to Canada's shores, bringing with them the rich gifts of their cultural traditions for all of them to share. Immigrants from different countries still keep their own cultures, religions, languages, and ways of life.

Walk down the streets of Canadian cities such as Vancouver, Montreal and Toronto, faces from all over the world greet you. The government encourages people to take pride in their language, religion, and culture. It also encourages all Canadians to treat each other with respect. People living in Canada also have a responsibility to take part in the society.

Because of the number of different ethnic groups in Canada, they've learned to appreciate many different kinds of cuisine. A Canadian family may enjoy Chinese food one night, Italian food the next—then Greek, or Ukrainian. When it comes time to eat, the choices are numerous. In Toronto, for instance, Polish, Italian, Greek, Chinese, Ukrainian and Vietnamese restaurants—to name just a few—are spreading all over the city.

As we know Canada is a multicultural society. There are many Italians, many Ukrainians, Finns, Japanese, Chinese, and Greek... It's a mixture of many different nationalities. The term "Multiculturalism" is used to describe the different ethnic groups in Canada. And when you turn on a television set or listen to radio in a Canadian city, you will hear programs in Spanish, Hindi or Mandarin, along with French or English. This is the face of Canada today—a multicultural society.

It's worth remembering that immigrants enrich the population in Canada, and the descendants of immigrants, from every part of globe. Around 1880, for example, thousands of Chinese arrived to work on the Canadian Pacific Railway. Today, more than 400,000 Chinese are in British Columbia.

After three or more years in Canada, immigrants may apply for Canadian citizenship. The Canadian government allows dual citizenship. To become a Canadian citizen, you must be 18 years old or older, and permanent resident. You must speak some English or French and you must know something about Canada's history, geography, and political system. Permanent residents must live in Canada for three years before applying for citizenship. Permanent residents who leave Canada or who live outside of Canada for more than half a year may lose their permanent resident status.

Since 1998, Canada Post and the Royal Canadian Mint have been proud to join Canada's Asian communities to honor the Lunar New Year through the issue of special edition stamp and coin sets. In 2003, for example, the Royal Canadian Mint continued production of the annual series with a coin commemorating the Year of the Sheep.

All 12 of the Lunar animals—the Rat, the Ox, the Tiger, the Rabbit, the Dragon, the Snake, the Horse, the Sheep, the Monkey, the Rooster, the Dog and the Pig—appear in a circular arrangement around the rim of each coin, with a different animal highlighted each year in a central cameo. The coin's obverse bears the effigy of Her Majesty Queen Elizabeth II.

The majority of Canadians are Christian. According to the census, Roman Catholicism has the most adherents, followed by Protestantism. Other religions include Judaism, Islam, Hinduism, Sikhism and Buddhism. About 3.4 million people stated that they had no religious affiliation whatsoever.

Generally speaking, Canada is obsessed with federalism and with law, and with using the law to try to create a nation state in which various communities, races and religious are not merely tolerated, but respected. Canada is a really peaceful nation, and it has avoided the worst excesses of intolerance and prejudice that have characterizes many nations where different nationalities and ethnic groups coexist.

译 文

　　加拿大是一个多民族国家。数百年来，许多国家的公民漂洋过海来到加拿大，为这里的人们带来了丰富多彩的民族文化传统。来自不同国家的移民仍然保持着自己的文化、宗教信仰、语言和生活方式。

　　沿着加拿大城市的街道行走，比如在温哥华、蒙特利尔和多伦多，你能看到来自世界各国的人的面孔。政府鼓励人们以自己的语言、宗教信仰和文化为荣，还鼓励所有的加拿大人互相尊重。居住在加拿大的人都有责任参与社会活动。

　　由于加拿大包含众多种族，他们学会了享受各种风味的饮食。一个加拿大的家庭可能是今晚吃中餐，明晚吃意大利菜，过后再吃希腊菜或乌克兰菜。到了吃饭的时候，你有很多选择。以多伦多为例，波兰人、意大利人、希腊人、中国人、乌克兰人和越南人开的餐馆——这里只列举了一部分——遍及全城。

　　我们知道，加拿大是一个多元文化社会，有许多意大利人、乌克兰人、芬兰人、日本人、中国人和希腊人等等，是一个多民族大熔炉。"多元文化"正是对加拿大各个不同种族融合的描述。而当你在加拿大的某一城市打开电视或收音机时，你会听到用西班牙语、海地语或中国普通话，以及用法语或英语播出的节目。这就是如今的加拿大——一个多元文化的社会。

　　值得记住的是，正是来自世界各地的移民以及他们的后代使加拿大的人口得以增长。例如1880年左右，有成千上万的中国人来到加拿大修建加拿大太平洋铁路。如今，已有超过40万的中国人居住在不列颠哥伦比亚。

　　在加拿大生活3年及以上时间的移民可以申请加拿大公民身份。加拿大政府允许双重国籍。要成为加拿大公民，你必须年满18岁并已经成为加拿大永久居民。你还必须会讲一些英语或法语，了解一些加拿大的历史、地理和政治制度。永久居民必须在加拿大居住了3年才可以申请公民身份，如果离开加拿大或有超过半年的时间不在加拿大居住，就有可能失去永久居民的身份。

　　自1998年起，为了与加拿大亚裔社区共同庆祝农历新年，加拿大邮政局和皇家铸币厂开始发行一系列特制邮票和纪念套币。举例来说，在2003年，加拿大皇家铸币厂继续制造发行了羊年纪念币。

　　每一枚纪念币的周边都刻有12生肖宫图，即鼠、牛、虎、兔、龙、蛇、马、羊、猴、鸡、狗、猪等的动物图像，纪念币中央的浮雕图案则凸显相关年份的特定生肖。在纪念币的正面是伊丽莎白二世女王陛下的头像。

大多数加拿大人信奉基督教。根据人口普查，罗马天主教教徒人数最多，新教教徒人数排在第二。其他宗教信仰还包括犹太教、伊斯兰教、印度教、锡克教以及佛教。大约有340万人宣称没有任何宗教信仰。

总的来讲，加拿大极为崇尚联邦主义和法律条文，并且依据法律来创建这个国家。在这样一个国家里，各种社会团体、不同种族成员和各种宗教信仰不同的民族生活在一起。他们不仅相互容忍，而且相互尊重。加拿大是一个爱好和平、生活安宁的国家。加拿大避免了多民族和多种族团体共存的国家最严重的不容忍和偏见，而这类的例子在许多国家里比比皆是。

Dialogue

Like a Fish out of Water

(Alan and Bill are walking down the street when they suddenly see a young man who is strangely dressed.)

Alan: Hey, Bill—*get a load of* that guy! Man, dressed like that, he must be a new landed immigrant.

Bill: Yeah, I guess so, but just because people are different from you, it doesn't mean you should *talk down on* them or laugh at them. I'm not surprised to see the new comers who are strangely dressed since Canada is a society of multiculturalism. Do you still remember what we learned in class last week the *Multiculturalism Act*?

Alan: Yes, I know what you mean, but sometimes, it's hard to be open-minded. I remember when I first arrived here, some of the things I did and said made people laugh.

Bill: Well, I'll admit that living in another new environment can make you feel *like a fish out of water*. Look at the people over there, different dressing and different manners. They are typical Inuit or Eskimos. Some of them are now still living in Igloos.

Alan: I see. Don't laugh at them. I had the similar experience—when they laughed at me for the way I was dressed, I really felt like *giving them a piece of my mind*.

Bill: You should have **taken it with a grain of salt**, Alan. You shouldn't let things like that bother you.

Alan: I suppose you're right, and I think people should be more tolerant.

Bill: OK, start by following your own advice! Alan, say, how are your Italian lessons coming along?

Alan: Well, to be honest, I still haven't made much progress. It seems to me that the classes aren't **paying off**.

Bill: How come?

Alan: Well, for some reason, I just don't seem to **get along with** the teacher. He's an Italian, you see, and he seems so strange and foreign. We're just not on the same wave-length.

Bill: Try to be patient, Alan, and don't take it so personally. It's quite possible to get along with people from all over the world, and learn from them, too, despite the cultural differences. Just **give it time**. I think, sooner or later, he'll **grow on you**.

Alan: That's what I'm hoping. I'm going to keep plugging away and I think I'll eventually make a lot of progress.

Bill: That's the spirit!

Vocabulary and Notes

• Canada is a society of multiculturalism.	加拿大是一个多元文化社会。
• *Multiculturalism Act*	《多元文化法》。1988年，联邦政府颁布的《多元文化法》提出，加拿大是一个多种族、多元文化的社会，每位国民都有保留和推广其文化遗产的自由，并强调各民族应该互相尊重各自的不同文化。这加强了多元文化政策在加拿大的地位，并使多元文化主义政策作为一项法律在全加拿大推行。
• but sometimes it's hard to be open-minded	可有时接受新事物并不容易
• living in another new environment	在另一个新的环境居住

- Inuit or Eskimos

因纽特人或爱斯基摩人，属蒙古民族，与美洲印第安人有明显区别，如手小、脚小。该民族的特点是狩猎时更多地使用海豹皮单人皮船和与此相关的其他工具。北极沿岸地区的因纽特人主要吃海豹肉、鱼，内陆地区的因纽特人吃驼鹿肉等。由于多年来的同化政策，土著民族的饮食习惯已经发生了很大变化。居住在北极地区的因纽特人还是住在北极的雪屋(Igloos)或叫做圆顶冰屋里。他们在平地上用雪砖垒成半球形的屋顶，屋内挖一深坑，坑前开一小窗。雪屋的门极低，必须爬行才能钻进雪屋。雪屋里藏有许多食物。因纽特人平时忙于狩猎，多在冬闲时进行婚配，青年男女以碰撞和摩擦鼻子的方式来互表爱慕之情。

- ... when they laughed at me for the way I was dressed, I really felt like giving them a piece of my mind.

……当他们笑话我的衣着打扮时，我真想回敬他们两句。

- You shouldn't let things like that bother you.

你不必为这类事而烦恼。

- I think people should be more tolerant.

我认为我们应该处处宽以待人。

- It seems to me that the classes aren't paying off.

对我来说这门功课似乎是白费力气。

- he seems so strange and foreign

他好像很怪，让人感到陌生

- don't take it so personally

不要只从自己的角度看问题

- That's the spirit!

这就对啦！

Idioms for Everyday Use

get a load of
注意看，仔细看（不寻常的、有趣的或令人赞美的人或物）

take a look at (something very unusual, interesting or admirable)

Unit 25 Multiculturalism 多元文化主义

- **Get a load of** that handsome guy! He must be an exchange student from Canada.
  看看那位英俊的小伙子！他一定是从加拿大来的交换生。
- **Get a load of** that pretty girl. She is from Canada, Thompson Rivers University.
  快看那个漂亮的女生。她是从加拿大汤姆逊河大学来的。

| **talk down on someone** 说某人不好；贬低某人的工作或观点 | speak badly of someone; belittle someone's work or ideas |

- No matter how hard the employees work, their boss always **talks down on them**.
  不管这些雇员多么努力地工作，他们的老板总是对他们不满意。
- Sarah's husband was always **talking down on her**—she was right to divorce him.
  萨拉的丈夫总是小看她——和他离婚是对的。

| **like a fish out of water** 因处于生疏环境而感到不自在；感到不适应 | feel uncomfortable because of unaccustomed surroundings; not fit in |

- She was the only German speaker in a room full of Japanese people—she couldn't communicate, so she felt **like a fish out of water**.
  屋里全是日本人，只有她讲德语——她不能和他们交谈，感到特别不自在。
- He was the only boy at the dinner party not in formal dress and he felt **like a fish out of water**.
  他是宴会上唯一没穿礼服的男孩，因此他觉得很不自在。

| **give someone a piece of one's mind** 指责某人；对某人直言不讳 | scold someone angrily; tell someone what you really think |

- The students had all done very poorly on the exam, so the teacher **gave them a piece of his mind**.
  学生们的考试很不理想，因此老师批评了他们一顿。
- He has been late for work three times this week. If he does that again, I'll **give him a piece of my mind**.
  这星期他上班迟到了三次。如果他再这样的话，我就说话不客气了。

| **take something with a grain/pinch of salt** 对所说的事不当回事；半信半疑 | not take too seriously what one hears or reads; believe or accept only in part |

- Uncle Tom has a great imagination. He can tell you all sorts of tales, but mind you, you have to **take them with a grain of salt**.

汤姆大叔有丰富的想象力，他能给你讲各种故事。可你得注意点儿，对这些故事切不可全信。

We **took** our grandfather's stories of the war **with** a **grain of salt**.
我们对爷爷所讲的战斗故事半信半疑。

| **pay off**
是值得的，有报偿；没有白费力气 | be worthwhile; bring rewards for one's efforts |

It has been rather costly to install the machinery, but it should **pay off** in the long run.
虽然安装机器费用很高，但从长远来看，这是值得的。

John studied hard before the examination, and it **paid off**—he get an A.
约翰在考试前学习很努力，他没白费力气——得了个A。

| **get along with someone**
与某人友好相处 | live or work together in a friendly way with someone |

I **get along very well with** Dan. We care for each other and help each other.
我和丹相处得特别好。我们俩互相关心、互相帮助。

I've never been able to **get along with** my mother-in-law.
我始终和我的婆婆合不来。

| **give someone/something time**
耐心点儿，别着急 | be patient; don't be in such a hurry |

I know Bill doesn't seem talkative, but **give him time**, he'll open up.
我知道比尔好像不爱讲话，耐心点儿，他会说的。

You must **give** your wound **time** to heal before practicing sports again.
你应该等你的伤口痊愈再参加体育锻炼。

| **grow on someone**
逐渐引起某人的喜爱；使越来越感兴趣 | gradually increase in favor; become likable |

I didn't like him too much at first but after working together for a while, he **grew on** me.
开始我特别不喜欢他，可跟他工作一段时间后，我越来越喜欢他了。

Life in a foreign country is often difficult at first, but if you give it time, it will probably **grow on** you.
在国外生活，一开始往往是困难的，但过一段时间，你也许就会习惯。

Unit 26
Niagara Falls
尼亚加拉瀑布

Niagara Falls is one of the greatest tourist attractions of the world. Each year 12 to 15 million visitors come to see this spectacular waterfall on the border between Canada and the United States. Niagara Falls stays open right through the year including the winter months, and the area is pleasantly illuminated in the evening.

Spectacular waterfall is the World's greatest waterfall by volume. It is split in two by Goat Island—the American Falls and the Canadian Falls. The American Falls are 64m high and 305m wide, with a flow of 14 million liters of water per minute. The Canadian Falls or Horseshoe Falls are 54m high and 675m wide, with a flow of 155 million liters.

It is exciting to board the Maid of the Mist, a boat for sightseers that carries passengers to the foot of the Falls. The roar of the water is fantastic and because you are so close to the Falls, you can't help getting covered by spray. However, you'll be given a hooked raincoat if you board the Maid of the Mist.

There are many ways to see the Falls.

The easiest way is to walk along or lean over the low wall right at the water edge above the Falls on the Canadian side.

Or if you like, you can take a ride in a Spanish aerocar and see the Falls from a distance.

You can also ride an elevator down 50 meters to some wet scenic tunnels to see the Falls or up 160 meters to the top of Skylon Tower for a spectacular view of the Falls and the surrounding areas.

There are many hotels in this region, which is a popular honeymoon spot. It draws in thousands of honeymooners each year. It is known as the "honeymoon capital of the world".

The Falls became known in Europe and the other countries through the paintings and descriptions of visitors in the early 19th century. The famous author Charles Dickens wrote, after the visit of the Falls, "I seemed to be lifted from the earth and to be looking into heaven."

The thunderous roar of Niagara Falls is truly awe-inspiring, shocking and stunning. As the massive volume of water rushes over the cliff edges, it creates a deafening sound that resembles nature's most powerful symphony. The sheer force and intensity of the falls produce a reverberating noise that can be heard for miles. The visitors are fully feeling the power of the nature. Accompanied by the roar of Niagara Falls, Shanzhige Choir sang the Chinese songs "I Love You, China" and "Song of the Yangtze River" in October 2024.

Driving leisurely through the Niagara region, you will see charming towns and enjoy the flavor of peaches, pears, cherries, apples, and plums and smell the fresh and green grass.

Driving leisurely through the Niagara region, you'll notice vineyards everywhere. With the ideal growing condition created by the Niagara Escarpment and Lake Ontario, along with the ideal mixture of soils and minerals, this area provides the superb grapes and superb grape wines.

There are more than 15,000 acres of vineyards in the Niagara area, which is recognized as one of the finest wine-grape growing regions of the world.

Niagara Falls is not only for adventures and tourism, but also for generation electricity. It's worth remembering that the incredible drop in water level made the Falls an ideal place for hydroelectric development. The first generation station opened in 1906.

译文

尼亚加拉瀑布是世界上最壮观的旅游胜地之一。每年有1200万到1500万的观光者前来欣赏这个奔流在加美边界的壮观瀑布。尼亚加拉大瀑布常年开放，也包括冬季，而且这里的夜晚更是灯火灿烂辉煌。

尼亚加拉大瀑布是世界上水流量最大的瀑布，它被戈特岛分隔为两部分——美国瀑布和加拿大瀑布。美国瀑布（又称为亚美利加瀑布）高64米，宽305米，每分钟流量达到1400万公升。而加拿大瀑布（又被称为霍斯舒瀑布）高54米，宽675米，每分钟流量达到15500万公升。

乘坐"雾中少女"号游艇是一件令人兴奋的旅行，那是一艘把游客带到瀑布脚下的观光船。水流发出的呼啸声大得令人难以置信，而且由于你与瀑布非常接近，你就会置身于水花喷溅的飞沫之中。不过，如果乘坐"雾中少女"，工作人员会给你发一件连帽雨衣。

欣赏大瀑布的方法很多。

最简便的方法就是沿着加拿大瀑布边上的矮墙溜达着看或俯身观看。

如果你有兴趣，还可以乘坐空中汽车进行远距离的观看。

你还可以乘坐电梯下降50米到达潮湿的观光隧道去欣赏瀑布，或者上升160米到达天伦塔的顶部，去欣赏瀑布的壮观景象和周围的景色。

这一地区有许多旅馆，这些旅馆是很受欢迎的度蜜月的场所。每年它都会吸引成千上万度蜜月的人来此观光。尼亚加拉大瀑布被称为"世界蜜月之都"。

19世纪早期，通过游客们的绘画和他们的描述，大瀑布逐渐被欧洲和其他国家所熟知。著名作家查尔斯·狄更斯欣赏大瀑布后曾写道："我好像从地面上腾身而起，似乎看到了天堂。"

尼亚加拉大瀑布的轰鸣声令人震撼和敬畏。巨量的水流从悬崖边缘奔腾而下，发出震耳欲聋的声响，宛如大自然最震撼的交响乐。瀑布的强大力量和猛烈冲击产生了回荡数里的轰响。游客们全身心地感受到了大自然的威力。伴随着瀑布的轰鸣声，2024年10月山之歌合唱团在那里演唱过《我爱你，中国》和《长江之歌》。

开车穿行于尼亚加拉地区，你会看到美丽的城镇，可以品尝到桃子、梨、樱桃、苹果和李子的美味，同时可以嗅到嫩草的清香。

开车行驶于尼亚加拉地区，你会发现到处是葡萄园。尼亚加拉陡崖和安大略湖为此地创造了理想的生长环境，还有理想的含有矿物质的土壤，为这个地区生产一流的葡萄和葡萄酒提供了资源。

在尼亚加拉地区大约有15000多英亩的葡萄园，这里被认为是世界上最棒的酿酒葡萄生长地之一。

尼亚加拉瀑布不仅仅是探险和旅游胜地，也为水力发电做了贡献。值得记住的是，大瀑布惊人的落差使之成为开发水力发电的理想位置。1906年这里的第一座水力发电站投入了使用。

Dialogue

Get a Bird's-eye View of the Falls

(Alice, Li's friend, asks Li to see Niagara Falls.)

Alice: Hi, Li, I have some *time on my hands*. I wonder if you would like to go to Niagara Falls tomorrow.

Li: By all means! I've heard a lot about it. It's one of the great natural wonders of the world. In my present *frame of mind*, I'd like to go there today.

Alice: Today? We have to do some preparations for the trip today.

Li: I'm only kidding. To tell the truth, I've been wanting to go there myself. Have you ever been there before?

Alice: Oh, yes, many times. It's splendid. Magnificent sight! Just imagine, every second of each day, ton after ton of rushing water pours into the Niagara River just below. I bet that's a sight to see. It *draws in* thousands of honeymooners each year. It is known as "the honeymoon capital of the world".

Li: I *got wind of* the fact that people should take raincoats, or risk getting soaked through.

Alice: We never take raincoats. People don't enjoy themselves to the fullest till they're covered by the spray. However, you'll be given a hooded raincoat if you board the Maid of the Mist.

Li: The Maid of the Mist—that seems to *ring a bell*.

Alice: Well, that's the name of the boat which carries sightseers to the foot of the Falls.

Li: Oh, I see. According to the Canadian Encyclopedia, there are two Falls: the Canadian or Horseshoe Falls, and the American Falls.

Alice: Yes, they're separated by Goat Island, on the American side of the border.

Li: Is it true that there are many ways to see the Falls?

Alice: Absolutely! The easiest way is to walk along or lean over the low wall right at the water edge above the Falls on the Canadian side.

Li: I've heard it's possible to get *a bird's-eye view* of the Falls from a helicopter up above the Falls.

Alice: That's true, or an elevator takes you down to the Niagara Gorge below the Falls, or up 160 meters to the top of the Skylon Tower for a spectacular view of the Falls and surrounding area. Or if you like, you can take a ride in a Spanish aerocar and see the Falls from a distance.

Li: So, which way should we take to see the Falls?

Alice: Oh, I'd rather *leave that up to you*. I've already tried several ways to see the Falls anyway. Well, the last point, *it goes without saying* that the Niagara Falls is not only for adventures and tourism, but also for generation electricity. It's worth remembering that the incredible drop in water level made the Falls an ideal place for hydroelectric development. The first generation station opened in 1906.

Li: Well, Alice, thanks for your kind description of the Falls. Say, when will we start tomorrow?

Alice: Six o'clock tomorrow morning. It's not more than two hours' drive from here *as the crow flies*.

Li: So we could get there by eight.

Alice: Definitely. We *made very good time* on our trip to the Falls last year. It took us less than two hours to get there.

Li: Sounds great. I'm all for that.

Vocabulary and Notes

- Niagara Fall
- It's one of the great natural wonders of the world.
- magnificent sight
- honeymooner
- the honeymoon capital of the world
- get soaked through
- spray
- Maid of the Mist

尼亚加拉大瀑布

这是世界大自然奇观之一。

壮丽辉煌的景色

度蜜月的人

世界蜜月之都

淋湿；使湿透

水花，浪花

"雾中少女"号游艇（取名于一个印第安人的传说）

- You'll be given a hooded raincoat if you board the Maid of the Mist.
  如果你登上"雾中少女"号游艇，工作人员会发给你一件带帽子的雨衣。
- encyclopedia
  book or set of books, giving information about every branch of knowledge, or on one subject, with articles in ABC order 百科全书
- Horseshoe Falls
  霍斯舒瀑布（加拿大瀑布）
- They're separated by Goat Island on the American side of the border.
  两个瀑布被在美国一方的山羊岛分割开来。
- lean over
  bent over gently 伏在……上面；弯身俯视
- helicopter
  直升机
- or up 160 meters to the Skylon Tower
  或（乘电梯）升到高于地面160米的天伦塔上（观赏）
- surrounding area
  周围地区的风景
- Spanish aerocar
  空中汽车（实际上是一种彩饰的高空缆车）
- generate electricity
  发电
- the incredible drop in water level
  惊人的大瀑布落差
- I'm all for that.
  我完全赞成。

Idioms for Everyday Use

time on one's hands
空闲时间，闲空 | leisure time; extra time

A: Why, Peter! What a surprise! What brings you out here?
B: Oh, I had some **time on my hands** and thought I'd take a little drive in town. And I wanted you to meet my guest from China.
A: 哎，彼得！真没想到！哪阵风把你吹到这儿来了？
B: 噢，我有些空闲时间，想到城里来转转。我也想让你见见我的中国客人。

As I had a good deal of **time on my hands**, I decided to explore Canada for another week.
因为有大量空闲时间，我决定再对加拿大考察一周。

frame of mind
心情，心思，心气儿 | the state or condition of one's mind at a particular time

A: What a washing machine! It's getting worse today. Look! Now it doesn't work at all. I think I need a new one.

B: Here's an ad about a big washing machine sale. Do you want to see it?

A: Of course! Let's have a look. Great! In my **frame of mind**, I'd like to buy one today.

A: 这台倒霉的洗衣机！今天更坏得不行了。你看，现在根本就不转了！我想我该买台新的了。

B: 这是一张有关洗衣机大促销的广告。你想看看吗？

A: 当然了！让我看看。太棒了！按我现在的心气儿，今天我就买一台。

There is no use talking to him while he is in that low **frame of mind**. We could talk to him when he is happy.

他心情不愉快的时候找他谈话是无济于事的。我们可以在他高兴的时候和他谈谈。

A: Here's an ad about an auto sale now at Canadian Tire. Do you want to see it?

B: By all means! In my present **frame of mind**, I'd buy the first car I looked at.

A: 这里有条广告，加拿大泰尔赛场正在出售汽车，你想看看吗？

B: 当然想看！按我现在的心气儿，我想买我刚看过的第一辆车。

draw in
吸引，使加入 | attract; induce to participate or enter

A: I hear you went to Dunhuang Grottoes during the summer vacation.

B: Yes. To make the most of the vacation, I went to visit the Caves of a Thousand Buddhas, Crescent Moon Spring and so on. That place really **draws in** lots of foreign guests.

A: 听说你暑假去参观敦煌石窟了。

B: 是的。为充分利用假期，我参观了千佛洞、月牙泉和其他别的地方。敦煌那个地方的确吸引着许多外国来宾。

The performances given by the Philadelphian Ballet Troupe in Beijing were really a big hit and **drew in** large crowds every night.

费城芭蕾舞剧团在北京的演出曾轰动一时，每天晚上都吸引着大批观众。

get wind of
听说，听到……风声 | hear about indirectly or by rumor

A: Sam **got wind of** the fact that Brian left his wife.

B: Yes, Susan told me that their marriage broke up. She didn't say much but I guess there must be a third person involved.

A: 萨姆听说布赖恩和他妻子离婚了。

B: 是的，苏珊告诉我说他们的婚姻已破裂。她没多说什么，不过我推测一定是有第三者插足。

If they **get wind of** our new plan for the Christmas party, they'll surely want to join us.

如果他们听说了我们圣诞节晚会的新计划，他们一定会来参加的。

ring a bell
听起来觉得耳熟 | sound familiar

I'm not sure I know who you are talking about, but the name **rings a bell**.

我不能肯定我知道你们在谈论谁，但是这个名字听起来耳熟。

A: Hey, Tom. Does the name Manfred mean anything to you?

B: Manfred. Let me see...um... That name **rings a bell**, but I just can't place it.

A: 嘿，汤姆。你知道曼弗雷德这个名字指的是谁吗？

B: 曼弗雷德。我想想……喔……名字听起来挺熟悉，可一时就是想不起来。

I don't think I know the professor you mentioned though the name seems to **ring a bell**.

我想我不认识你提到的那位教授，虽然他的名字听起来挺熟的。

a bird's-eye view
鸟瞰 | a view that you see from high above

We got **a bird's-eye view** of the whole campus from the fourteenth floor of the library building.

从图书馆的14层我们可以鸟瞰整个校园。

A: How was your one-day trip yesterday?

B: Really great! I've never had so much fun in all my life. It was unforgettable. We visited the CN Tower, the Provincial Parliament Building, and the Art Gallery and finally we boarded a helicopter and got **a bird's-eye view** of the whole city.

A: 昨天的一日游怎么样？

B: 太好了！有生以来我还没有玩得这么开心过。真是令人难忘。我们参观了多伦多CN塔、省议会大厦、美术馆，最后我们坐上直升机，鸟瞰了城市的全景。

leave something up to someone
把某事交给某人处理；让某人决定处理某事 | let someone decide

A: Where would you like to go for dinner?

B: Oh. I'd rather **leave that up to you**. Remember, you promised to surprise me.

A: 你喜欢到哪儿去吃饭？

B: 噢，这由你来决定。记住，你可是答应要让我大吃一惊的。

A: Professor Smith, I gave out the textbooks to the students, but there are still five extra copies. What should I do with them?

Unit 26　Niagara Falls 尼亚加拉瀑布

B: I don't know. I'll **leave that entirely up to you**.
A: 史密斯教授，我把教科书都发给了学生，可这里还剩下五本。怎么处理？
B: 我也不知道。你看着办吧。

| **It goes without saying**
不言而喻；不用说 | Something is so obvious that it doesn't have to be mentioned. |

A: **It goes without saying** that good health is very essential. Don't sit in the room reading the books all day long. Why not come out with us for a walk?
B: I guess you're right. Let's go.
A: 谁都知道好的身体是非常必要的。不要整天关在屋里看书。出去跟我们散散步，好吗？
B: 我想你说得对。走吧。

Lilian's an excellent pupil. She got full marks for mathematics and English in the final exam. **It goes without saying** that her parents are very proud of her.
莉莲是个聪明的学生。她数学和英语的期末考试都得了满分。不用说她父母都在为她而骄傲。

| **as the crow flies**
走直线，直线地；最短距离地 | along a straight line between two places; by the most direct way |

A: Excuse me, but can you tell me how long it'll take us to Okanagan College.
B: It's eight miles to Okanagan College **as the crow flies**, but it's eleven miles by the road, which goes around the mountain.
A: 劳驾，您能告诉我一下到奥科内根学院还有多远吗？
B: 如果直接走过去，到奥科内根学院还有8英里。如果走绕山的那条公路，还得走11英里。

Actually, it's not far, only three miles from here **as the crow flies**.
实际上并不远，从这儿一直走，不到3英里。

| **make good time**
在较短的时间内赶到；开车开得快 | go at a speed that is satisfactory or better than expected; travel rapidly at good speed |

A: How was your trip to Montreal?
B: Fascinating! There was little traffic, so we **made good time** driving to Montreal.
A: 蒙特利尔之行怎么样？
B: 太棒了！路上的行人和车辆不多，因此，我们很快就开到了蒙特利尔。

Unfortunately, it rained all the time and so we didn't **make good time** on our trip to Toronto.
不幸的是，一路上雨下个不停，因此，我们没有很快到达多伦多。

Unit 27
Quebec
魁北克

In 1608, Frenchman Samuel de Champlain set up a fur trading post on the St. Lawrence River at the place the people called Quebec. By 1700, there were 25,000 French people living in Quebec. Under British control, this French province gradually grew into a major commercial center. Today, 90 percent of Canadians whose native language is French live in the Province of Quebec. Although laws guarantee the right of French Canadians to their own language and culture, many Quebecois want to be separate from the rest of Canada.

Quebec is the largest province in Canada. It has an area of 1,450,680 square kilometers, three times that of France and seven times that of Great Britain.

Quebec is the seat of French culture in Canada. Out of a total population of about seven million, Quebec has more than five million people of French origin, 350,000 of British origin. French is the mother tongue of 82.2 percent of Quebecers, while 9.7 percent cite English as their mother tongue.

The province is almost entirely surrounded by water. Almost 80 percent of Quebecers live in urban centre located along the St. Lawrence River.

Quebec's forests are equal in area to those of Sweden and Norway combined. Quebec exports 40 percent of its total production, mainly from the forest industry—printing, lumber, and paper.

It is also famous for its mining, such as aluminum and iron ore. The electronics products and engineering know-how and equipment are sold to different countries of the world.

In many areas in Quebec, the sap of the maple tree is still tapped each spring. It is made into a confection that is sold throughout the world.

Founded in 1608, Quebec City is the province's capital. It is the only walled city in North American. It embodies much of the allure of old Quebec.

Montreal, the province's commercial capital, had developed competitive industries in space, telecommunications, energy and transportation.

Montreal and its suburbs have a population of three million and it is the second largest French-speaking city in the world, after Paris.

Montreal is also an important university centre, with two French-speaking universities and two English-speaking universities—McGill and Concordia.

Montreal is also a center for international competitions in amateur sports, the most famous held so far being the 1976 Summer Olympics.

译　文

　　1608年，法国人塞缪尔·尚普兰在圣劳伦斯河河畔开始了皮草贸易，人们把这里叫做魁北克。到1700年，有25000法国人居住在魁北克。在大英帝国的统治下，这个法裔省份逐步变成了一个主要的商业中心。今天，90%说法语的加拿大人居住在魁北克省。尽管法律允许这些讲法语的魁北克人沿用自己的语言和文化，许多魁北克人仍试图从加拿大分离出来。

　　魁北克省是加拿大最大的省份，面积为1450680平方公里，相当于法国3倍或英国7倍的面积。

　　魁北克省是加拿大的法国文化中心。在700万总人口中，有超过500万人是法国血统，35万人是英国血统。82.2%的魁北克人以法语为母语，只有9.7%的人认为英语是他们的母语。

　　魁北克省几乎四面环水。将近80%的魁北克人居住在圣劳伦斯河沿岸的市中心。

　　魁北克省的森林覆盖面积相当于瑞典与挪威森林面积之总和。该省40%的产品用于出口，出口产品主要是林业——印刷、木材和纸张。

　　魁北克的矿产也闻名遐迩，比如铝矿和铁矿。魁北克省的电子产品、工程技术和电器设备销往世界不同的国家。

　　在省内许多地区，人们每年春天仍然采集枫树糖浆。他们制作枫糖食品，远销世界各地。

　　魁北克市建立于1608年，是魁北克省的省会。它是北美唯一的以城墙围起的城市。它是古老魁北克省的魅力所在。

　　蒙特利尔市，作为魁北克省的商业中心，在航天科学、电信、能源和交通方面已颇具竞争力。

蒙特利尔及其郊区拥有300万人口，是继巴黎后世界上第二大说法语的城市。

蒙特利尔市还是一个重要的大学中心，建有两所法语大学和两所英语大学——麦吉尔大学和康考迪亚大学。

蒙特利尔也是国际业余体育爱好者比赛竞技的中心，至今最为著名的赛事是1976年的夏季奥运会。

Fancy Meeting You Here

(Susan is running into an acquaintance on the street of Montreal. She was very much surprised.)

Susan: Hey, I've seen you somewhere before, haven't I?

Li: Yes, your face looks familiar.

Susan: McGill, 2015, wasn't it?

Li: That's right. We were in the same class studying American Literature. Your name is...Gee, it's **on the tip of my tongue**. Oh, yes, Susan.

Susan: You are Li something, right? Fancy meeting you here in this restaurant. **Isn't it a small world**? We haven't seen each other for about ten years. What are you doing here in Montreal?

Li: I won a national competition for a grant being offered by the Canadian government. I'll be traveling in Canada for about three months. I'll meet Canadian educators and do some academic research.

Susan: That's wonderful. Anything I can do for you? I'd love to show you around Montreal and Quebec City if you have time.

Li: Thanks a lot. I'm dying to know the new look of Quebec City and Montreal. You will see lots of changes in the Province of Quebec. How have you been?

Susan: Well, I haven't found a permanent job yet. First, I was a teacher in a language center at McGill, and afterwards I taught English in a French school. Tow years ago, I was offered an opportunity at a big company, and I **jumped at** it. I was hired as a secretary. However, I only worked there for one year.

Li: How come?

Susan: Too much work to do there. I *was* absolutely *snowed under with work.* I couldn't do the work in regular working hours; very often I had to work overtime, so I gave it up.

Li: I'm sorry to hear that. What are you going to do next?

Susan: Well, I went to Quebec City for an interview a few days ago. I applied for a position in the Quebec Museum. I'm now waiting for a response. But I think my age, sex and my poor French *work against* me.

Li: Why don't you come to China to teach English?

Susan: That's a good idea. Li, you know I'm very interested in Chinese Culture, so please *keep me posted* about any job opportunities!

Li: Absolutely. I've got some information about our language institute in my hotel. Drop in any time and I'll show it to you.

Susan: Thanks a lot, Li. I'll visit you tonight. I think teaching English in China will be a new experience for me.

Vocabulary and Notes

- McGill — 麦吉尔大学，加拿大一所著名大学（设在蒙特利尔市）
- fancy meeting — 巧遇（指非常惊讶地见到某人）
  Fancy meeting you here in this restaurant. — 在这个饭馆里见到了你，真是巧遇。
- competition — 竞争
- grant — something granted, especially money 赐予之物；奖金
- academic research — 学术研究
- Montreal — （加拿大）蒙特利尔市
- permanent job — 固定工作；永久性工作
- I was hired as a secretary. — 我作为秘书受雇。
- Quebec City — 魁北克城（魁北克省的首府）
- Quebec Museum — 魁北克博物馆
- drop in (drop by, drop over) — pay a casual visit (to) 顺道拜访

Idioms for Everyday Use

on the tip of one's tongue
差一点就想起；某事就在嘴边；随时可记起某事

be about to remember (a word, name or expression); on the verge of being uttered; something you might remember at any moment

- A: Quick, Chris. What's the name of the guy who gave the talk at this morning's meeting?
  B: Gee, let me see. It's an unusual name. It's **on the tip of my tongue** but I just can't get it out.
  A: 克里斯，快想想，今天上午在会上讲话的那个人叫什么名字？
  B: 哎呀，让我想想，是个挺特别的名字。就在嘴边，可说不出来。

- I've got that expression right **on the tip of my tongue**, but I just can't remember it.
  那个词就在嘴边，可我就是想不起来。

Isn't it a small world?
没想到你在某地见到了你认识的人；世界到底不大，我们又见面了。

This expression is used when you meet someone you know whom you did not expect to see there.

- A: Oh, my god! Chris! Fancy meeting you here in Vancouver.
  B: It's unbelievable! I thought you'd be taking the summer courses in McGill. I didn't know you were taking a vacation. I couldn't imagine that we would meet here in Vancouver. **Isn't it a small world?**
  A: 哎呀，我的天哪！克里斯！在温哥华怎么遇上你了呢！
  B: 这可真是想不到的事！我以为你正在麦吉尔大学上暑期班呢。我不知道你在度假。没想到在温哥华碰上你。世界到底不大，我们在这儿又见面了。

- A: What a surprise! Meeting our professor while we were climbing the mountain in Tibet.
  B: Really? **Isn't it a small world?**
  A: 真令人惊讶！当我们在西藏爬山时，遇到了我们的教授。
  B: 真的吗？世界到底不大。

jump at
欣然接受建议或急切地抓住机会

accept an offer or opportunity eagerly as soon as it has been offered to someone; accept suggestions

- When someone suggested a dip in the cool stream, we all **jumped at** the idea.
  有人建议到清凉的溪水里去洗个澡，大家都欣然接受了这个主意。

- I know that he would **jump at** such an offer.
  我知道他会欣然接受这个建议的。

- We should **jump at** the chance to buy the house at that price, but Mother isn't sure whether she likes it.

以这个价钱，我们应该抓住时机买下这座房子。可妈妈还不能肯定她是否喜欢它。

be snowed under with work
工作过多忙不过来；超负荷

it means that someone has a large amount of work to do; overloaded

- We've got a pile of rush jobs to do today so we're absolutely **snowed under with work**.
  今天我们有一堆急活要干，所以肯定忙不过来。
- A: Would you like to go swimming this weekend?
  B: Oh, no. I've been **snowed under with work** ever since my boss was away on business.
  A: 这周末你愿意去游泳吗？
  B: 噢，不去。自从老板出差，工作压得我抬不起头来。

work against
在某方面造成不利因素

If something works against you, it causes problems for you in some way.

- Her appearance **works against** her chance of success as a dancer.
  她的外貌影响了她成为舞蹈家。
- His poor pronunciation **works against** his English study.
  他糟糕的发音给他的英语学习造成了不利的因素。

keep someone posted
不断为某人提供最新信息

continue to give someone all the latest news about something

- A: Good luck on your trip to Canada, Li Yue. Write to me and **keep me posted**.
  B: No problem. I'll write to you by email twice a month and let you know how things are going.
  A: 李悦，祝你旅途平安，顺利到加拿大。给我来信，及时告知你的情况。
  B: 没问题。我一个月给你写两封电子邮件，让你了解那儿的情况。
- A: You know I'm very interested in this project, so please **keep me posted**.
  B: Don't worry. I'll call you every other week to let you know how things are going.
  A: 你知道我对这个项目非常感兴趣，请你常给我提供新情况。
  B: 别担心。我每隔一周给你打一次电话，让你了解项目进展情况。
- A: Hello, professor Li. I can't write to you by email. The homestay's wires do not work. I have to **keep you posted** by telephone.
  B: Don't worry. I will contact the TRU World right away and the teachers there are ready to help you.
  A: 喂，李教授。我不能给你发邮件。寄宿家庭的线路有问题，我只好给你打电话来汇报这里的情况。
  B: 别着急。我马上和汤姆逊河大学国际部联系，那里的老师随时给你帮助。

Unit 28
Education in Canada
加拿大教育

In Canada today it is increasingly necessary to have a college diploma or university degree. The education industry—schools, textbook publishers, teachers, enrollment and educational administrations, and the tuition fees—has become big business catering to the new reality of modern life.

Education in Canada used to be centered on the ages of 6 to 18. They were required to attend public schools. However, today, day-care centers, nursery schools and kindergarten education programs respond to social pressure to get an early start in those all important early childhood years. And youth are encouraged to continue their education by not only completing high school but going on to college and university. And it doesn't stop there.

Business Markets and society encourage and even demand that employees be involved in on-going upgrading programs by taking additional degrees and training courses. Therefore, many schools in Canada have provided the continuing education programs for those who need this kind of education platform.

Education in Canada is a provincial responsibility under Canadian Constitution. Therefore, instead of a federal ministry of education, there are provincial ministries of education. However, the federal government is also deeply involved in the national education. The federal government supervises education in federal penitentiaries, and it provides financial support for post-secondary education, adult occupational training and the teaching of the two official languages.

Unit 28 Education in Canada 加拿大教育

In addition, it is responsible for the education of Aboriginals, and inmates of federal penal institutions. The provincial ministries of education set standards, draw up curriculum and give grants to educational institutions.

There are mainly three kinds of schools in Canada: the public school, the separate school and the private school.

Public schools are usually provincial-supported, nondenominational schools. All the Canadian children are entitled to free education in public schools. Public schools mainly accept local students because they do no have boarding facilities. In recent years, some public schools enroll overseas students and they are taken good care of by the hospitable homestay parents.

Separate schools, also called religious schools, are run by the Roman Catholic Church and in turn, for its service.

Private schools are set up for specific educational or social purposes. And they are subsidized by private sources and various degrees of public funding.

The secondary schools in Canada do not have specific requirements. Each individual secondary school uses the primary school reports to decide on the admission. Public education in Canada is co-educational and free up to and including secondary school. The student pays tuition for most other post-secondary education.

Since the provincial government has its sole responsibilities for its own education system, there is no national entrance examination across Canada. Each institution decides its own standard and assessment of applicants' qualification. Except for Quebec, students study for grade one to grade twelve before entering into a university. In Quebec, students who have completed a grade eleven must also study on a two-year preparatory course in a community college before progressing to a university.

Most colleges in Canada provide university preparatory courses or transfer programs for students. Colleges and universities also come under provincial jurisdiction. Prior to the 1960's, a relatively small number of universities existed in Canada. They primarily served the upper middle and upper classes who could financially afford to have their children educated at such institutions. But the creation of government funded student loan programs, the establishment of numerous community colleges and the expansion of universities in the latter 1990's changed all this.

The opportunity to receive a college or university education is now pretty well available to anyone who wants one. As a result, the number of students attending colleges and universities has grown tremendously. Colleges in most provinces offer 1, 2 and 3 year diploma programs in the applied arts, sciences and technology. In some provinces, such as British Columbia, university credit courses can be taken at community colleges. Generally speaking, Canadian Universities offer undergraduate, graduate and doctoral degrees in the sciences, arts and humanities.

译 文

如今在加拿大，拥有大专或大学的文凭越来越必要了。教育产业，包括学校、教科书出版、老师、招生与教育行政和学费已经成为迎合现代生活新形势的一个重要行业。

过去，加拿大受教育年龄集中在6岁到18岁，而且要求学生们到公立学校学习。但是现在不同了，由于来自社会上早教的压力，全日制托儿中心、托儿所和幼儿园教育早在重要的孩提时代就开始了。而且家长不但鼓励孩子们完成高中学业，还希望他们接着读大学，甚至继续深造。

目前的商业市场和社会都提倡甚至要求各自的员工融身于专业技能提高的热潮中，比如辅修其他学位或者参加培训课程。因此，加拿大的许多学校通过举办一些继续教育项目为那些有需要的人提供了一个教育平台。

根据加拿大宪法，加拿大教育归省一级管理。因此，省级教育部代替了联邦教育部。尽管如此，联邦政府也非常关注国民教育。联邦政府负责监督指导那些联邦政府教养所或负责监狱的教育，并为职业中等教育、成人职业培训和两种官方语言的教学提供财政支援。

另外，联邦政府还负责土著居民和联邦刑事机构罪犯的教育工作。而省级教育部制定标准、草拟课程并为教育机构提供补贴。

加拿大的学校主要有3种：公立学校、教会学校和私立学校。

公立学校通常是由省级教育部门支持的且与宗教宗派无关的学校。所有的加拿大儿童都有资格免费进入公立学校读书。因公立学校不设寄宿，所以公立学校以招收本地学生为主，但近年来亦逐渐录取海外学生，并且这些学生在当地的居民家里能得到很周到的照顾。

教会学校（也被称为宗教学校）是由罗马天主教会管理并为之服务的学校。

私立学校是为了满足专门的教育或社会需求而成立的，这些学校通常由个人资助，也有政府不同程度的资助。

加拿大的中学没有固定的入学条件，录取与否主要取决于申请人的小学成绩报告单。加拿大的公立教育是男女合校的，而且是免费的，这一直包括到中学阶段。其他的职业中等教育多数需要学生支付学费。

因为加拿大教育由各省负责，所以加拿大没有全国性的入学考试。每一个省政府均执行该省自行设计的教育制度，评估录取资格。除了在魁北克省，学生们需要读完12年级以后才能进入大学。在魁北克省，学生完成第11年级的学习后，必须转到社区学院继续两年的预科课程，才能申请升读大学。

加拿大的大部分学院都开设大学预科和大学转读课程，为同学提供深造机会。学院和大学同样是在各省的权限范围内。20世纪60年代前，加拿大大学的数目相对比较少，而且它们主要是为那些在经济上可以支付其教育费用的中上层或上层阶级服务的。但是，政府筹办的学生贷款基金项目的出台、更多大学的建立以及20世纪90年代后期大学的井喷，使得这种形势大大改观。

现在，只要你想得到大专和本科教育的机会，你就能得到。其结果是进入大专和本科读书的学生数量以惊人的速度在增长。大部分省里的专科学院在文科和理工科方面提供1年、2年或者3年的证书项目。在某些省份，诸如不列颠哥伦比亚省，大学本科学分的课程也可以在社区学院获得。总的来说，加拿大正规大学在理科、文科和人文学科方面为本科生、硕士研究生和博士研究生提供学位。

I Got off to a Flying Start

(Li meets his Canadian friend Karen on campus after he had some academic meetings with some Canadian professors.)

Karen: So, how's it going?

Li: Not bad. I *got off to a flying start* on the research of Canadian Studies. John D. Redmond, a Canadian Studies professor, *showered me with* lots of materials. He patiently explained to me the ins and outs of the Quebec Independence problem and I'm also impressed by his sense of humor.

Karen: I agree. I sat in on his class the other day, and just before class ended, he told us a great joke. All the students really *cracked up*.

Li: The professors from the Canadian Studies Section were very generous and the valuable materials they gave to me will certainly do me good in my future Canadian Studies.

Karen: Wonderful! I also have some books about education in Canada. They give some information about different educational systems in Canada and the introduction to some famous universities.

Li: Which of the universities in Canada are most prestigious? Is the University of Toronto the top-notch university?

Karen: That's a very difficult question to answer. Universities in Canada have their respective advantages. Some universities may be well known for some of their faculties, while other universities may be famous for a particular college. University of Toronto, for example, has been regarded as one of the leading universities. Founded in 1827, it has now 5 colleges and dozens of faculties and departments, some of which have distinguished themselves in scientific and technological achievements.

Li: What about McGill and Concordia in the French-speaking Quebec area.

Karen: Well, McGill, chartered in 1821, is known for its humanities departments and medical college. Concordia University, located in the centre of Montreal, has achieved much in its academic pursuit and distinguished itself as a vigorous multi-disciplinary urban university. Li, please come with me, and I'll show those books about education in Canada and you may keep them. These are good materials for your Canadian Studies Program. Being a Canadian, I should *do my bit* in your research of Canadian Studies.

Li: That's very kind of you.

Karen: You're always welcome.

Vocabulary and Notes

- Canadian Studies — 加拿大学研究
- generous — 慷慨的，大方的
- valuable materials — 有价值的资料
- University of Toronto — 多伦多大学，1827年建校，目前有三个校区，是加拿大在学生数量上最多的大学。其主校区位于多伦多市中心。它是一所世界著名、顶尖的研究型大学之一，不仅在学术上有着卓越的声誉，其教育国际化的程度也非常高。多年来，多伦多大学与中国多所著名大学合作办学。

- McGill University　麦吉尔大学，1821年建校。是一所位于魁北克省蒙特利尔市的世界著名公立研究型大学，被誉为"北方哈佛"或"加拿大哈佛"。该校不仅在学术界享有盛誉，还培养了众多杰出校友，包括斯坦福大学校长和剑桥大学校长。其他知名校友包括多位加拿大总理、诺贝尔奖获得者、著名发明家、经济学家。白求恩大夫也是在麦吉尔大学下属的蒙特利尔皇家医院里开始他的医学研究生涯的。

- Concordia University　康考迪亚大学，1974年建校。全校共有60多幢建筑物。该校在美术、电影以及传播方面的课程吸引了大批的国内外学生前来就读。

Idioms for Everyday Use

get off to a flying/good start
成功地开始；出师告捷 | begin very successfully

A: How's the joint project?

B: We **get off to a flying start** on that project because the Chinese side provided us with the names and addresses of all the people we needed to see.

A: 合作的项目进展如何？

B: 我们这项工作一开始就很顺利，因为中方给我们提供了所有需要拜见的人的姓名和地址。

A: That was a great game last night, wasn't it?

B: Sure was. It was the best one I've seen so far this season.

A: The Lions did play well today. They really **got off to a flying start**.

B: And they beat the tar out of the Ravens.

A: 昨晚是一场精彩的比赛，是吧？

B: 可不是吗。这是我这段时间看到的最好的一场球赛。

A: "雄狮队"今天的确打得不错。他们可真是旗开得胜。

B: 把"乌鸦队"打得一败涂地。

shower someone with something
大量的给予某人（礼物、金钱等） | give a great deal of something to someone

Those famous singers **showered** the hospital **with** contributions.

那些著名的歌唱家给那家医院捐助了一大笔钱。

- As soon as the peddler finished his story, the king **showered** him **with** lots of gifts.
  当小贩刚一讲完故事，国王就给了他很多的礼物。
- During his singing, he was **showered with** different kinds of fresh flowers.
  当他演唱时，观众们向他送上了各种各样的鲜花。

crack up	(for a plane, boat, car, etc.) crash;
使飞机、船舶或车等爆炸、冲撞；弄碎；	(for someone) break out in laughter;
使人开怀大笑，捧腹大笑；发疯；精神崩溃	go crazy; have a nervous break down

- He flew into the side of a mountain and **cracked up**.
  他因飞机撞到了山侧而遇难。
- The whole room **cracked up** when he finished the joke.
  他讲完笑话后，全场捧腹大笑。
- It is mysterious that the car **cracked up** when he started engine.
  真是令人费解，他刚一发动，汽车就爆炸了。
- The stress of her son's divorce and her husband's death was too much. She **cracked up** finally and had to be admitted to a hospital ward.
  儿子离婚、丈夫去世给她带来了巨大的精神压力。最后她终于倒下了，住进了医院。

do one's bit / part	do one's share of the work; do
尽自己的本分，尽自己的职责	whatever one can do to help

- I'm the person that always tries to **do my bit**. How can I help you this time?
  我是那种尽职尽责的人。这次我能给你帮点儿忙吗？
- If everyone who offered to help would come and **do their bit**, we could finish this job in half a day.
  如果每一个愿意帮忙的人都来，并尽最大的努力，我们就能在半天内完成这项工作。
- A: How's the preparation for the annual conference?
  B: Well, everyone in the Association has agreed to **do their bit** in the preparation for the annual conference.
  A: 年会的准备工作如何了？
  B: 啊，协会的每一位成员都同意为年会的准备工作尽力。
- Remember that in every situation, each person must **do his bit**.
  记住，无论在任何情况下，每个人都应该尽自己的职责。

Unit 29
Weather Conditions
气候状况

Many people in the world think of Canada as a land of cold and snow. However, there are hot summers as well as cold winters. Many Canadians take pride in their ability to cope with adverse weather conditions.

Spring begins in Canada in mid March and ends in mid May. In many parts of Canada, the first sign of spring is the trickling of sweet sap from thousands of maple trees. It is in spring that farmers reap this special harvest-maple syrup, and tourists are invited to taste the delicious maple syrup. It is also a time for them to go skiing in mountain areas and strolling in parks as flowers bloom.

Summer in Canada is warm and sunny, but not hot. It is regarded as the best season for fun and relaxation. People are fond of going in for water sports, tennis and sunbathing.

In the clear, cloudless weather of autumn leaves turn into millions and millions of shades of gold and scarlet against a background of azure sky.

Winters along the coast, like in Vancouver, are usually very rainy. You will need an umbrella, raincoat and rain boots.

In the interior and northern regions, winters can be extremely cold. Most people wear thick coats or jackets, scarves, hats and gloves or mitts. Many people wear boots outside and take shoes to wear indoors at work or school.

Winters are long and cold, and when the snow falls, snow plows and salt trucks are out making sure the roads are safe. Winter is fun for children, who can play ice hockey on temporary rinks in the streets as well as on frozen lakes and ponds.

Canadians would never deny that they have got lots of ice and snow. But they will never admit that their winter is gloomy. In fact, it is a golden time for skiing, skating, ice fishing and tobogganing.

Canada is a northern country. However, there are many climate differences among the various regions of Canada. The west coast of British Columbia has the most temperate climate. That's probably due to warm, moist Pacific Ocean airstreams. Snow seldom falls there, and when it does, it usually melts the same day. The southwest coast of British Columbia is labeled Canada's "banana belt" for its year-round temperate climate.

But here in Toronto or Montreal, winter brings heavy snowfalls. Spring can be fleeting. Temperatures of −15℃ have been recorded even in April. And that's why some people jump ship and escape winter's cold by spending holidays in warm southern climates. Florida, California, Hawaii, and Mexico are popular winter vacation areas.

It is said that climate influences the personality of a people. It is generally thought that people from northern climates are cold and unfriendly, and that people from southern regions are hot-tempered and passionate. That is an oversimplified and inadequate notion. Actually, Canadians at all places are warmhearted, hospitable and truthful.

Generally speaking, Canadian weather is very unpredictable, from season to season, and from day to day. It's enough to boggle the mind! When it's a mild, wet day in Vancouver, it can be −20℃ degrees and snowing in central Ontario or in Montreal.

译 文

世界上许多人都认为加拿大是一个被冰雪覆盖的国家。然而，加拿大不仅拥有寒冷的冬天，同时拥有炎热的夏日。很多加拿大人都以能够应对不良的气候条件而感到自豪。

在加拿大春季从3月中旬开始，一直到5月中旬结束。在很多地方，春天带给人们的第一印象就是从那些枫树上流出的甜美欲滴的枫浆。正是在春天，农夫们前来采集收获这种特别的枫浆，并且邀请游客品尝美味的枫糖汁。春天也是人们去山区滑雪的季节，还可以漫步在公园盛开的花丛中。

夏季的加拿大气候温暖，阳光充足但并不炎热，是公认的娱乐和休闲的最佳季节。人们喜欢参加各种水上运动、打网球或晒日光浴。

秋天的加拿大天气晴朗、天高云淡，茂密的树叶渐呈无尽的金色、红色，在蔚蓝天空的映衬下煞是好看。

冬季在温哥华这样的沿海城市会湿润多雨。你需要准备的是雨伞、雨衣以及雨鞋。

在内陆和北部地区，冬天极其寒冷，大多数人都穿戴起厚厚的外套或是夹克，还有围巾、帽子和手套或者防冻皮护手套。很多人外出时穿上棉靴，并且随身带着上班或上学时室内需要换上的单鞋。

冬季是漫长又寒冷的。下雪的时候，雪犁和撒盐车就会出动以确保路面安全。孩子们是喜欢冬季的，因为他们既可以在街面上暂时的溜冰场里玩冰球，也可以在结冻的湖面或池面上玩。

加拿大人从不否认他们拥有许多的冰雪，但他们并不认为他们的冬天是阴郁的。事实上这正是一个滑雪、溜冰、冰钓、乘雪橇的黄金季节。

加拿大是一个北方国家，然而加拿大各地的气候迥异。不列颠哥伦比亚省的西海岸气候最为温和。可能是由于受到了太平洋暖湿气流的影响，那里几乎不下雪，即使下了也通常在当天就融化。不列颠哥伦比亚省的西南沿海就是因四季如春而被称为加拿大的"香蕉地带"。

但在多伦多或蒙特利尔，大雪随冬季而至。春天可能非常短暂，甚至在4月份都曾有过气温在零下15度的纪录。这正是为什么有些人纷纷逃避冬天的寒冷，到温暖的南部度假的原因。佛罗里达、加利福尼亚、夏威夷和墨西哥都是冬季度假的热门地区。

有人说气候对人们的性格有影响。人们通常认为来自北部地区的人冷漠、不很友善；而来自南部地区的人脾气急、充满热情。这是一种过于简单而且不全面的看法。实际上，在任何地方的加拿大人都待人热情、好客和坦诚。

总的来说，加拿大的天气难以预测，不论是各个季节还是每一天。你总会有惊喜！当温哥华舒适而多雨的时候，安大略中部或蒙特利尔则有可能是零下20摄氏度的雪天。

I Was Frozen Stiff

(Linda comes back from her work and is talking to her guest, Li, from China.)

Linda: It's freezing! What unusual weather! I could hardly start my car. It was so cold this morning!

Li: ***I was frozen stiff*** when I came in! How come it's so cold even in the middle of May? Does it often get that cold around here in Toronto at this time of the year?

Linda: Not really. I don't remember having snow in mid May before. That's a real disaster.

Li: That's strange, worrying ever. Am I a Jonah?

Linda: You must be joking. A few days ago, before you came, it was a lot colder.

Li: The weather in Toronto is ***a far cry from*** the weather in Vancouver. When I was in Vancouver and Victoria last time, I enjoyed a cool and relatively dry summer and a mild, wet winter there.

Linda: Yes, that's true. There're many climatic differences among the various regions of Canada. For example, when it's a mild, wet day in Vancouver, it can be −20℃ degrees and snowing in central Ontario or in Montreal.

Li: The west coast of British Columbia has the most temperate climate. That's probably due to warm, moist Pacific Ocean airstreams.

Linda: Yes, you said it! Snow seldom falls there, and when it does, it usually melts the same day. But here in Toronto or Montreal, winter brings heavy snowfalls. Spring can be fleeting. Temperatures of −15℃ have been recorded even in April.

Li: Many people in China think of Canada as a land of cold and snow.

Linda: Well, there're hot summers as well as cold winters in Canada. We Canadians ***take pride in*** our ability to cope with adverse weather conditions.

Li: But I sometimes also hear people grumble about the cold weather.

Linda: Yes. So that's why some people ***jump ship*** and escape winter's cold by spending holidays in warm southern climates. Florida, California, Hawaii, and Mexico are popular winter vacation areas. Generally speaking, Canadian weather is very unpredictable, from season to season, and from day to day. It's enough to ***boggle the mind***!

Li: Yes. I agree. I heard the radio announcer say today: "***Take heart***. The snow is not here to stay. We can expect clearing skies tomorrow and a warm and sunny weekend."

Linda: That's great! This cold is *for the birds*. Speaking of cold, how about going for a cup of coffee to take the chill off?

Li: *I'm right behind you*!

Vocabulary and Notes

- Jonah — 约拿，基督教《圣经·旧约》中的先知。喻指给同伴带来厄运或灾难的人、不祥之人。
- It's freezing. — It's very cold. 这天气真冷。
- relatively — quite; in comparison with other persons or things 相当地；相对地；比较
- mild, wet winter — 温暖、湿润的冬天
- climatic differences — 气候差异
- region — 地区
- the west coast — 西海岸
- temperate — moderate; free from extremes of hot or cold （气候）温和的
- due to — because of; caused by 因为；由于……而……
- moist Pacific Ocean airstreams — 潮湿的太平洋气流
- You said it! — You can say that again! 你说对了！我完全同意！
- melt — cause to become liquid 使融化；使熔化
- fleeting — (of time or periods) short; passing quickly 短暂的；飞逝的
- adverse — going against; unfavorable 不利的
- grumble about (something) — complain about (something) in a bad-tempered way, usually in a low voice 咕哝，嘟囔着抱怨，发牢骚
- Florida — 佛罗里达
- California — 加利福尼亚
- Hawaii — 夏威夷
- Mexico — 墨西哥
- take the chill off — warm up 去去寒；暖和暖和；热一热；烫一烫

Idioms for Everyday Use

be frozen stiff
冻僵；冻得要死 | so cold that one cannot move

- A: I hear you went skating yesterday. Did you have a good time?
- B: Oh, no, not at all. It was very windy and I **was frozen stiff** when I was on the ice.
- A: 听说你昨天去溜冰了。玩得痛快吗？
- B: 噢，真没意思。风太大了，我站在冰上冻得要死。

- A: This cold wave is severe enough to freeze over all the rivers and ponds.
- B: Yes, I **was frozen stiff** when I came out of the room this morning.
- A: 这次寒流很厉害，河流和池塘都得结冰。
- B: 是的，今天早晨我出屋时，快给我冻成冰棍儿了。

a far cry from
和……完全不同 | very different from

- The student residence of McGill University is **a far cry from** what it was ten years ago.
  麦吉尔大学的学生宿舍与10年前相比大不一样。
- Nowadays the world situation is **a far cry from** that of the 1940s.
  当今世界的形势和20世纪40年代的世界大不相同。
- Robert is very talkative and is **a far cry from** his brother. His brother is very quiet. Still waters run deep.
  罗伯特很健谈，与其弟弟相比，大不相同。他弟弟寡言少语。沉默者深谋。

take pride in
以……而自豪；对……感到骄傲/满意 | feel pleased and satisfied with oneself about something

- A: I hear Bob's son has been accepted by Harvard. He's really a brilliant student.
- B: Yes, we all **take pride in** the success of his son.
- A: 听说鲍勃的儿子被哈佛大学录取了。他儿子确实是一个优秀的学生。
- B: 对，我们都为他儿子的成功而骄傲。

- We all **take pride in** the great achievements of our country.
  我们都为我们国家所取得的伟大成就而自豪。

jump ship
逃跑；开小差；变换工作或环境来躲避困难 | desert; change a job or situation to avoid hardship

- A: Have you heard from Morris lately? I haven't received any letters from him since last November. Does he still serve in the army?
- B: Oh, no. He **jumped ship**, and went to Florida, "the Sunshine State".
- A: 你最近收到莫里斯的信了吗？自去年11月份以来我一直没收到他的信。他还在部队服役吗？
- B: 噢，没有。他早躲开那儿，跑到"太阳城"佛罗里达州去了。

- He **jumped ship** when we were about to ask him to sing some songs.
  当我们正要让他唱几首歌时，他溜掉了。

boggle the mind
使人不理解；不可思议 | make one confused

- It **boggles the mind** that the Brazilian peasant said that he did see a flying saucer flying over his head.
  那位巴西农民说他确实看到了一个飞碟飞过他的头顶，真令人不可思议。
- The questions raised by the newly-arrived biologist really **boggle the mind**.
  新来的那位生物学家提出的问题真令人费解。

take heart
振作起来；鼓起勇气 | be encouraged

- I'm afraid he's about to give up. I wish we could do something to make him **take heart**.
  我担心他会灰心丧气。但愿我们能做些努力使他振作起来。
- A: I've been given the axe. Our company has made across-the-board reductions in the work force. Every department had to let two people go. I was one of them.
- B: Well, that's bad news, but **take heart**. I'm sure you'll find another job. You're young and talented.
- A: 我被解雇了。我们公司对雇员进行了大裁减。每个部门要解雇两个人。我就这样被刷了下来。
- B: 这可真是件倒霉的事，但你不要灰心。我相信你会找到另一个工作的。你年轻，而且又有才干。

for the birds
对某物或某事不喜欢；没意思 | something or situation someone does not like; not interesting

- A: Did you go to see the movie last night?
- B: Yes, but I didn't see it through to the end. I think it's **for the birds**.
- A: 昨天晚上你去看电影了吗？

B: 去了，可我没看完。我觉得真没意思。

I didn't take the history course this term. I think it's **for the birds**.
这学期我没选修历史课。我觉得这门课枯燥无味。

I'm right behind you!
好主意；走吧！

Good idea. Let's go.

A: I don't feel like cooking. Let's eat out tonight.

B: **I'm right behind you**.

A: 今晚我不想做饭。我们到外面吃一顿吧。

B: 好主意，我们走吧。

A: Let's go to the smack bar to buy some sandwiches first and then we'll go to the movies.

B: **I'm right behind you**.

A: 我们先去快餐馆买些三明治来，然后我们再去看电影。

B: 行，是个好主意。

Unit 30
On Our Own
独立自主

    Canadian parents always encourage their children to develop their potential to the fullest extent. They try to provide with the conditions for their children's dreams. Fathers and mothers frequently instill their children both ambition and confidence. The children are given all awards for being a hard worker by their parents, and have been educated to establish their reputation as an authority in their fields. Canadian parents usually speak highly of their children, never criticize them before strangers, and let them grow up freely. They concentrate on what their kids can do, not what they cannot. As a result, thousands of Canadian boys and girls are working very hard towards their goals and they grow up hoping to become actors, athletes, diplomats, professors, doctors, lawyers and government high officials. Some even want to become Ministers, Premiers, or even Prime Minister.

    Canadian parents also encourage their children to become involved in extracurricular activities of all types at school, such as going for an outing, playing sports and singing and dancing parties organized by the student union. They believe that only through involvement in these activities can their children become mature young adults.

    Besides the activities in school, the parents make conscious efforts to take their children participate in some social activities outside school. Canadian parents have realized that the social skills their children learn from natural interaction with the others in non-scholastic settings more closely approximate the skills they will need in the "real world". Generally speaking, Canadian parents wholeheartedly support their children's work outside school, never criticize their children for spending too much time on an activity unrelated to their schoolwork.

The parents praise and celebrate their children's creativity and enthusiasm. The "hands-off" education is a fundamental characteristic of Canadian education. Canadian children grow up with the notion of "self-reliance". That's why people respect for individual effort and contempt for over-relying on others. That has become a basic concept in Canadian society.

In Canada, children are encouraged to be independent. Many young adults leave their family home between the ages of eighteen and twenty-three and live on their own or with their pets. They choose their own career and their own spouse. Sometimes they will ask their parents for help, but they usually don't want to be protected by their parents.

Canadian families tend to place more emphasis on the needs and desires of the child. Since World War II, so much emphasis has been placed on the psychological needs of children that the number of experts in this field has increased enormously; child psychologists, counselors and social workers are employed to help children with problems at school or in the family. Many books on how to raise children have become best-sellers, and almost all of them share the emphasis on the development of the individual as their primary goal.

North Americans are constantly urged to be on their own, to be individualistic. There is a strong cultural pressure to be self-supporting, to leave home. By the time you're 18 years old, you usually finish high school and you're expected to leave home, to go out and make it on your own. It is said that if a young man of 22 years old is still living with his mother and father, for any reason, all of his friends will think he is very strange. They may think that he has mental problems since he is still looked after by his parents.

Many senior high and college students hold at least one part-time job. They do lawn and garden chores; mop and clean buildings; work in factories, restaurants, swimming pools, and libraries; work as tutors, salespersons, doing whatever work they can find. They spend some money they earned for pocket money, and some money is accumulated for the purchase of a used car since Canadian young people can get a driver's license soon after their sixteenth birthday.

Canadian young people think that the significance of doing a part-time job means more than money and experiences. It broadens their outlook and exerts a profound influence on their personality and life. Their concept is that a man needs to be independent first and then to be successful. And taking a part-time job may be a good way to realize their dream.

The job will offer them opportunities to cultivate independence and develop a sense of competition. It also makes them feel mature and help to build up their confidence. And more important, they can learn what they cannot learn from books. That is why Canadian youth who were born in very rich families also prefer to support themselves and be independent. In addition, doing a part-time job can relieve the financial burden on their parents.

The independence of the elderly is emphasized in Canadian society. A problem may result if a parent is ill and in need of care, however. The children often find it difficult to take an elderly parent into their own home. In Canada, many elderly people live in nursing homes or homes for the elderly and are supported by social security.

译 文

在加拿大，父母总是鼓励子女最大限度地发挥他们的潜能。他们尽可能地为孩子提供平台去实现梦想。爸爸妈妈经常给孩子灌输既要有雄心又要有信心的思想。孩子的工作干得出色就会得到父母的奖励，而且孩子一直被灌输要在自己的领域中功成名就。加拿大父母经常表扬自己的孩子，从不在陌生人面前批评孩子，让他们自由自在地成长。他们关心的是孩子们能做什么，而不是他们不能做什么。这种教育的结果是，成千上万的加拿大孩子都在积极地朝着自己的目标而努力。他们怀着当演员、运动员、外交官、教授、医生、律师和政府高官的希望长大成人。有些孩子甚至想成为部长、省长甚至首相。

加拿大父母还鼓励孩子参与学校各种各样的课外活动，诸如学生会组织的郊游、体育活动以及音乐与舞蹈晚会。他们认为孩子只有通过参与这类活动才能成熟起来。

除了校内组织的活动，父母还有意识地带孩子们参加一些校外的社交活动。加拿大的父母们意识到，在校外环境中孩子们从与其他人自然交往中学到的社交能力会更接近"现实世界"所需要的能力。总之，加拿大的父母真切支持孩子们校外的工作，从不责备孩子们花了过多时间用于与学校功课无关的活动。

他们对孩子们的创造性和热情奔放给予高度评价和祝贺。这种"放手"教育的方式也是加拿大教育的一个基本特点，加拿大的孩子在"一切靠自己"的观念下成长起来，这是他们崇尚个人奋斗、鄙夷依附他人的原因。这构成了加拿大社会的一个基本观念。

加拿大社会鼓励孩子们独立自主。许多年龄在18岁到23岁的年轻人离开父母，独自或者带着他们的宠物生活。他们自己确定职业发展方向、选择配偶。有时他们会向父母求助，但通常不会生活在父母的保护伞下。

加拿大家庭更加注重孩子的需求和期望。二战结束后，孩子们的心理问题需求越来越被社会广泛关注，这一领域的专家也以惊人的数目增加。社会上出现了大批儿童心理学家、顾问和社会工作者，来帮助在学校或家庭里有问题的孩子。许多育儿书成了抢手货，几乎所有的热销书都强调个人发展这个首要目标。

北美人经常被敦促要独立和自主。离开父母实现自立是一种强大的文化压力。当你18岁时，通常情况下你完成了高中学业，应该离开父母走向社会，自力更生。如果一个22岁的年轻人还和父母生活在一起，不管什么原因，他所有的朋友都会认为他是个古怪的人。因为他仍然受到父母照顾，朋友们可能会认为他精神上有问题。

许多高中生和大学生手头都至少有一份兼职工作。他们有的修理草坪，看管花园，帮人拖地，清扫楼房；有的在工厂、饭馆、游泳馆或者图书馆打工；也有的做家教或者推销员，做着各种各样他们能找到的兼职。挣来的钱一些被当做零花钱，也有一些被攒下来买辆旧车，因为加拿大年轻人到了16岁即可取得驾驶执照。

加拿大的年轻人认为，兼职的重要性不仅限于报酬和经历，它更多的是开阔了他们的眼界，并对他们的个性塑造和生活习惯产生深远的影响。他们的理念是，一个人只有先独立，才能获得成功；而兼职则是他们实现自己梦想的一个很好的途径。

兼职可以帮助培养他们的自立能力和竞争意识。同时，也帮助他们走向成熟，使他们更加自信。更重要的是，他们能够学到书本上学不到的东西。正是出于这种原因，即使是出生在富有家庭里的加拿大年轻人，也选择自力更生，独立自主。另外，年轻人做兼职也可以减轻家长们的经济负担。

加拿大社会同样强调年长者的独立，可如果父母生病需要儿女照顾时就会出现问题。儿女很难把父母接到自己的家里来照顾。在加拿大，很多老人住在社会保障机构提供的疗养院或者敬老院里。

Unit 30   On Our Own 独立自主

 **Dialogue**

We Don't Usually See Eye to Eye on Many Things

(Ann and Li are talking about the noise in the student residence.)

Li: Hey, Ann, you look depressed today, *down in the mouth*. What's up?

Ann: All the racket in res' makes it hard to study. Last night a group of students kept making so much noise that we couldn't sleep. A friend of mine finally *blew a fuse*. To be frank, I'd prefer some peace and quiet for a change.

Li: It sounds like you're thinking of moving off campus. I saw some ads for apartments the other day that *didn't sound half bad*. I'm also thinking of moving out of the noisy residence.

Ann: How would you like to be roommates? It's not so hard if you share. And I may also be able to help you to *get into the swing of* things in Montreal.

Li: Not a bad idea. But the problem is the furniture and dishes. It'll *cost a mint* just to get set up.

Ann: Don't worry. I'll talk to Chris, the director of the residence. He will be willing to help us. He's the kind of guy that's always willing to *go the extra mile*.

Li: And why don't you talk to your parents? They may give us some help, too.

Ann: That's a good idea. I guess they would let me have some of their old stuff in the basement. I'm sure my parents will help me out a bit—anything if it gets me *out of their hair*.

Li: Please call them and we could take some action tomorrow.

Ann: No problem, as quick as we can.

Li: Ann, do you have a bedroom in your home?

Ann: Oh, yes. Since families are generally small, many Canadian children enjoy the luxury of their own bedroom. We Canadians enjoy the comfort of a large amount of living space.

Li: Then why don't you stay with your parents?

Ann: Well, you don't know my parents. They've got such old-fashioned ideas. We disagree all the time and we don't usually *see eye to eye* on many things. For instance, they want me to be home by 11 o'clock on Saturday nights.

Li: That seems a little strict but, you know, if you want them to give you more freedom, you've got to be willing to *meet them halfway* sometimes. You can't expect to get your own way in everything.

Ann: Well, the main reason for leaving home is that we North Americans are constantly urged to be on our own, to be individualistic. There is a strong cultural pressure to be self-supporting, to leave home. By the time you're 18 years old, you usually finish high school and you're expected to leave home, to go out and make it on you own. It is said that if a young man of 22 years old is still living with his mother and father, for any reason, all of his friends will think he is very strange. They may think that he has mental problems since he is still looked after by his parents.

Li: Oh, I see. Thanks, Ann. You really gave me a lesson about social life in Canada. We have a lot of work to do if we rent the apartment. Let's go and check the ads first.

Ann: Good. Let's go.

Vocabulary and Notes

- racket 　　　　　　　　loud noise 吵闹声；喧哗
- res'　　　　　　　　　　（residence的缩写）（对话中指）学生住处
- ads　　　　　　　　　　（advertisements的缩写）广告
- It'll cost a mint just to get set up.　　　　　配齐这些（家什）要花费很多钱。
- the director of the residence　　　　学生宿舍负责人
- old stuff　　　　　　　　旧家什
- basement　　　　　　　　地下室
- luxury　　　　　　　　　奢侈；豪华
- old-fashioned ideas　　　旧的传统观念
- That seems a little strict...　　看起来（他们）管得有点严……
虽然加拿大的父母主张给孩子较多的自由以培养少年儿童的独立能力，但是对孩子的关心和教育也是挺严格的，尤其对孩子的安全特别在意。政府规定，家长不得让12岁以下的孩子一个人留在家里，儿童上街或去公园都得有成人陪同。家长们也往往建立一些家庭规则，要求孩子必须遵守。例如，宵禁（curfew）就是一条加拿大家庭中最常见的规定。未成年的孩子晚上外出时必须在规定的时间前回家，不得逾时不归。如果孩子去参加通宵晚会（all-night party）或在朋友家过夜（sleep-over），都必须得到家长的同意。在加拿大，16岁是一个十分关键的年龄，被称为"神奇16岁"（magic age of sixteen）。从16岁开始，孩子获得了更大的自主能力。

- individualistic 独立的；个人主义的
- go out and make it on one's own 走向社会，依靠自己奋斗
- mental problem 精神不正常

📖 Idioms for Everyday Use

down in the mouth /dumps
神色沮丧，垂头丧气 | be depressed

- The children looked very **down in the mouth** when I told them that I couldn't take them to the Kites Fair during the May holiday.
  我对孩子们说五一放假期间我不能带他们去风筝会了，他们一个个就像泄了气的皮球似的。
- Even since he lost his job, John has been looking very **down in the mouth**.
  约翰失业后，一直垂头丧气。
- He's one of those people who can't stand his own company. As soon as he finds himself alone, he gets **down in the mouth**.
  他就是那种不能忍受孤独的人。一旦发现自己独自一人的时候，他就郁郁寡欢。

blow a fuse
勃然大怒；用强烈的语言发泄愤怒 | become very angry; express one's anger using strong words

- A: Tim has decided to transfer to another section. Do you know why?
- B: It's the section manager, David Wright. He got angry with Tim the other day and they

argued for about ten minutes. Finally, Mr. Wright **blew a fuse**.

A: 蒂姆已决定要调到另一个部门了。你知道为什么吗?

B: 是因为部门经理大卫·赖特。那天他跟蒂姆生气了,他俩吵了大约10分钟。末了,赖特先生发脾气了。

I never saw him so angry. He **blew a fuse** when I mentioned his former girlfriend.

我从来没有见过他这样生气。当我提起他以前的女朋友时,他勃然大怒。

| **not half bad** 挺不错的,很好 | quite good |

A: Let's go and check that house after lunch. It does look like a buyer's market right now.

B: I went there myself this morning. It does have all the modern conveniences—central heating, hot water supply, two bathrooms and the price **doesn't sound half bad**.

A: 午饭后我们去看看那栋房子。看来现在确实是买房子的好时机。

B: 我今天早晨已经去过了。那栋房子确实具备所有的现代化设备,如中央暖气、热水供应、两个洗澡间,而且价钱还很不错。

He may seem rather standoffish at first acquaintance, but he's **not half a bad fellow** when you get to know him.

当你初次与他结识时,他看起来有些冷淡,但是当你开始对他有所了解的时候,你就知道他是个挺不错的人。

| **get into the swing of (something)** 逐渐习惯或适应新环境;积极投入并爱好(某活动) | adapt or adjust oneself to a new environment; become very involved in (something) and enjoy what you are doing |

It didn't take that American student very long to **get into the swing of** things at McGill University.

那位美国学生没多久就熟悉了麦吉尔大学的环境。

A: Well, it's difficult for me to master a computer. I can't keep up with the others though.

B: It's certainly not easy work, but when you **get into the swing of** it, you should be able to work with it quite quickly.

A: 对我来说,使用计算机太难了。我怎么也赶不上其他人。

B: 这当然不是一件容易的工作,不过当你熟悉了以后,你就会干得很快。

| **cost a mint** 花费高,很贵 | be very expensive |

Unit 30　On Our Own 独立自主

- A: Let's buy a house near Catherine Street. Since that part of town has become fashionable, and people are flocking to it.
- B: But the prices are going up. It'll **cost a mint** to buy a house in that area.
- A: 咱们在凯瑟林大街附近买一幢房子吧。因为那片城区越来越现代派了，人们蜂拥而至。
- B: 可是房价正在上涨。在那个地区买房子花费太大。

Students from outside Canada would be wise to seek accommodation in a university residence because it would **cost a mint** to rent an apartment off campus.
来到加拿大的留学生在学校宿舍寻找住房是明智的，因为在校外租房很贵。

go the extra mile
做额外工作；主动承担工作；想尽办法去完成（某事） | do more than is necessary; go out of one's way to do (something)

- A: Do you think I should call Stan? Would he be willing to help?
- B: No problem, I think. You know Stan. He's the kind of guy that's always willing to **go the extra mile**.
- A: 你说我该不该打电话给斯坦？他肯帮忙吗？
- B: 我看没问题。你是了解斯坦的。他是个有求必应的人。

Professor Redmond is always willing to **go the extra mile**. He gave up three days of vacation to help Tom out with the problems of trigonometric function.
雷德蒙教授做事总是过于热心。他放弃了三天的休假，主动帮助汤姆解决了三角函数问题。

out of one's hair
使某人不受打扰 | in a position not to bother someone

- A: Peter! Why don't you keep the children of the guests occupied and **out of their mothers' hair**.
- B: Good idea. I'll take them outside and we can fly a kite together.
- A: 彼得！你能不能让客人的孩子有点事儿干，别让他们打扰自己的母亲。
- B: 好主意。我带他们到外边一起去放风筝。

Barbara finally got the boys **out of her hair** so she could concentrate herself on study.
芭芭拉终于摆脱了那些男孩子，这样她就可以集中精力学习了。

see eye to eye (with someone)
同意（某人），赞同（某人） | agree

Your father and I **see eye to eye** about taking the family camper to the Yellow Stone National

Park.

关于你把家里的野营旅游车开到（美国的）黄石公园去一事，我和你父亲都不赞同。

A: What do you think of the Canadian Prime Minister?

B: Well, I agree with him on domestic issues but I don't **see eye to eye** with him on foreign policy.

A: 你认为加拿大总理怎么样？

B: 哦，我赞成他在国内事务上的做法，但我对他的外交政策持不同意见。

A: How's married life treating you? Have you had any fights?

B: Not at all. We sometimes disagree on small things but we usually **see eye to eye** on the major issues.

A: 婚后的生活怎么样？你们俩人吵过架吗？

B: 从来没有。有时候我们在一些小事上有不同意见，可在大事上我们的意见总是一致的。

meet someone halfway
向某人妥协，向某人让步 | compromise with someone in a situation where the opinions differ

She was always ready to **meet him halfway** when they had an argument.

每当他们争吵时，她总是让着他。

A: How was the negotiation yesterday? Did you compromise with Edal Company?

B: No, we didn't reach any agreement. Well, we would certainly **meet them halfway**, if they would give a little ground on their side.

A: 昨天的谈判怎么样？你们有没有对埃戴尔公司做出让步？

B: 没有，我们没有达成任何协议。实际上如果他们那方稍做点让步的话，我们当然愿意同他们妥协。

Unit 31
The Meech Lake Accord
米其湖条约

The Province of Quebec differs from other provinces of Canada, because it has a strong French culture. Their language, traditions, culture and institutions set Quebec apart from all other provinces.

The European history of Quebec began with the arrival of the French explorer Jacques Cartier in 1534. The establishment of a thriving fur trade, relatively friendly relations characterized the succeeding era with the aboriginal people and a continuous rivalry between French and English colonists.

In the early 1960s French Canadians became more vocal in their protests. In particular, they complained that they were kept out of jobs in government and in some large businesses because they spoke only French. Some French Canadians felt that the only way for them to maintain their unique identity was to separate completely from Canada.

Quebec is Canada's French province as about 80% of the population is descendants of the original settlers of New France. Most people speak only French. With the adoption of *Bill 101* in 1977, French is the sole official language in Quebec.

In 1982 Canada got a new constitution. Nine provinces signed the constitution, but Quebec Province didn't. Quebec said the constitution didn't give it power to protect French culture and language. They say that the policies are hard on Quebeckers. So they went out of their way to make the government change the constitution.

It was in 1987 that the premiers of Canada's 10 provinces met with Prime

Minister Mulroney at Meech Lake, Quebec. After the serious debates, they agreed to change the constitution of 1982. So this time Quebec signed *the Meech Lake Accord*.

Don't take it for granted that Canada is a peaceful country. *The Meech Lake Accord* in fact rubs some of the provinces the wrong way. Since the Accord called Quebec a "distinct society" and gave Quebec special power to protect French culture and language, some provinces, such as Manitoba and New Brunswick didn't sign *the Meech Lake Accord*.

In June 1987 Canada's top politicians reached an agreement offering the province special status within the country and privileges to promote its French culture and language. That agreement called *the Meech Lake Accord* was abolished in June 1990 because of strong opposition from Canada's English-speaking majority.

On October 30, 1995 a referendum on Quebec's future status was held in the province. The result was that those who were against independence defeated advocates of independence by a slender majority (50.6% to 49.4%), thus temporarily bringing to an end the lasting debate on the province's future. It is now estimated that of all the 82% French-speaking Canadians, 60% are for independence. This growing nationalism means that Quebec's future status has remained unresolved.

译 文

魁北克省在加拿大独树一帜，这是因为它拥有浓郁的法国文化。这里的语言、传统、文化及其制度使它与其他的省份存在较大的差异。

在1534年，一位名叫雅克·卡蒂埃的法国探险家踏上了加拿大的土地，造就了魁北克省的欧洲历史。随后开始了以日益增长的皮毛生意为特征的时期，法国定居者与当地人保持着相对友善的关系，同时继续与英国竞争，掠夺殖民地。

自20世纪60年代起，法裔加拿大人的反抗声音表现得日益明显。抗议的焦点是由于只讲法语，他们被排除在政府部门以及一些大公司之外。有些法裔加拿大人认为，保持他们独特身份的唯一办法就是让魁北克彻底脱离加拿大管辖。

魁北克是加拿大法语占主导的一个省份——大约80%的人口是新法兰西定居者的后裔。大多数人只讲法语。自1977年颁布了《101法案》以来，法语是魁北克省唯一的官方语言。

1982年加拿大出台新宪法。九个省份签署了该宪法，而魁北克没有。魁北克表示该宪法没有授予魁北克保护法国文化和语言的权利。他们说这个政策是在为难魁北克人民，所以他们尽力要求政府修改宪法。

1987年，加拿大10个省份的省长们与马尔罗尼总理在魁北克的米其湖见面。经过认真的争论后，他们同意修改1982年宪法。因此，魁北克当时签订了《米其湖条约》。

不要想当然认为加拿大是一个相安无事的国家，《米其湖条约》事实上造成了有些省份的不满。自从该条约规定魁北克为一个"特别地区"并授予魁北克特殊权利保护法国文化和语言以来，有些省份比如马尼托巴省和新不伦瑞克省就没有签署《米其湖条约》。

1987年6月，加拿大最高政府领导达成一致，给予魁北克省特殊地位并授以特权，使其发扬法国语言和文化。该协议名为《米其湖条约》，但因为大部分英语为母语的加拿大人的强烈反对，这个协议在1990年被终止了。

1995年10月30日，加拿大在魁北克举行全民公投来决定魁北克的前途。结果，反对魁北克独立的一派仅仅以微弱优势取胜（50.6% 对 49.4%），这场旷日持久的有关该省的未来的争论暂时告一段落。据估计，占魁北克82%的讲法语人口中，60%的人支持独立。这场持续增长的民族主义情绪标志着魁北克的发展前景仍然没有答案。

Smooth Things Over

(Li is curious about *the Meech Lake Accord*, and is asking his friend Angela about it.)

Li: Angela, many people in Canada are talking about *the Meech Lake Accord*. I also hear people here in Toronto are debating and arguing about it. It seems that it's a serious national problem. What's it all about? Could you explain **the ins and outs** of it to me?

Angela: Well, let's tell you from the very beginning. In 1982 Canada got a new constitution. Nine provinces signed the constitution, but Quebec Province didn't. Quebec said the constitution didn't give it power to protect French culture and language. They say that the policies ***are hard on*** Quebeckers. So they ***went out of their way to*** make the government change the constitution.

Li: Was the constitution changed finally?

Angela: Yes. It was in 1987 that the premiers of Canada's 10 provinces met with Prime Minister Mulroney at Meech Lake, Quebec. After the serious debates, they agreed to change the constitution of 1982. So this time Quebec signed *the Meech Lake Accord*.

Li: So Quebec is now happy and the problem of Quebec separation is solved. Right?

Angela: No. Don't *take it for granted* that Canada is a peaceful country. *The Meech Lake Accord* in fact *rubs some of the provinces the wrong way*. Since the Accord called Quebec a "distinct society" and gave Quebec special power to protect French culture and language, some provinces, such as Manitoba and New Brunswick didn't sign *the Meech Lake Accord*.

Li: I see. That's why the Prime Minister says he wants to change the Accord. What if the Accord dies by the way?

Angela: Quebec may separate from Canada.

Li: So it puts the Prime Minister into a *catch-22* position. I hear some provincial governments objected, arguing that all Canadians should have their rights protected equally. Thus *the Meech Lake Accord* failed in 1990 and the problem of Quebec remained.

Angela: Yes, after many attempts to meet Quebec's demands, Brian Mulroney failed as well. He has to do something special to *smooth things over*. Well, Li, that's a rough idea of *the Meech Lake Accord*.

Li: Thanks a lot, Angela.

Vocabulary and Notes

- accord — formal agreement 协定；协议
- *the Meech Lake Accord* — 《米其湖条约》，是加拿大联邦政府总理布赖恩·马尔罗尼（Brian Mulroney）与10个省的省长于1987年6月就魁北克省加入联邦统一宪法问题时达成的协议。这次会议是在魁北克省米其湖举行的，《米其湖条约》由此得名。会上接受了魁北克省的五项条件。但由于纽芬兰省、新不伦瑞克省和马尼托巴省的反对，该协议于1990年终止。
- constitution — the body of laws and principles according to which a country is governed 宪法
- protect French culture and language — 保护法国文化和语言
- premier — the head of the government in certain countries（一些国家的）总理，首相（对话中指加拿大各省省长）

Unit 31　The Meech Lake Accord 米其湖条约

- Prime Minister　　政府总理
- distinct　　clearly marking a person or thing as different from others 不同的，特殊的，个别的

- distinct society　　特殊社会，特别社区
- Manitoba　　马尼托巴省。该省是加拿大三大草原省之一，人口123万，首府温尼伯（Winnipeg）。该省是加拿大的农业大省，重要的粮食产区。马尼托巴省有三所大学：马尼托巴大学（the University of Manitoba）、布兰登大学（Brandon University）及温尼伯大学（the University of Winnipeg）。马尼托巴大学成立于1877年，规模最大。因为该大学历史悠久并拥有众多的农业、科学、法律、医学、教育等资深教授而成为马尼托巴省的中心大学。该大学的理工和法律专业的研究生培养都很著名。布兰登大学和温尼伯大学以文学和科学著称，也均为一流大学，其学科恰好弥补了马尼托巴大学的不足，开设的专业分别有历史、经济、政治科学、艺术、音乐及戏剧等。

- New Brunswick　　新不伦瑞克省。该省位于大西洋东部沿岸，与新斯科舍接壤，濒临爱德华王子岛，再加上纽芬兰，成为"大西洋四省"。新不伦瑞克省人口80万，省会为弗雷德里克顿（Fredericton）。该省人口约55%为欧洲后裔，约40%的人口是法裔。该省有三所大学：新不伦瑞克大学（University of New Brunswick）建于1785年，位于弗雷德里克顿；蒙特爱里森大学（Mount Allison University）建于1858年；蒙克顿法语大学(University de Moncton)建于1963年。新不伦瑞克省教育局管理着600余所公立学校的课程，其中许多学校用法语上课。新不伦瑞克省拥有众多的景点，被称为加拿大最适宜拍照的省份。最为出名的是两座国家公园。

- It puts the Prime Minister into a catch-22 position.　　这件事使得总理处在一个左右为难的尴尬局面。

Idioms for Everyday Use

the ins and outs　　all the details and complexities of (something)
（某事的）详细情况；原委始末或来龙去脉

A:　Peter really is a remarkable expert! There is very little he doesn't know.

B: I have exactly the same feeling. This afternoon he explained **the ins and outs** of the stock market to me. He knows a lot about investments.

A: 彼得真是个了不起的专家！他知识渊博。

B: 我有同感。今天下午他给我解释了股票市场的来龙去脉。他在投资方面见多识广。

My father told the police **the ins and outs** of what had happened.

我父亲把事情发生的来龙去脉都告诉了警察。

be hard on (something or somebody)
（对人）刻薄的或过分严厉的；用东西费 | treat unkindly or roughly

A: It**'s hard on** Karen, having to work when the rest of us are enjoying ourselves.

B: It serves him right. He's been late for work recently.

A: 我们大伙都在玩，而凯伦却不得不去干活，这对他未免太刻薄了吧。

B: 他自作自受。他最近上班一直迟到。

Peter's parents **were hard on** him, so he left home for New York without telling them.

彼得的父母对他过于严厉，因此他没告诉他们就离家到纽约去了。

My son **is hard on** shoes. Look at this pair. I bought them for him only a month ago.

我儿子的鞋穿得太费了。看看这双鞋，我一个月前刚给他买的。

go out of one's way to do something
尽最大努力去做某事；想尽办法或不怕麻烦做某事 | make a special effort to do something; take pains to do something

A: Her restaurant business is extremely good, isn't it?

B: That's right. She always **goes out of her way to** please her customers.

A: 她饭馆的生意太好了，是吧？

B: 那还用说。她总是尽力来使顾客满意。

A: You should try volunteering for the questions in class next time, and take the initiative.

B: Thank you for your advice. From now on, I'll **go out of my way to** answer questions willingly.

A: 下次你应在课堂上试着主动回答问题，要争取主动。

B: 谢谢你的劝告。从现在起，我一定争取主动回答问题。

Mr. Bridge **went out of his way to** invite his boss to the party tonight.

布里奇先生特意邀请了老板来参加今晚的晚会。

take something for granted
把某事认为是理所当然的；认为某事不成问题 | assume something without question

She spoke French so well that I **took it for granted** she was French.

她的法语讲得真好，我想她一定是法国人。

(B is waiting for the bus at a bus-stop. A is coming towards him.)

Unit 31　The Meech Lake Accord 米其湖条约

A: Hi! Have you been waiting long?
B: No, only a few minutes. I **took it for granted** that we wouldn't have to wait too long this time.
A: 嘿！你等了好长时间了吗？
B: 没有，只有几分钟。我想这次我们当然不会等太长时间的。

rub someone the wrong way
激怒某人；触犯某人；得罪某人；惹某人生气 | irritate someone

A: Susan, I'm bending over backwards to make you happy, but you're always **rubbing me the wrong way**.
B: You're too sensitive, David—grow up and be an adult.
A: 苏珊，我一直在尽力让你高兴，可你总是惹我生气。
B: 你太敏感了，大卫——别孩子气，拿出大人样来。

Father's friend called Tom a little boy, and that **rubbed Tom the wrong way**.
父亲的朋友叫汤姆是小毛孩子，这可得罪了汤姆。

catch-22 (situation or position)
左右为难；进退维谷；使某人处于尴尬的局面 | A situation in which you cannot do one thing until you do another thing, but you cannot do the second thing until you do the first thing. It is therefore impossible to do anything.

You can't get a job in that wine factory if you haven't got the experience; and you can't get the experience if you haven't got a job in that factory—it's a **catch-22**.
如果你没有经验，你就不能在那个酒厂工作；可是你不在那个酒厂工作，你就得不到那种经验——这可真让人为难啊。

If he quits his job, his boss will be angry; but if he doesn't, his wife will be even angrier. It's a real **catch-22** situation.
如果他辞掉工作，老板会生气的；可如果他不辞掉工作，他妻子会更生气。这可真让他左右为难呐。

smooth things over
使不愉快的局面平息下来；消除分歧 | make an unpleasant situation seem better; try to excuse

A: Well, just take it easy. I'll have a word with her to try to **smooth things over**. But don't make a mistake like that again. OK?
B: I'll try not to, believe me!
A: 别着急，我来跟她谈谈，想办法消除隔阂。但你可别再犯这样的错了，好吗？
B: 我尽力吧，请相信我！

No matter how hard he tried, he was unable to **smooth over** their differences.
不管他怎么努力，也未能消除他们之间的分歧。

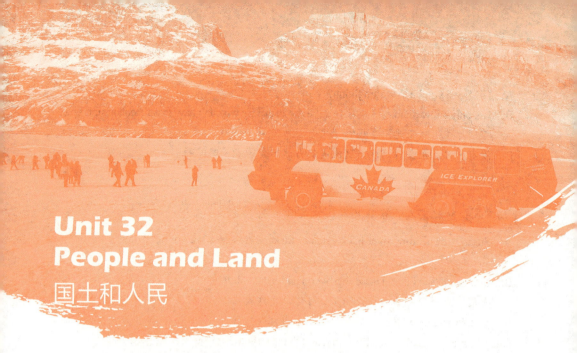

Unit 32
People and Land
国土和人民

At 9,970,610 square kilometers, Canada is the second largest country in the world. It is more than forty times the size of Britain, or eighteen times the size of France; Ottawa, in the Province of Ontario, is the capital of Canada.

Ottawa was chosen as Canada's capital city in 1855 by Queen Victoria. Today the city boasts many magnificent copper-roofed government buildings, museums, and art galleries. On both sides of the Ottawa River, a cluster of Federal laboratories and offices have been built. The administrative headquarters of Canadian Broadcasting Corporation and the Federal departments of public works and postal services stand now on the southern edge of the city. High-rise offices and apartment buildings go up faster than old buildings disappear. The capital is not a large city, but it is a nice city to live in. There is a cool and comfortable shopping mall, a block from the parliament buildings where every summer's morning the guard is changed to the stirring music of a military band. The city echoes the pageantry of its past.

Canada has ten provinces and three territories, each with its own capital city (in brackets): Alberta (Edmonton), British Columbia (Victoria), Prince Edward Island (Charlottetown), Manitoba (Winnipeg), New Brunswick (Fredericton), Nova Scotia (Halifax), Ontario (Toronto), Quebec (Quebec City), Saskatchewan (Regina), Newfoundland (St.John's), Northwest Territories (Yellowknife), Yukon Territory (Whitehorse), Nunavut (Iqaluit).

Unit 32 People and Land 国土和人民

Canada's nearly 10 million square kilometers of territory comprises mountains, forests, tundra, prairies, lakes and rivers.

Under the earth's surface is a storehouse of petroleum, natural gas and minerals and its riches are still uncounted. Canada is one of the world's leading producers of nickel and zinc.

Canada's water resources are remarkable. Its lakes account for one-half of the world's fresh water, and oceans, lakes and rivers abound with a variety of life. Highways of exploration for early settlement, complex river systems today transport the products of processing and manufacturing industries, as well as provide hydroelectric power for domestic use and export.

The astonishing natural beauty of Canada—its mountains, lakes, plains and lure of its vast wilderness areas—attracts visitors from around the world.

Canada's wilderness areas are protected well by the government; there are over 100 national parks and hundreds of provincial parks. Canada is beautiful. Indeed Canada contains an overwhelming variety of natural beauty. No matter where you live in Canada, interesting and even breathtaking landscapes are usually just a short walk or bus ride away.

In 1964, Canadians thought that they should have a flag of their own. So the government asked everyone to draw pictures of flags and send them in. The best picture would be chosen as Canada's flag. So the people drew thousands of different flags.

There was a heated flag debate in Parliament in fact, and, after many discussions and debates, on 15 Feb. 1965, Queen Elizabeth II proclaimed the maple leaf Canada's national flag.

Why did they choose a maple leaf as Canada's flag? The maple leaves look beautiful, especially in autumn. The color is so bright and red. Besides, maple trees are good for making houses and furniture, and, last but not least, you can get sugar from the maple tree.

Canada is one of the most sparsely populated countries. Its population is over 30 million (2002). The total population in 2023 is over 40 million, with more than half of the people living in the Southern part of Canada and within 400 kilometers of the U.S. border.

Canada's people are as diverse as its land, tracing their origins from all over the world. Different languages, ethnic origins, histories and environments have made for regional differences across Canada.

According to the statistics in 2022, most Canadians are of British (44.65%) or French (28.7%) ancestry. The Indigenous Peoples make up 1.5% of the country's population. Canadians of other ethnic backgrounds comprise about 25% of Canada's population, including large groups of Italians, Indians, Germans, Chinese and Ukrainians.

Canada has one of the world's highest living standards. For example, according to the World Bank, the per capita PPP (Purchasing Power Parity), which is a parity coefficient between currencies calculated based on different price levels in various countries, was estimated at $47,567 in 2022. In the same year, Canada is projected to have a median after-tax income of $54,630.

The Vancouver Sun says that the average Canadian car owner drives his car 2,000 miles each year on vacation trips alone. Many Canadians own cars not only for business but also for pleasure traveling. Nowadays in Canada the major part of their traveling is done in cars. We've got a boiling sea of bicycles in China and they've got a boiling ocean of cars in Canada. Every family here has a car, or two or even three. Statistics shows that more than half the populations know how to drive an automobile and have licenses to drive.

译 文

加拿大的国土面积为9970610平方公里，是世界第二大国家。其面积要比英国大40多倍，相当于18个法国。渥太华是加拿大的首都，位于安大略省。

渥太华在1855年被维多利亚女王命名为加拿大的首都城市。今天，这座城市以其很多壮丽的铜顶政府办公大楼、博物馆和美术馆而享有盛誉。渥太华河两岸各种联邦政府实验大楼和办公大楼鳞次栉比。现在在渥太华市南边，耸立着加拿大广播公司总部大楼、联邦市政工程部门大楼和邮政大楼。随着高耸入云的联邦政府办公楼和住宅楼如雨后春笋般建起，城市中的古旧建筑逐渐减少。首都虽小，但居住环境优雅。离议会大厦一街之隔，有条凉爽且舒适的商业街。在大厦前，每天夏天的上午都有禁卫军在军乐队激动人心的音乐伴奏下换岗的场面，这座城市再现出昔日的盛观。

加拿大由10个省和3个管辖区组成，每个都有自己的省会城市，具体如下（括号内为省会）：阿尔伯塔省（埃德蒙顿）、不列颠哥伦比亚省（维多利亚）、爱德华王子岛省（夏洛特敦）、马尼托巴省（温尼伯）、新不伦瑞克省（弗雷德里克顿）、新斯科舍省（哈利法克斯）、安大略省（多伦多）、魁北克省（魁北克）、萨斯喀彻温省（里贾纳）、纽芬兰省（圣约翰斯）、西北地区（耶洛奈夫）、育空地区（怀特霍斯）、努纳武特地区（伊卡卢伊特）。

加拿大将近一千万平方公里的领土由山脉、森林、苔原、牧场、湖泊与河流组成。

地表之下蕴藏着丰富的石油、天然气以及矿物资源，储量之丰富无法估计。加拿大是世界上镍矿和锌矿的主要生产国之一。

加拿大的水资源极为丰富。湖泊蓄水量占世界淡水总量的一半，海洋、湖泊和河流的生物种类繁多。早期移民开拓的公路和现代开发的错综复杂的水运系统传送着加工业以及制造业的产品，同时也提供了水力发电，以满足国内外需求。

加拿大的自然之美令人惊叹——山川、湖泊、平原以及充满诱惑的野生环境吸引着世界各国的游客。

加拿大的野生环境受到政府的严格保护；全国拥有100多个国家公园和成百上千个省级公园。加拿大风景如画，令人无法抗拒的自然奇观比比皆是。无论你住在加拿大的什么地方，通常只需稍微步行或者乘直通巴士就可一睹风格奇异甚至令人叹为观止的美丽风景。

1964年，加拿大人认为他们应该有属于自己的一面旗帜，因此政府向全民征集旗帜图样，最佳设计会被采用为国旗的图案。人们因而上交了上千份各种各样的旗帜图片。

事实上，国会也展开了一场热烈的旗帜争论，经过多次讨论和争论，在1965年2月15日，女王伊丽莎白二世宣布画有枫叶图案的旗帜为加拿大国旗。

为什么他们会选择一片枫叶为国旗图案呢？因为枫叶外形美丽，特别是在秋天的时候，颜色明亮鲜红。而且，枫树还是建造房屋和制作家具的良好材料。当然，还有最后一点，也是同样重要的一点，就是你可以从枫树那里获得枫糖。

加拿大是世界上人口密度最低的国家之一。2002年人口总数为3千多万。2023年人口总数超过4千万，其中超过半数的人口居住在南部与美国边境接壤的400公里之内。

就像它的复杂地表结构一样，加拿大人民也来源于世界各地。各种各样不同的语言、种族、历史和环境构成了加拿大鲜明的地域特色。

根据2022年的统计数据，大部分加拿大人的祖先是英国人（44.65%）及法国人（28.7%）。土生土长的当地土著占人口总数的1.5%。加拿大其他种族背景的人大约占25%，其中大量来自意大利、印度、德国、中国和乌克兰。

加拿大是世界上生活水平最高的国家之一。举例来讲，根据世界银行的数据，2022年人均PPP（Purchasing Power Parity，购买力平价，一种根据各国不同的价格水平计算出来的货币之间的等值系数）估计为47567加元。同年，加拿大人的税后收入中位数为54630加元。

据《温哥华太阳报》报道，每个会开车的加拿大人平均每年独自旅行度假要驾驶两千英里。许多加拿大人买车既为了工作需要也为了畅快旅行需要。现在，加拿大人旅行大部分是用自驾车的方式。我们中国是自行车的海洋，而加拿大是汽车的海洋。每个家庭都有一辆、两辆甚至三辆汽车。有数据显示，有一半以上的人会开车并持有驾照。

Dialogue

They'll Come in Handy

(Li has been in Montreal for about 20 days, and he's saying good-bye to his host Dr. Hilda Stephen, a professor who teaches Canadian History.)

Li: The time has come to say goodbye. Tomorrow I'll be on the road and back to China.

Hilda: So soon. It seems as if you just arrived yesterday.

Li: I feel that way, too. The scene of leaving China is still fresh in my mind.

Hilda: Time flies fast. You've been *on the job* here in Montreal for about three weeks. You've done a great deal since you came here.

Li: I think so. It's been most rewarding to visit Montreal compared to what I did in Toronto and Ottawa *a while back*. Here in Montreal, I visited not only universities, but also high schools. I collected a great deal of materials and made many contacts.

Hilda: Well, all good things must come to an end. Li, here are some books from my bookcase. I *picked them out* for you. I think they'll *come in handy* in your English teaching.

Li: Great! How thoughtful of you! These are very practical books.

Hilda: And here's something you've been wanting to get. Look! Silly Putty!

Li: That's wonderful! How nice of you to get Silly Putty. My daughter would give you a thousand thanks. Where did you get it, by the way?

Hilda: I bought it in a little shop that's far *off the beaten track*, a shop called Toys.

Vocabulary and Notes

- The scene of leaving China is still fresh in my mind.　　离开中国的情景我还记忆犹新。

Unit 32　People and Land 国土和人民

- Time flies fast.
- Well, all good things must come to an end.
- How thoughtful of you!
- silly putty

时间过得真快。
任何好事都会有尽头的。

你想得真周到！
a children's toy, something like putty 橡皮泥

Idioms for Everyday Use

on the job
努力工作着；忙碌着 | working hard; not wasting time

The boss gave him a raise because he's a good worker and always **on the job**.
老板给他增加了工资，因为他是个好工人，一向努力工作。

A: Look, we've been **on the job** the whole day and we're all tired. I don't think we're going to solve all these problems today.
B: I agree. Let's work them out tomorrow.
A: 你看，整整忙了一天，我们俩都筋疲力尽了。我想我们今天处理不完这些问题了。
B: 我同意。我们明天再干吧。

a while back
在过去的几周或几个月的时间里 | at a time several weeks or months in the past

We had a good rain **a while back**, but we need more now.
前几周我们这里下了不少雨，可我们现在还缺少雨水。

A: Your grandfather looks healthy and energetic.
B: He's well now, but **a while back** he was quite sick and was in the hospital for two weeks.
A: 你爷爷看上去很健康且精力充沛。
B: 他现在是不错，可前几个月他病得很厉害，住院了两个星期。

pick out
选出，挑出，拣出 | choose, select by picking

A: This room is in a mess. What are you doing there?
B: I'm trying to **pick out** some books to send to some friends in Tibet.
A: 这间屋子太乱了。你在那儿干什么呢？
B: 我想挑出一些书来，寄给西藏的几位朋友。

I want to **pick out** some new ties to give my brother as a Christmas present.
我想给弟弟挑几条新领带，作为圣诞礼物。

come in handy
可能有用；会用得上

serve a purpose

A: Wang, please help me get rid of this empty box.
B: Don't throw it away; it might **come in handy** another time.
A: 王，请帮我把这个空盒子扔掉。
B: 别扔了它，说不定什么时候会用得上。

I always take this pocket dictionary along, as it may **come in handy**.
我总是把这本小字典带在身边，因为常常会用得上。

off the beaten track
不出名的；人迹罕见的；偏远的

not well known or often visited; not gone to or seen by many people

A: I've never seen the antique chair like this before. Where did you buy it?
B: I bought it in a little shop that is far **off the beaten track**.
A: 我从来也没见过这种古式椅子。你在哪儿买的？
B: 我在一家很偏僻的小店里买到的。

A: The summer vacation is coming. Shall we go to the sea shore in Dalian?
B: I don't want to go there. It's very crowded during summer. Let's go somewhere **off the beaten track**.
A: 暑假来到了。我们去大连海滨度假，好吗？
B: 我不想去那儿。夏天那里人太多。我们到人们不常去的地方吧。

Unit 33
Camping in Nature
大自然野营

Few countries have such a varied and tempting "outdoors" as Canada. As for the landscape in Canada, it is enormously varied and spectacular. There are great Rocky Mountains with the snow-capped peaks and the wild vast and spacious forest-covered area.

There is an abundance of waterfalls, gentle rivers, and lakes that are small and intimate or vast like the Great Lakes. Lake Superior is the largest freshwater lake in the world and the waves that break on its shores are like the waves of the sea.

In winter and in spring, the clean water, sky and dazzling multi-colored rocks of the mountains tempt thousands of campers. The fascinating and dynamic beauty of the landscape has been attracting many visitors from different countries of the world.

Almost everywhere in Canada you can see campers, picnickers and vacationers. All roads can lead you to the wilderness. Once in the wilderness, you can feel refreshed and get to know the real beauty of nature.

The unique contributions of Canada to those who love the great outdoors are the National Parks and Provincial Parks. These parks are beautifully organized with particular thoughts to campers. There are some campsites by the sea that are hidden from the beach by a line of sand dunes, or a thick belt of trees. Wherever you go, you can nearly always find picnic sites complete with wooden tables and benches, garbage cans, washrooms or even cooking facilities.

Many Canadians, young and old, prefer camping in vehicles called "campers". There are many different kinds from the extremely luxurious to pick-up trucks with a tent or sleeping module. There are monster campers, the size of busses, with enough imaginable luxury from deep freezes and microwave ovens to plush carpets and color television sets. They can accommodate four people comfortably. Remember, "campers" do not necessarily belong to rich people. Many low-income families in Canada also enjoy camping regularly.

Some retired couples put a large part of their savings in these "homes on wheels" and spend half of the year roaming all corners of the country. It satisfies a craving for the great open spaces that some of them still have, even in their advanced years, and it is at the same time a cheap way to live. Some senior citizens, I have met, in Canada expressed their camping desire and no matter how far the price of gas goes up, they will still make the roaming plans.

Those who are adventurous often strap bicycles or motorbikes to the front of their campers. They could be used to follow the smallest track up the mountains, or across the deserts or into the forests if the camper cannot negotiate the steeper and more tortuous roads which lead far into the wilderness.

In Canada, not all the people travel by the "campers". Some people travel the countryside in a four-wheel-drive vehicle. They may carry with them canoes or kayaks in which they travel down rivers controlled by the National Park Service. These rivers flow through wildernesses. The adventurous can camp on the river banks, but they are forbidden to go inland. They cannot hunt, but they are allowed to fish. Fishing in Canada in fact is both a job and a form of recreation.

Canada is also a place where eagles, bears, and whales outnumber Canadian people. To my surprise, I saw several beavers swimming with us when once paddling on the river in Fredericton, New Brunswick. Outdoor adventure tours vary greatly and a preferred method of wilderness exploration is by boat. Whether you paddle or cruise, the spectacular geography and remote location will long be remembered. Kayaking is easy to master and is the perfect way to explore the coastal environment, allowing you to quietly study the wild coastline. On many rivers, your canoe or kayak will be surrounded by some of the most stunning wilderness scenery in Canada.

The excitement of hiking, camping, picnicking, canoeing, kayaking, fishing along with exceptional wildlife viewing, top-notch enjoyment, and extensive outdoors activities make Canada the ideal choice for visitors' vacation.

译　文

很少有国家拥有像加拿大这样多样化、极具诱惑力的户外活动场所。就加拿大的风景而言，它是极其多样而且美丽壮观的。这里有雄伟的落基山脉，峰顶白雪皑皑，也有广袤的原始森林，植被郁郁葱葱。

这里有数不尽的瀑布飞流直下，有轻柔的小河潺潺流淌，有小型的湖泊让你倍感亲切，也有浩瀚的大湖让人叹为观止。其中，苏必利尔湖是世界上最大的淡水湖，它那冲向岸边的浪头犹如大海的巨浪，汹涌澎湃。

在冬春两季，清澈的湖水、湛蓝的天空和那令人眼花缭乱的五光十色的山石吸引着成千上万的野营者。这里的风景引人入胜、充满活力，使得世界各地观光者为之向往、憧憬。

几乎在加拿大的任何一处你都可以看到野营房车、野餐者以及度假的人。你可以轻而易举地找到一条通往大自然的路，而一旦你置身旷野，真正的自然美让你心旷神怡。

对于喜好野外活动的人，加拿大独一无二的贡献便是那些国家级公园和省级公园。这些公园错落有致，还特殊考虑到野营者的需要。也有一些野营地，被海边的沙丘或者是茂密的丛林遮掩。无论走到哪里，你几乎都能找到野餐的木桌、长椅、垃圾箱、洗手间，甚至连做饭用的炊具也应有尽有。

不管是年轻的还是上了年纪的加拿大人，他们都喜欢在一种叫"野营房车"的车里野营。野营车多种多样，从最豪华型到带有帐篷或睡舱的小型两用货车。有些巨型的野营车载着你难以想象的奢侈品：从冷冻柜、微波炉、舒适的地毯，到彩色电视机。这些野营车里能轻松地容纳四口人。记住，在加拿大，"野营房车"并不是有钱人的专利，许多收入不高的家庭也能有规律地享受这种乐趣。

一些退休的夫妇把一大部分积蓄投入到这些"车轮上的家"，花上大半年的时间周游全国。这种野外活动满足了退休之后还希望感受广阔野外空间的人们的渴求，同时，这也是一种节约的生活方式。在加拿大，我见过的一些长者们这样表述他们对野外活动的渴望：不管油价往上涨多高，都阻挡不了他们制定漫游计划。

那些喜欢冒险的人往往在野营车头上用绳子捆绑上自行车或摩托车。当野营车无法安全通过通向旷野深处的更陡峭、更崎岖的道路时，自行车或摩托车就可以沿着最陡峭的道路爬上高山，或者穿过沙漠深入森林。

在加拿大，并不是所有人都在野营房车里旅行，也有一些人乘着四轮汽车在乡村旅行。他们也许会带着独木舟或橡皮艇，这样他们就可以坐在其中沿着由国家公园管理局管控的河流顺水而下，而这些河流往往流经荒无人烟的地方。冒险者可以在河岸上野营，但是不允许到内陆去；他们可以钓鱼，但是不允许打猎。实际上，在加拿大，钓鱼既是一项工作，也是一种消遣方式。

同时，加拿大也是一个动物比人还多的国家，比如鹰、熊、海鲸。更有甚者，有一次我在新不伦瑞克省的弗雷德里克顿划船的时候还见到了几只海狸，它们与我们相伴而游。户外的冒险活动多种多样，而船是人们比较热衷的一种野外探险工具。不管你是划船还是巡游，壮观的地理景观总能让你流连忘返。划皮船就非常简单，也是去感受沿海风景的最佳选择，这样你就可以轻而易举地领略海岸风光。在加拿大很多河流上泛舟时，你都会沉浸在这无比美妙的自然美景中。

激动人心的徒步旅行、野营、野餐、泛舟、划皮船、钓鱼，以及不同寻常的野外风景观光、顶级的享受、丰富多彩的户外活动，使得加拿大成为游客们度假的理想天堂。

 Dialogue

We Canadians Love the Great Outdoors

(Mr. Thomas Bridge, a Canadian Professor, teaches Canadian Literature and Language at Trinity Western University in Canada. He bumps into his Chinese friend Li on campus.)

Thomas: Hey, Li, how are you? You look so happy and cheerful today.

Li: Correct! I'm feeling on top of the world! Peter has arranged some touring activities for me during our four-day holidays. He promised me to go out on a picnic, camping in vehicles called "campers".

Thomas: Fascinating! We Canadians love the great outdoors. Wherever you're traveling in Canada, you can always find picnic places complete with wooden tables and benches, restrooms and all necessary camping facilities.

Li: Would you like to come with us? There will be a four-day holidays anyway.

Thomas: No, I can't. I'm in a dilemma right now. I'd like to **take advantage of** the holidays to do some academic activities. I've got to choose between attending a four-day academic conference at University of Victoria and attending a four-day ESL methodology training course at Trinity. What would you do if you **were in my shoes**?

Li: That all depends. If you want to meet with the Canadian Studies educators, the conference would probably *do you good*. However, if you want to learn present-day ESL methodology, the intensive training course is probably *the best bet*. Well, why don't you *sleep on it*? Maybe you'll be able to make up your mind more easily tomorrow morning.

Thomas: Yeah, that's a good idea. I may join the academic conference and I'm certain that I could meet with some Canadian Studies experts from University of Ottawa, McMaster, Waterloo and so on. Dr. Mike Jefferson, the Dean of Sociology Department at Waterloo will give a speech. He's been doing Canadian Studies for about ten years, and there is no doubt that he is *the cream of the crop* in this field...

Li: So, you should come to meet with him and I'm sure he is available to assist you with your academic goal.

Thomas: Thank you. I'll take your advice. By the way, when are you leaving for your camping?

Li: Tomorrow afternoon. We'll shop for some necessities tomorrow morning.

Thomas: Remind Peter that you should travel to Whistler. Because of the natural surroundings, Whistler has always been one of the world's favorite resorts.

Li: Yes, Peter actually promised me to go canoeing there and also told me that in 2005, the United Nations Environmental Program recognized Whistler as one of the most livable communities in the world.

Thomas: Don't forget some fishing lakes if you're going to Kamloops, and boat rentals there are also available.

Li: Thanks a lot. I'll take some pictures and we'll share our outdoor trip when I'm back from the nature.

Vocabulary and Notes

- Trinity Western University 　西三一大学，位于加拿大不列颠哥伦比亚省的兰里市。1962年建校，是一所国际认可的综合性大学，也是加拿大最大的私立教会综合性大学。它还是加拿大大学联盟及加拿大皇家科学院的重要成员，且受到美国教育部的认证。

- University of Victoria

  维多利亚大学，1963年成立，是一所多学科的综合性大学。该大学在加拿大大学评定中一直名列前茅，许多专业，尤其是工商管理、经济学和理工科等，在北美及全世界都享有很高的声誉。

- I've got to choose between attending a four-day academic conference at University of Victoria and attending a four-day ESL methodology training course at Trinity.

  我拿不准是参加在维多利亚大学举行的四天学术会议，还是去西三一大学参加为期四天的英语作为第二种语言教学法的培训课。

- That all depends.

  那得看情况而定。

- Maybe you'll be able to make up your mind more easily tomorrow morning.

  明天早晨再拿主意也许更容易些。

- University of Ottawa

  渥太华大学，是北美最大的双语教学的学校，创建于1848年。该校旨在多元文化环境中促进双语（英语和法语）发展，开展各种灵活多样的英法双语相结合的教学与科研项目。独特的双语课程设置使得学生可以自由地用其中任何一种语言完成学习任务。该大学积极为商界和政府提供咨询、科研成果以及合作项目，同时也是一所国际型的大学，与世界上的许多著名高校都有合作项目。

- McMaster

  McMaster University麦克马斯特大学，该大学是为纪念银行家、政界领袖、慈善家威廉·麦克马斯特（William McMaster）而命名的。这是一所研究性大学，学校教师中拥有博士学位的比例是全加拿大最高的。学校还拥有国际一流的实验室和各种先进的设施，是北美仅有的少数拥有自己核反应堆的大学之一。其材料制造为北美第一，机械专业在加拿大首屈一指，数字通讯和电脑硬件在北美也处于领先地位。麦克马斯特大学同时还拥有一流的商学院和医学院，能与麦吉尔大学相媲美。由于它一百多年来在工业界声名卓著，被美国同行和工业界称做加拿大的"麻省理工学院"。

- Waterloo

> University of Waterloo 滑铁卢大学，成立于1959年，是加拿大发展最快的高校，曾连续多年排名加拿大综合类大学第一。滑铁卢大学以外向型和合作教育项目而著称，并拥有世界上最大的合作教育项目。

Idioms for Everyday Use

be in a dilemma
左右为难，处于进退两难的境地

be in an awkward predicament; be in a quandary

A: National Holiday is coming. My parents asked me to go back home to have a family reunion; but my friend in Beijing insisted that I go to visit the Olympic Park with her. I've no idea how to deal with this tough situation. I'm really **in a dilemma**. What would you do if you were in my shoes?

B: Well, it's hard to say. If you miss your family members very much, just go back home. Your parents must be dying to see you. By the way, how often do you go home?

A: Once in half a year.

B: Then, you must go back home to get together with your family. You could visit Olympic Park during the weekend.

A: 国庆节到了，我爸妈想让我回家和家人团聚，可是，我北京的朋友坚持叫我和她去北京参观奥林匹克公园。我不知道如何处理这个棘手的问题，真让我为难啊！如果是你，你会怎么办呢？

B: 很难说。如果你特别想念你爸妈，就回家吧；他们肯定也非常想你。对了，你多长时间回一次家？

A: 半年一次。

B: 那么你赶紧回家团聚吧。你可以周末再去奥林匹克公园。

She **was in a dilemma** when her friend asked her for shopping instead of preparing for the test.
她本想准备考试，可被朋友邀请去逛街，她左右为难，不知如何是好。

take advantage of
利用时机；抓住机会

make good use of the occasion; take the opportunity to do something

A: We're planning to see the totem poles there. Why don't you **take advantage of** it and practice to be a shutterbug?

B: Sounds great! Thanks a bunch for your advice.

A: 我们准备去参观图腾柱，作为一名摄影迷，你是不是可以好好利用这次机会锻炼自己呢？

B: 你说得太对了。谢谢提醒！

be in one's shoes/boots
处于某人的地位或位置 | be in one's place or position

If you had **been in my shoes**, would you have behaved any differently?
假如你处于我这种地位，你做的和我会有什么两样吗？

A: Poor Bob! I'd hate to **be in his shoes**. He just lost his job again. He made some serious errors in his book-keeping, and the company lost a lot of money.

B: So it isn't easy to be an accountant.

A: 可怜的鲍勃！我可不愿意处于他那种情况。他刚刚又丢了工作。他的账目上出现了一些严重错误，致使公司损失了很多钱。

B: 所以说当会计并不容易。

He is always in debt; I wouldn't **be in his shoes** for anything.
他老是向人借钱，无论如何我也不愿过他那种日子。

do someone good
对某人有好处（或有利） | be beneficial to someone

A: I'm sorry to cancel the party I planned to give on Saturday. I've been very exhausted lately. I want to take a vacation for a week.

B: It doesn't matter. You need some rest. The trip will certainly **do you good**.

A: 对不起，我把原计划星期六要开的晚会取消了。我最近太疲惫不堪了。我想度假一周。

B: 没关系。你需要休息。这次旅游一定会对你有好处。

A: You don't look hot today, Bob. What's up?

B: Well, I've got a cold again, coughing, sneezing and aching all over.

A: You could do with a rest or it will be worse and worse. Listen! Drink plenty of hot tea with lemon. It will **do you good**.

B: Thank you for your suggestion and I'll try your recipe.

A: 鲍勃，你今天看上去不那么兴高采烈。你怎么了？

B: 我又感冒了，咳嗽，打喷嚏，浑身疼。

A: 看上去你应该好好休息了，要不会越来越严重。记住！多喝柠檬热茶，对你感冒有好处。

B: 谢谢你的建议，我会试一下你的药方。

Running around the track regularly will **do you a lot of good**.
坚持有规律地在跑道上跑步会对你大有益处。

the best bet
最好的选择；最好的措施，上策

the best choice; the best solution; the best way

- Suddenly the engine broke down. The pilot realized that **the best bet** was to make an emergency landing.
  发动机突然出了毛病。飞行员意识到最好的措施是紧急降落。
- There was a train at 3:20 and another at 3:40. But the 3:40 was a express train, so it was **the best bet**.
  3:20有趟火车，3:40也有一趟。但3:40的是趟快车，因此，乘坐这趟车是上策。

sleep on it
暂时搁一搁；改日再处理，把……留待第二天解决

delay making a decision until the next day; spend a night considering what to do

- A: Have you made up your mind when we're going to Dunhuang?
  B: I'll **sleep on it** and let you know tomorrow.
  A: 你拿定主意我们什么时候去敦煌了吗？
  B: 我今晚好好考虑一下，明天告诉你。
- We asked Judy if she would join our club and she answered that she would **sleep on it**.
  我们问朱迪是否愿意参加我们的俱乐部，她说第二天再答复。

the cream of the crop
最好的、最精选的部分；精华

the best of a group; the top choice

- That university accepts only students who are **the cream of the crop**.
  那所大学只招收最优秀的学生。
- The students had drawn many pictures and the teacher chose **the cream of the crop** to hang up when the parents came to visit.
  学生们完成了许多绘画作品，当家长们来学校参观时，老师挑选了最优秀的悬挂起来。

Unit 34
Privacy
隐私

Canadians often declare publicly their intention to protect their privacy. Their understanding of privacy is that others have no right to pry into things which belong to themselves alone and have nothing to do with others. One who is too nosy and who spreads around what they find is said to violate the right to privacy.

Canadians—males, females, old and young, are all paying close attention to "personal space". They need much more distance than Chinese do. As long as you get in touch with Canadian people, you will surely encounter the problems of some Canadian privacy: the privacy of photographs, letters, study notes, price, marriage, salary, body and so on. The multifarious privacies make you sometimes become an irresponsible idiot.

Canadians would be unlikely to pick up anything from someone else's desk or bed to read, even if only a newspaper. If one is visiting a friend at her or his home, some papers and magazines are laid out on a coffee table, it is acceptable to pick them up to read. The presumption is that anything displayed on "public" furniture is available to be picked up. But anything on private furniture, a desk or bed, for example, is definitely private and should not be touched.

Even though two persons take the same course, but they cannot share the notebooks. The notes that one took are based on the professor's lectures and his own understanding. They represented his own interpretation of what he had heard and read. Thus, they were essentially private and should not be looked at by anyone without his permission.

A picture album in Canada is private and not something that one should assume is open to the strangers. You must ask permission to look at one's album since some of their pictures are thought to be private. Canadians are sometimes overly sensitive about their privacy and automatically assume an innocent interest in somehow an unwelcome invasion of their privacy.

Canadians regard that decent people do not ask someone how much something costs, therefore, asking the price of something of a friend or colleague shows that it is considered to be an invasion of privacy, and marks the person asking as being coarse, too interested in money. In general, personal finances are very private, and how much one spends is normally seen as part of personal finances. It would be equally unacceptable to ask someone how much money they earn or how much they have in their bank accounts or stock portfolio.

Canadians find many things about their bodies to be sensitive to, such as being overweight, going bald and going grey. It is the fact that negative body images are a serious psychological problem for many Canadian women. Graying hair, especially premature graying in a lady, can cause her to feel old and thus unattractive. Getting older has so many negative connotations for Canadian women. Therefore, it is a taboo topic for people to talk about the privacy of the negative body images.

There is still privacy between husband and wife. A Chinese lady who is a good friend of mine married a talented Canadian gentleman, but recently her husband became so angry that he wanted a divorce. The reason is that his Chinese wife opened one of his letters and looked through his wallet. The Chinese wife did not realize that this is not tolerated in Canadian. She thought being a couple was like being one person. Why couldn't she see the letter or the contents of the wallet? Truly, everyone, even though living as a couple, needs personal space.

If you are in a social gathering, such as "potluck" or "coffee hours" or "open house", it is polite to talk about your work, your country, your trip to Canada or other countries and what you like about Canada, but not in detail.

Do not ask Canadians how old they are, how much money their house or other possessions cost or whether they are married. Questions about adults' age and money are considered private and rude.

译 文

  加拿大人时常公开宣扬要保护他们的隐私。他们对该词的理解是：凡是属于我自己的与他人无关的事，别人就无权过问。如果谁蓄意打听并传播，便是侵犯了他们的隐私权。

  加拿大人，无论男女老少都非常注重"私人空间"。加拿大人需要的私人空间比中国人要多。只要你和加拿大人来往，你肯定会遇到与加拿大人隐私相关的一些问题：相册的隐私、信件的隐私、笔记的隐私、价格的隐私、婚姻的隐私、工资的隐私、身体的隐私，等等。各种各样的隐私有时让你显得不负责任且非常愚钝。

  加拿大人一般不太随意从别人的书桌上或者床上拿起书来读，哪怕是一张报纸。如果你去一位朋友家里做客，拿起摊放在咖啡桌上的报纸杂志阅读是可以的，前提是那些东西放在一些可拿起的"公用的"家具上。然而，放在私人家具上，比如桌子上、床上，便绝对属于隐私，是不能乱动的。

  即使两个人听同样的课，也不能分享彼此的笔记。一个人记录的笔记是基于老师的讲授和他自己的理解，是他听课和看书的所得，代表了他自己的所感所思。从根本上讲，这些笔记是私人的东西，未经本人同意，任何人都无权去看。

  在加拿大，相册是私人物品，外人是不能想当然地随意翻看的。必须征得人家的同意才能翻看相册，因为一些照片被认为是隐私。有些时候，加拿大人对于他们的隐私过于敏感，总不自觉地以为别人不经意的好奇在某种程度上是对他们隐私的一种侵犯，让他们反感。

  加拿大人认为有教养的人不问别人东西的价钱，所以，向朋友或同事打听他们买的东西的价钱是对别人隐私的一种侵犯，并认为提问者粗鲁，对金钱太感兴趣。一般来说，个人财务是很隐私的事，一个人花多少钱通常被视为个人财务的一部分。同样地，别人挣多少钱，或者拥有多少银行存款以及股票投资都是不该问及的。

  在加拿大，肥胖、秃顶、白头发等关于身体的许多问题也属于隐私，他们对此非常敏感。事实上，身体上的缺陷已经成为很多加拿大妇女的严重的心理问题。对女人来说，白头发，尤其是少白头，很容易使她们觉得自己老了，或者失去魅力了。变老对她们有很多消极影响。所以，人们避讳谈论负面身体形象的隐私。

  夫妻之间同样也存在隐私。我的一位中国好朋友嫁给了一位才华出众的加拿大绅士，但是，最近那位丈夫因为极其生气而要离婚，原因是这位中国妻子拆开了她丈夫的一封信并翻看了他的钱夹。而这位中国妻子不知道这样的行为对于加拿大人来说是不能容忍的。妻子觉得，夫妻俩就像一个人似的，为什么她就不能看看他的信或者看看钱夹里装的是什么呢？的确，即使是朝夕相处的夫妻，彼此之间也需要个人的空间。

如果你参加一个社交聚会，比如说聚餐会、茶话会或者家庭招待会，出于礼貌，你们可以讨论你的工作、你的国家、你的加拿大之旅或者其他国家以及你对加拿大的感受，但是别太详细。千万别问加拿大人他们多大年纪、房子多少钱或者拥有多少其他资产、是否结婚。而且，涉及成年人年龄和钱财的话题也被看做是一种隐私，探听被认为是粗鲁的。

I'm Really Fed up

(Mary and Chinese Li have just finished the dinner party held at her house for the Chinese delegation. Mary is talking to Li when the delegation has left. She is a bit upset.)

Mary: Well, Li, I don't like that group of people very much. They again and again asked me some awkward questions—my marriage, the amount of rent paid and my salary earned. It is simply to show unfriendliness and pry into my own life. They should respect for my privacy and personal space.

Li: Sorry, that's probably my fault. I didn't give them cultural orientation beforehand. However, our Chinese traditionally are warmhearted and care for the livelihood of the friends. Forgive them, different cultural communities have different ideas about topic boundaries. They actually wanted to help you settle down and establish a safe and sound family.

Mary: Didn't you remember that when we toured SFU campus yesterday, that one of them even introduced his Chinese friend to be my boyfriend? It's really ridiculous. Whether I'm going to get married or not has nothing to do with him. It seems that my privacy is invaded in some way. *I'm really fed up*. We Canadians do not talk about personal marriage even between family members.

Li: Well, take it easy. Don't *get them wrong*. They advise you to get married *with the best of intentions* anyhow. They are truthful, honest and sincere people.

Mary: Are they? You'd better give them a piece of your mind that they cannot take the pictures of the Native Indians in the Museum of Anthropology of

UBC. They could take the picture with the Indians' permission. Otherwise, that would be a serious violation of their right to privacy.

Li: Correct! I'll certainly give them more information about Canadian privacy—do not take pictures without permission, do not ask Canadians how old they are, how much money their house or other possessions cost. And the most important thing, I'll remind them, is that do not ask Canadians why they haven't got married. Mary, believe me, my Chinese friends are innocent. They're surely nice people. Believe it or not, if you come to Tianjin, China, they'll be hospitable to you and *wait on you hand and foot*.

Mary: I'll be expecting then! You are probably right. The choice of which topic to talk about among strangers can also be tricky. It all depends on one's cultural differences. I'll certainly come to China to explore more about Chinese customs. I'm getting more curious about Chinese people from our conversation. Please give me some orientation about Chinese customs before I leave for China. I hope I won't offend them.

Li: My pleasure. China has a long history with five thousand years. Chinese culture is a broad and complex topic. It isn't a word to fill you in on the details. Shall we do some cleaning first and get rid of those leftovers? And then we will talk about different manners between China and Canada.

Mary: That's a good idea. Let's *roll up our sleeves* and do thorough cleaning.

Vocabulary and Notes

- I didn't give them cultural orientation beforehand.

  我没提前给他们文化方面的介绍。

- Forgive them, different cultural communities have different ideas about topic boundaries.

  别怪他们，不同的文化区域对话题的界限有不同的看法。

- They actually wanted to help you settle down and establish a safe and sound family.

  实际上，他们就是想帮助你安顿下来，建立一个祥和、安定的家庭。

Unit 34　Privacy 隐私

- SFU

  Simon Fraser University 西蒙菲莎大学，是一所以加拿大19世纪探险家Simon Fraser的名字命名、创建于1963年的综合性大学。共设有三个校区，均位于"全世界最适于人类居住的地方"——加拿大BC省温哥华市。三校之间有世界上著名的温哥华"空中火车"连接，交通十分便利。大学设有应用理学院、文学院、工商管理学院、教育学院、理学院和健康科学学院。它是加拿大少数几个一年设置三个学期、三次开学的大学。它注重教学的实用性，课堂教学与课外实践紧密结合，帮助学生在专业相关领域参加带薪实习以扩大知识面，为将来适应社会做好准备。

- UBC

  University of British Columbia 不列颠哥伦比亚大学，始建于1915年，位于温哥华市。其人类学博物馆（the Museum of Anthropology）由亚瑟·艾里克森（Arthur Erickson）设计，珍藏着丰富的西北海岸印第安文化艺术珍品，于1976年开放。

- Otherwise, that would be a serious violation of their right to privacy.

  不然的话，这样做就是对他们隐私权的一种严重侵犯。

- innocent

  天真的；没有恶意的，无冒犯之意的

- The choice of which topic to talk about among strangers can also be tricky.

  在陌生人之间，选择什么样的讨论话题也是比较棘手的。

- It isn't a word to fill you in on the details.

  不是一句话就能说明白的。

- Shall we do some cleaning first and get rid of those leftovers?

  让我们先打扫一下卫生，清除那些厨余垃圾好吗？

Idioms for Everyday Use

be fed up
受够了；厌倦或厌烦；不愉快或沮丧 | tired or bored; unhappy or depressed

A: I'm really **fed up**! The speaker has been talking on and on for 2 hours and the audience has been murmuring from the beginning to the end. I didn't learn anything from it.

B: Well, take it easy. We'll try another lecture given by the CEO from the insurance company. I believe that will be an attractive one.

A: 我真受够了！那个发言者喋喋不休地讲了两个小时了，观众从头到尾一直抱怨。我也什么都没学到。

B: 别那么认真，我们去听听这家保险公司的首席执行官的讲座吧。我觉得那个讲座肯定特别好。

I'm fed up with waiting for her to telephone.
我等她的电话都等得不耐烦了。

I'm fed up with talking to you. You never listen to me.
我腻歪跟你讲话了。你从来都不听我说。

get someone wrong
误会或误解某人 | misunderstand somebody

A: Please don't **get me wrong**. I'm not criticizing you. I only tell you to be polite to her since she's a sensitive person.

B: I'm sorry I misunderstand. I thought that you wanted to put me in the wrong.

A: 你别误会我啊，我不是批评你。只是提醒你对她礼貌些，因为她是一个比较敏感的人。

B: 对不起，我错怪你了。我以为你把错都栽给我呢。

A: Can you prove that I'm wrong? That's where you're wrong. You must admit that you **get me wrong**.

B: I'm sorry I've already realized that I had said the wrong thing.

A: 你能证实我错了吗？在这一点上是你的过错，你必须承认你误会我了。

B: 对不起，我已经意识到我说错了。

They really **got me wrong**, but I think the whole truth will come out tomorrow.
他们真的误会我了，但是我相信明天就会真相大白。

with the best of intentions
好心好意，出于一片好心

intending only to help or do good

- A: I've done everything for Tom **with the best of intentions**, but he didn't appreciate my favor and took my good will for ill intent.
- B: Don't worry. That's different culture. I'll explain it to Tom later.
- A: 我一片好心为汤姆做了一切事情，他非但不领情，还把我的好心当做恶意。
- B: 别担心，那是因为文化不同。以后我会跟汤姆解释的。

- Don't get me wrong. It was done **with the best of intentions**.
  别误会我，我也是出于一片好心才那么做的。

wait on somebody hand and foot
照料或伺候某人（尤指进餐时）

act as a servant for somebody especially by serving food and drink at a meal

- He expected his wife to **wait on him hand and foot**.
  他希望他妻子像佣人那样伺候他。
- At home the boys never lifted a finger. We girls had to **wait on them hand and foot**.
  男孩们在家里什么都不干，总是我们女孩伺候他们。
- Professor Wu had a major operation and her son has been **waiting on her hand and foot** for two days.
  吴教授做了一个大手术，这两天她的儿子悉心照料，无微不至。

roll up somebody's sleeves
卷起袖子准备工作或战斗

prepare to work or fight

- A: What a mess! Why don't you **roll up your sleeves** and clean them all?
- B: No problem! But why don't you give me a hand?
- A: 太乱了！你怎么不把这些东西都收起来打扫干净呢？
- B: 没问题！但是，你帮我一起整理，好吗？

- Hey guys, the race begins at 11:30. Let's **roll up our sleeves!**
  朋友们，赛跑11点半开始。让我们准备"战斗"吧！
- The travel begins tomorrow. Let's **roll up our sleeves** and put the stuff into the trunk.
  明天就要去旅行了。让我们做些准备，把东西放在卡车里。

Unit 35
The Happy Life of Seniors
老年人的幸福生活

People often describe western capitalist society as "a Paradise for Children, a Battlefield for Young, and a Graveyard for Elderly". However, this is not always the case. Together our Canada friends, we especially visited some Nursing Homes in Greater Vancouver, Canada. Most of the elderly, we saw with our own eyes, lived a happy life. I have worked actually in a Canadian Nursing Home for the elderly before. What we saw was that they were very much satisfied with their living conditions and the variety of foods. Generally speaking, Canadian Seniors are living a carefree life with the government subsidies and welfare policies and they have a wide range of hobbies.

One hobby of the elderly is that they spend time at the Mall. The Mall is comfortable and convenient: there are fountains and flowing water, flowers and trees. The space is large and the facilities are complete, with benches to sit on. You can see the Food Courts, Coffee Bars, Beauty Salons, and various brand shops everywhere. Many elderly people treat the Mall as a sort of Chinese senior citizens' activity centre. They drive there in the morning, have breakfast, drink coffee, and start physical exercises, walking, swinging their arms, and doing chest expansion exercises. Then, they read newspapers or play with their phones. They have their lunch in the Food Court at noon. Finally, they buy vegetables and fruits in the afternoon or evening and then go home. With something to eat, something to drink, and something to doing the Mall, their life is quite carefree.

Another hobby is that many elderly people love flowers. They also love to grow flowers. They take great care of their own gardens, making them beautiful and elegant, with a rainbow of colours. Since Canadians have good housing conditions, many elderly people have their own garden houses or villas. In spring, summer, and autumn, they decorate their gardens around their homes with vibrant explosion of colors. Whether in the suburbs or the city, the outlook of Canada is just like a big garden.

Many Canadian seniors are willing to keep dogs. They are willing to spend money and effort on their dogs. Besides feeding them well, they brush and bathe their dogs every day. They must take their dogs for a walk every day, and what is more interesting is that if someone's dog is mistreated, neighbours will report it to the police.

In many communities in Canada, there are independent sports facilities and activity sites specifically designed for the elderly. For example, the Senior Ice Hockey Arena in Vancouver often has the senior ice hockey teams training and matches. Some local stores also organize discount days specifically for seniors to allow as many seniors as possible to enjoy the discounts.

Many elderly people also go outdoors to exercise in parks. In Richmond, Vancouver, there are two large parks that are particularly popular with elderly people. They walk in the park, play football, skate, throw frisbee and other sports training activities. Especially with the increase of Chinese immigrants, many elderly people will go to the park to participate in collective activities, singing Chinese songs with enthusiasm, such as "I Love You, China" "Song of the Yangtze River". When it snows, they will sing "I Love You, Snow in Saibei". Sometimes, the group can grow to hundreds of people, who practice singing in the park, regardless of wind and rain. And their exciting singing attracts people of other races and to sing along with them.

译 文

人们常常把西方资本主义社会描述为"儿童的天堂、年轻人的战场、老年人的坟墓"。然而，事实并非总是如此。与加拿大的朋友们一起，我们特别参观了加拿大温哥华的一些养老院。我们亲眼所见的是大多数老年人都过着幸福的生活。实际上，我曾在加拿大的一家养老院工作过。当时我们看到的是，他们对自己的生活条件和各种食物非常满意。总的来说，加拿大老年人在政府补贴和福利政策的支持下过着无忧无虑的生活，并且他们有广泛的爱好。

老年人的一个爱好就是去商场里消磨时间。购物商场里面舒适便利，有喷泉流水、花草树木。里面空间大，设施齐全，有长椅可坐。到处可见美食角、咖啡吧、美容店、各种名牌店铺。许多老年人把购物商场当成了像中国的老年人活动中心。他们早上开车来，吃过早饭，喝过咖啡，开始锻炼身体；有竞走的、甩胳膊踢腿的，扩胸运动的。然后呢，看报纸或者玩手机。中午时去美食角吃午餐。最后，下午或晚上，他们买上蔬菜和水果回家。有吃有喝，还有玩儿，生活也是比较潇洒的。

好多老年人的另一个爱好是痴迷花卉，也爱种花。他们把各自的花园整修得漂亮典雅，色彩斑斓。由于加拿大人的住房条件普遍较好，好多老年人有自己的花园洋房或是别墅。在春天、夏天、秋天里，他们把住宅的花园点缀得生机盎然。无论是郊区还是市区，给人的印象就是加拿大整个国家就像一个大花园。

加拿大有好多老年人愿意养狗。他们在狗身上舍得花钱、花精力。除了给狗吃好，每天都要给狗刷毛、洗澡。必须每天遛狗。更有趣的是，如果别人的狗受了委屈，邻居还会报告给警察。

在加拿大的许多社区里，都有独立的专为老年人设计的体育设施和活动场地。比如在温哥华的老年人冰球馆，经常会有老年冰球队伍在那里进行训练和比赛。一些当地的商店也会组织一些针对老年人的折扣日，来让尽可能多的老人能够享受优惠。

好多老年人也去公园进行户外活动。在温哥华列治文市，有两个大型公园就很受老年人喜欢。他们在公园里散步、踢球、滑冰、扔飞盘，以及进行其他体育锻炼活动。特别是随着华人移民的增多，很多老年人都会去公园里参加集体活动，兴致勃勃地唱起中国歌曲，比如《我爱你，中国》《长江之歌》。下雪的时候，他们触景生情，会唱起《我爱你，塞北的雪》。有时这一规模甚至能达到几百人，他们在公园里放声歌唱，风雨无阻，甚至带动了不少其他种族的人加入到他们的队伍中一起歌唱。

I Was Completely Captivated by Shanzhige Performances

(Dr. Philip Laird from Trinity Western University was very emotional and excited after watching the performances given by Shanzhige Choir.)

Philip: Awesome! Your show, Professor Li, was fascinating. That was incredible! I *was* completely *captivated by* Shanzhige performances. Your show left

Unit 35 The Happy Life of Seniors 老年人的幸福生活

me in awe.

Li: Thank you for your kind compliment and enthusiastic encouragement. As you know, Phil, the members of Shanzhige Choir are all seniors aged over 60. A few of them are octogenarians, take Professor Jin Meilin as an example.

Philip: Wow! Unbelievable! Professor Jin is very active for an octogenarian. Shanzhige Choir is *full of vitality*, singing with a strong sense of rhythm and passion of the voice. The singing of Shanzhige Choir is majestic and powerful, with strong penetrating power. That was gorgeous, marvellous.

Li: The average age of Shanzhige Choir is 72 years old and they really create beautiful and powerful voices. We all cherish singing in this harmonious big family. Professor Li Lin once said: "It is like a big family with everyone supporting each other and have a happy time. It is like we are all connected by our love for singing, and the music builds the harmonious atmosphere and strengthens our sense of collective belonging." By the way, Phil, Canadian universities have retired teacher choirs? Almost all the universities in Tianjin have retired teacher choirs.

Philip: It is hard to say. Some of them have, not all. The retired teachers in Canada join different singing and dancing groups or symphony orchestras, as you know Doctor Deane Downey. He *is crazy about* music and he is a violinist in Vancouver symphony orchestra. He is very much *alive and kicking*.

Li: Congratulations to Doctor Deane Downey. *If my memory serves me right*, I think Doctor Deane Downey is a man of nonagenarian.

Philip: Absolutely right! He is now over 90 years old. But he is still active in the field of music, enjoying a happy retirement life.

Li: Phil, we are planning of coming to Canada, to Trinity Western University to sing together with your Choir. That is our dream to sing together with Canadians. And I believe that the different voices must blend into a cohesive, beautiful harmony.

Philip: Yes. It is the harmony that is essence of a choir to bring people together and create society larger than themselves.

Li: You know, Phil, my singing experience is that whether you are an experienced singer or just starting out, being in a choir, provides a unique opportunity to improve your vocal skills.

Philip: Correct! We are on the same wavelength. Through regular rehearsals and performances, you will have the chance to refine your musical abilities and grow as a good singer. Success comes from hard work, discipline, and dedication.

Li: What an exciting moment it is! I very much enjoy our *pep talk* today, and I have a faith in our future of Shanzhige Choir.

Vocabulary and Notes

I was completely captivated by Shanzhige performances.	我完全被山之歌的节目表演所迷住。
Your show left me in awe.	你们的表演让我感到震惊。
Thank you for your kind compliment and enthusiastic encouragement.	感谢你友好的赞美和热情的鼓励。
Shanzhige Choir	山之歌合唱团（由天津理工大学组织）
The singing of Shanzhige Choir is majestic and powerful, with strong penetrating power.	山之歌合唱团的演唱雄壮有力，穿透力极强。
octogenarian	八旬老人；尤指80至89岁的老年人
nonagenarian	九旬老人；尤指90至99岁的老年人
septuagenarian	七旬老人；尤指70至79岁的老年人
sexagenarian	六旬老人；尤指60至69岁的老年人
centenarian	百岁老人；尤指百岁以上的老年人
cherish	珍爱，珍视；怀念
We all cherish singing in this harmonious big family.	我们都珍惜在这个和谐的大家庭里歌唱的机会。
It is like we are all connected by our love for singing, and the music builds the harmonious atmosphere and strengthens our sense of collective belonging.	我们都因热爱歌唱而紧密相连，音乐营造出和谐的氛围，增强了我们的集体归属感。

- symphony orchestra
- And I believe that the different voices must blend into a cohesive, beautiful harmony.
- We are on the same wavelength.
- Through regular rehearsals and performances, you will have the chance to refine your musical abilities and grow as a good singer.
- Success comes from hard work, discipline, and dedication.
- I have a faith in our future of Shanzhige Choir.

交响乐团
我相信，不同的音乐之声一定会融合成一个和谐、美丽的整体。
我们在同一频率（波长）上；我们的看法是一致的。
通过定期的排练和演出，你将有机会提升自己的音乐能力，成为一名优秀的歌手。
成功源于不懈的努力、自律和奉献。
我对我们山之歌合唱团的未来充满信心。

Idioms for Everyday Use

be captivated by
被……迷住了；沉迷于……

something or someone attracts you so much that you are crazy about it; be intensely attracted or fascinated by something or someone

- A: Are you going to leave office? It is not the time we get off work.
  B: Well, I **was** completely **captivated by** hiking. So I put in an early break.
  A: 你要离开办公室了吗？我们还没有到下班时间。
  B: 嗯，我对徒步旅行完全着迷了。所以我提前休了假。
- One hundred years later, people **are** still **captivated by** this mysterious story.
  一百年过去了，人们仍然被这个神秘的故事所吸引着。

full of vitality
充满活力的；生机勃勃的；朝气蓬勃的

being energetic, lively, and full of life

- In the cold winter, daffodil foliage is still lush, **full of vitality**, to bring people the spring.
  在寒冷的冬天，水仙花依然枝叶繁茂，生机盎然，给人们送来了春意。
- The sculpture is true to life and **full of vitality**.
  这件雕塑品很逼真，富有生气。
- The basis of a strong, young professorial, and creative thing of the team allow the company

full of vitality, continue to develop.

以雄厚的实力为基础的、年轻专业化的和富有创造力的团队，让企业充满活力，不断发展。

| **be crazy about**
着迷于；狂热爱好 | be very much enthusiastic about something; be extremely interested in something or love someone very much |

- A: Look! This is a beautiful doll I picked out of a blind box.
- B: We had better not **be crazy about** blind boxes, or we can't stop buying them.
- A: 看！这是我从一个盲盒里抽到的很漂亮的玩偶。
- B: 我们最好不要对盲盒着迷，否则我们会不停地买。

College students can pursue fashion, but they should not **be crazy about** it. They need to measure their situation and make the wise choice.

大学生可以追求时尚，但是他们不应该痴迷于此。他们需要衡量自己的处境，做出明智的选择。

| **alive and kicking**
健康活跃：状态良好且充满活力 | be very healthy and active if someone is alive and kicking, which means he or she is not only alive or in existence, but very active and lively; continue to live or exist and be full of energy |

- A: Look, he is **alive and kicking** again.
- B: Good for him! Maybe this experience will teach him something.
- A: 瞧瞧他，又活蹦乱跳的了。
- B: 为他感到高兴！希望这次的经历能让他长长记性。

I do think this is a very, very useful reminder that our enemies are out there, that they are **alive and kicking** and they wish to do us harm.

我真的认为这次事件提醒了我们，敌人依然存在，他们正磨刀霍霍，想要伤害我们。

- A: By the way, how's your father nowadays?
- B: Oh, he is still **alive and kicking**.
- A: 顺便问一下，您的父亲最近怎么样？
- B: 哦，他依然充满活力。

| **If my memory serves me right...**
如果我记得没错的话……（一种委婉语的用法） | I believe I'm remembering correctly, but I'm not entirely sure. |

- A: I am sorry. I didn't go to the cinema last weekend.

B: But **if my memory serves me right**, you were determined to go.
A: 对不起。我上个周末没有去电影院。
B: 如果我没有记错的话，你当时已决定要去的。

- **If my memory serves me right**, it happened in the winter of 1987.
如果我没记错的话，这件事发生在1987年的冬天。

| **pep talk** 鼓舞士气的简短演讲 | a motivational speech intended to boost someone's confidence and enthusiasm |

- It was my brilliant **pep talk** that convinced my students to give up their silly superstitions and finally they believed themselves.
正是我的精彩的鼓舞士气的讲话使我的学生们放弃了愚蠢的迷信，最终相信他们自己。
- The university president gives the graduates a **pep talk**.
大学校长给毕业生们做了一次动员讲话。
- It is a great pity that you did not participate the mobilization meeting this morning. The coach was very excited and gave our team a **pep talk**.
很遗憾你没有参加今天上午的动员会。教练当时非常兴奋，给我们团队做了鼓舞士气的讲话。

Unit 36
The Roots of Canadian English
加拿大英语的根

Because Canada used to be a colony of Great Britain and is now a member country of the British Commonwealth, many people assume that Canadian English is merely a dialect or branch of British English.

That is an oversimplified and inadequate notion. Actually, the first batch of English speakers coming to Canada was not from Britain but from the United States. Canadian history tells us that many characteristics of present-day Canadian English can be traced back to the events that followed American Revolution of 1776. When the British Army was defeated by the Washington Troops, those who had supported Britain found themselves unable to stay in the United States and, led by William Howe, several thousand of these New England refugees fled to Halifax in Canada in March, 1776. These people were called, according to Canadian history, "Empire Loyalists" because, after the American Revolution, they remained loyal to the British crown.

Soon after the arrival of the first batch of "Empire Loyal" immigrants, many others, one group after another, moved to Canada from the eastern coastal areas of the United States. Within 50 years, by 1826 or so, the population of the eastern part of Canada had reached more than 100,000. These settlers spoke the dialect of 18th century New England with a Pennsylvanian accent. This dialect bore little similarity to what was often called Standard British English.

Supplementing this influx of United Empire Loyalists into Canada was

Unit 36 The Roots of Canadian English 加拿大英语的根

a significant number of emigrants from Britain itself. Between 1825 and 1846, more than half a million British people moved to Canada. Because it was not until 1880 that education became compulsory in Britain, most British immigrants to Canada in the early 19th century had received just a little schooling and had no opportunity to acquire an education in so-called Standard British English. So the language of even the immigrants directly from Britain themselves was by no means standard written English. It was almost all spoken English only.

Because the new settlers did need new words to describe unfamiliar things, many new English words and expressions were created. The word "skid road" originated in B.C. lumber camps in 1852. It means a road of greased skids, over which logs were dragged by teams of oxen or horses. The loggers who built such trails were called "skidders". From this Canadian lumbering slang expression sprang several unique Canadian English verb phrases:

"hit the skids" (be broke);

"be on the skids" (be unemployed or fail utterly);

"grease the skids" (make things easier);

"put the skids under" (topple or cause to fail).

"Crummy" is another lumbering slang created in the late 1930s in B.C.'s logging area. A "crummy" was then an old truck or van in which loggers were transported back and forth downtown to logging camp. Now in British Columbia, a "crummy" can mean a "school bus". Interestingly, "crummy" can also be employed as an adjective meaning "inferior" or "awful".

When you as a foreigner first arrive in Canada, it might be very hard for you to guess the meaning of "hydro bill". The prefix "hydro" means "running water", but "hydro bill" in Canada means "electricity bill" because for a long time electricity in Canada has been generated by hydro power stations, especially cheap electric power from Niagara Falls. As a result, Canadians created the adjective "hydro-electric". It was first officially used when the Hydro-Electric Power Commission of Ontario was established in 1910. Later on, "electric" was dropped, so it became "hydro service" "hydro serviceman" "hydro wires", and so on. If a Canadian asked an Englishman or an American "Has your hydro ever been turned off?" (meaning "Has your electricity ever been turned off because of your failure to pay your electricity bill?") I suspect that most such persons would be puzzled because this is a completely Canadian usage.

The word "Mounties" is also of Canadian origin. It stands for "Royal Canadian Mounted Police", the police troop whose duty is to safeguard the country's security. When it was first established, the members of the force rode horses in the pursuit of their duties.

You can only find the words "Anglophone" and "Francophone" in Canadian English dictionaries since these words have been especially coined to distinguish people in Canada whose native language is English from those whose native language is French.

There are many English words originating in Canada, often borrowing from native Indians, Eskimos, and other ethnic groups. *Gage Canadian Dictionary* lists more than 10,000 words that originated in Canada.

If you are not quite familiar with Canadian English, it is difficult for you to understand some sentences which are carried in the Canadian newspapers. For example:

"Be careful on a snowmobile or you could disappear down a *rot hole*."

"Winter causes *frost boil*, and with spring comes the *slob ice* drifting down from the North."

"I like the beauty of *silver thaw*."

"I fell down because of the *black ice*."

A *rot hole* is a soft spot in a frozen lake; *slob ice* is the partially melted kind, chunks of which float in the ocean; *frost boil* is what happens to roads and pavement in winter; and *silver thaw* is a freezing rain that leaves trees, roads, etc., covered with a coat surface; *black ice* (glare ice) is the rain frozen on pavement, leaving a sheet surface that is difficult to see.

Canadian people have been trying hard to maintain the unique characteristics of Canadian English which can be easily noticed by people from other countries. Canadian people are very much proud of their unique Canadian expressions. The growth of the determination not to be Americans can be seen in many areas in Canada (except Quebec).

Although Canadian people have created many unique expressions and the special usages in the past 200 years, and try to be careful of using American English, they still follow the American English usage in general, not British English usage.

I think that in an age of quick travel and strong trade ties—the differences in the two strains of Northern American English are slowly disappearing. Sounds are moving both ways across the border. And Canada has now lost some of its words. But likewise, Americans, according to some studies, are more frequently pronouncing words like "cot" and "caught" as if they were the same as [ɔ]—a long standing trait of Canadian pronunciation.

译 文

因为加拿大曾经是英国的殖民地,而且现在是英联邦的一个成员国,许多人认为加拿大英语只是属于英国英语的一种方言或是它的一个分支。

这是一种过分简单而且不全面的看法。实际上第一批来加拿大定居的讲英语的移民并非来自英国,而是来自美国。加拿大历史告诉我们,当代加拿大英语的许多特点都可以追溯到1776年的美国独立战争期间的那些事件中。当那些亲英分子被华盛顿部队打败后,他们感到不能继续留在美国了。因此,在威廉·豪的带领下,几千名新英格兰难民于1776年3月逃到加拿大的哈利法克斯地区。据加拿大历史记载,这些人被称为"英帝国保皇派"。因为美国独立战争结束后,他们仍然效忠于英国王室。

第一批"英帝国保皇派"抵达后不久,其他人一批接一批地从美国东部海岸地区移民到加拿大。50年间,大约到1826年左右,加拿大东部人口已经达到10万多人。这些定居者讲的是带有美国宾夕法尼亚口音的18世纪新英格兰方言。这种方言在当时和所谓的标准英国英语几乎没有相同之处。

对"英帝国保皇派"大批涌入加拿大的增加和补充的则是那些相当数量的来自英国本土的移民。1825年至1846年期间,有50多万英国人移民到加拿大。由于英国直到1880年才实行义务教育,所以,大多数19世纪初来到加拿大的英国移民没有受过多少教育,他们也没有机会接受所谓标准英国英语的教育。因此,就连直接来自英国的移民也并不是使用标准的书面英语,几乎所有的人使用的只是口语式英语。

由于新定居的移民的确需要新的词汇来描述不熟悉的事物,许多新的英语单词和词组孕育而生。"skid road"一词源于1852年B.C.省的伐木场。该词的意思是(伐木场的)"横木滑道"，由一组牛或马把横木拖走。建造滑道的那些伐木工人被称为"集材工人"。由这个伐木业的俚语派生出几组独一无二的加拿大英语动词短语：

　　hit the skids（身无分文）；
　　be on the skids（失业或彻底失败）；
　　grease the skids（使事情进展顺利）；
　　put the skids under（使倒塌或失败）。

　　"crummy"是另一个伐木业的俚语，它产生于20世纪30年代末B.C.省的伐木地区。"crummy"是指旧时的卡车或面包车，它运载那些从城镇到伐木场上下班的伐木工人。现在"crummy"在B.C.省也指接送孩子上下学的班车。有趣的是，"crummy"还被当形容词来用，意思是（质量）"劣等的"或是"糟糕的"。

　　当你作为一个外国人刚刚来到加拿大时，你可能不容易猜出"hydro bill"是什么意思。前缀"hydro"是"流水"的意思，但是在加拿大"hydro bill"却指"电费账单"。因为在过去很长的时间里，加拿大所用的电是水力发电站提供的，尤其是利用廉价的尼亚加拉大瀑布的水力发电。最终，加拿大人杜撰了"hydro-electric"这个形容词。这个形容词在1910年安大略省水力发电站委员会成立时第一次被官方正式使用。后来"electric"被省略了。因此，"电业服务""电业服务人员""电缆"等也都变成了"hydro service""hydro serviceman""hydro wires"。如果一位加拿大人问一位英国人或美国人，"Has your hydro ever been turned off？"（意思是说："你是否因没付electricity bill而被停电？"）我认为他们大都会迷惑不解，因为这是一个纯粹的加拿大英语用法。

　　"Mounties"一词也是源于加拿大的单词。这个单词代表的是"加拿大皇家骑警"（Royal Canadian Mounted Police），这是一支保安部队，它的任务是保卫国家的安全。当这个组织刚刚在加拿大建立时，队伍的成员骑着马履行他们的职责。

　　你只能在加拿大的英语词典中才能找到"Anglophone"和"Francophone"这两个单词，因为这两个单词是专门用来区别在加拿大的那些"以英语为母语的人"和"以法语为母语的人"而创造的。

　　有好多英语单词源于加拿大，这些单词常常是从当地印第安人、爱斯基摩人以及其他少数民族语言中借用的词。《盖奇加拿大英语词典》列出了一万多源于加拿大的英语词条。

　　如果你对加拿大英语不太熟悉，你在看加拿大报纸时，要想明白其中的文章里句子的含义就比较困难。例如：

　　使用摩托雪橇滑雪时要当心，否则你可能掉进冰窟窿（rot hole）里。

　　严寒造成公路翻浆（frost boil），而春天来了，海面冰块（slob ice）则会从北部一路漂流下来。

我喜欢美丽的冰挂（silver thaw）景色。

我因为暗冰而（black ice）滑倒了。

rot hole指结冻河面上的冰窟窿；frost boil指冬天道路由于严寒而发生的翻浆情况；slob ice指流入海洋的半融化的大冰块；silver thaw指冰雨落在树上和路面上形成的冰包雪裹的冰挂；black ice（或glare ice）指雨水落在路面冻成冰，形成了人们肉眼很难发现的冰面。

许多国家的人已注意到加拿大人一直在努力保持着加拿大英语的独特风格。加拿大人对自己独特的加拿大英语词汇深感自豪。在加拿大（除魁北克省外），许多地方的人不情愿当美国人的决心越来越大。

虽然加拿大人在过去的200年里创造出了许多具有加拿大特色的词汇及用法，而且在英语使用上试图和美国英语保持距离，但是总体上讲，加拿大人还是基本上遵循美国英语的习惯用法，而不跟随英国英语。

我想随着日渐繁盛的旅游和日渐浓郁的纽带关系，北美地区两种英语间的差异在逐渐消失，不同的英语发音在两国边界穿梭。如今，加拿大的一些词语逐渐在流失，同样地，研究表明，越来越多的美国人在cot和caught发音上效仿加拿大的发音特点，即两个词都发成[ɔ]。

I'd Better Stop Talking Shop

(Li is about to leave Canada. Connie prepared some gifts for him.)

Connie: Now that you are leaving for China tomorrow, I collected some newspaper article concerning ESL teaching, and also some buttons for your colleagues. That's a Canadian flag. It's a maple leaf. The maple leaf *stands for* Canada.

Li: That's very kind of you. I hear that in the past, Canada used to have the British flag.

Connie: That's right. But later, in 1964, we thought we should have a flag of our own. So the government asked everyone to draw pictures of flags and send them in. The best picture would be chosen as Canada's flag. So the people drew thousands of different flags.

Li: Finally the maple leaf was chosen. Right?

Connie: Well, it wasn't that easy to *pull off*. There was a heated flag debate in Parliament in fact, and, after many discussions and debates, on 15 Feb. 1965, the maple leaf was proclaimed Canada's national flag by Queen Elizabeth II.

Li: Oh, I see, it sounds like it was a big event. Why did they choose a maple leaf as Canada's flag?

Connie: The maple leaves look beautiful, especially in autumn. The color is so bright and red. Besides, maple trees are good for making houses and furniture, and, *last but not least* you can get sugar from the maple tree.

Li: Connie, you've given me a vivid Canadian history course.

Connie: Oh, sorry, I'm talking too much. I'd better stop *talking shop*.

Li: Well, Connie, thank you for these wonderful gifts, and I really appreciate your spending so much time showing me the sights. You've sacrificed many weekends and you have *leaned over backwards* to make the contacts and collect the materials for my Canadian Studies while I've been here. I've had a delightful time during my visit here in Montreal.

Connie: Don't mention it. All in a day's work.

Li: You'll be coming to China to visit me next summer as you promised, right?

Connie: Oh, yes. Unless something unusual crops up, that's my present plan. I will be in Tianjin City sometime next August.

Li: Sounds wonderful. I'll be expecting you then.

Vocabulary and Notes

- button 纽扣形的小徽章；纽扣；按钮
- maple leaf 枫树叶
- a heated flag debate 一场热烈的关于国旗的辩论
- Parliament the lawmaking body of Canada made up of the House of Commons and the Senate 加拿大议会，由上议院和下议院组成
- proclaim 宣布，宣告；声明

- Queen Elizabeth II

  英国女王伊丽莎白二世（1926—2022），1952年2月6日继承其父英王乔治六世的王位，1953年6月2日加冕，是英国在位时间最长的君主。她在皇家受教育，研读历史、语言和音乐。

- All in a day's work.

  习以为常；不足为奇。

 Idioms for Everyday Use

stand for
代表；象征；意味着 | represent; symbolize; be a sign of

- A: T stands for temperature in this equation. The sign X usually **stands for** an unknown number.
- B: Thank you for your help.
- A: 在这个方程式中，T代表温度。符号X一般代表一个未知数。
- B: 谢谢你的帮助。

- A: Could you tell us something more about the American flag?
- B: Well, each stripe in the American flag **stands for** one of the original thirteen colonies; each star stands for one of the fifty states.
- A: 你能再谈谈有关美国的国旗吗？
- B: 好的，美国国旗上的每一长条代表着最初的13个殖民地之一；每一颗星代表50个州中的一个。

- Dictatorship **stands for** the denial of individual freedom.

  独裁意味着否认个人自由。

pull off
实践；实现 | (in this context) accomplish

- He's been a salesman for only about one month, but he **pulled that deal off** beautifully.

  他当推销员仅仅一个来月，但他出色地做成了那桩交易。

- The trick looked impossible, but she **pulled it off**.

  这个戏法看上去不可能，但她却成功了。

last but not least
最后一点，但并不是最不重要的 | in the last place but not the least important

- Peter will bring sandwiches, Alice will bring cakes, Susan will bring cookies, John will bring potato chips, and **last but not least**, Shally will bring the lemonade.

  彼得带三明治，艾丽丝带蛋糕，苏珊带饼干，约翰带炸土豆片，最后，同样重要的是莎莉要带柠檬汁来。

- New York is one of the leading industrial centers in the US as well as its business headquarters. And **last but not least**, it is the place where the United Nations has its headquarters.

  纽约不仅是美国的商业中心，而且是美国重要的工业中心之一。最后一点，也是最重要一点，纽约还是联合国总部所在地。

talk shop
谈论本行的事情；三句话不离本行 | talk about things in one's work or trade

- A: Come on, you guys. This is a party, not a meeting. You've been sitting there talking about work for nearly an hour. Come on and join the party.
- B: OK. We're coming.
- A: But you have to promise you'll stop **talking shop**.
- A: 过来吧，几位。这是聚会，可不是在开会。你们坐在那儿商量工作近一个小时了。过来参加晚会吧。
- B: 好的，我们就来。
- A: 可你们得保证别谈工作的事了。

- As they were all school teachers, they sat together and began to **talk shop**.

  因为他们都是教师，于是他们坐在一起议论起学校的事来。

lean/bend over backwards
尽全力做某事，拼命做某事 | try as hard as one can to do something

- Tim is **leaning over backwards** to please his wealthy aunt.

  蒂姆竭尽全力讨好他那阔气的姨妈。

- We **leaned over backwards** to persuade him to change his mind, but in vain.

  我们已经竭尽全力说服他改变主意，可是完全无用。

Afterword
后　记

论加拿大英语的特点

作为国家交换留学生，我于1976年赴加拿大留学，随后作为访问学者又多次出访加拿大。多年来，我的同事和学生们不断询问我有关加拿大英语特点的问题。"加拿大人的英语发音和他们的邻居美国人是不是一样？""加拿大英语使用的是英国人的词汇还是美国人的词汇？""加拿大英语的拼写是遵循英国英语还是美国英语？""加拿大英语有什么独特之处吗？"

每次出访加拿大，我都会带着这些问题去咨询加拿大的学者、学生和同事，而且每次我都确实从加拿大朋友们那里、加拿大的书籍和词典中受益匪浅。根据我和加拿大朋友的接触、40多年来英语教学的亲身体验和有关加拿大英语发展的最新资料，我来谈一谈加拿大英语的特点。

加拿大英语，它既不同于英国英语，又不同于美国英语，在很大程度上是这两种语言的融合体，而且在这种混合中又具有许多自身的特点。因此，我们可以确切地说，加拿大英语是有着自身鲜明个性的英国英语和美国英语的集合体。加拿大英语的这种融合性和自创性实际上来源于200多年以来美国和英国对它持续不断的影响。

由于加拿大曾经是英国的殖民地，而且现在是英联邦的一个成员国，许多人认为加拿大英语只是属于英国英语的一种方言或是它的一个分支。这是一种过分简单的、不全面的看法。实际上，第一批来到加拿大定居的讲英语的移民并非来自英国，而是来自美国。根据加拿大历史的记载，1776年3月，在美国独立战争中被击败的几千名亲英分子，也就是所谓的保皇党人（loyalists），在威廉·豪的带领下，逃到了加拿大的哈利法克斯地区（Halifax）。第一批"英帝国保皇派"抵达加拿大后不久，大约在1812年，第二批移民移入，也就是英美战争后来到加拿大的爱尔兰人。由于当时的加拿大总督担心民间的反英情绪，所以鼓励英国人、爱尔兰人移民加拿大。

在1825到1846年之间，有超过50万的英国人到加拿大定居，这些人再加上那些"英帝国保皇派"，对加拿大英语的影响是最大的，他们构成了维系加拿大英语保守性的主体。

实际上，加拿大人讲英语当然也受到了英国英语的很大影响。加拿大历史表明，除了大批的"英帝国保皇派"从美国涌入加拿大外，大量英国本土的居民也争先恐后地移居到加拿大。这些从英国本土来的英国人自然地把大英帝国的文化和英国式英语带入了加拿大。

1857年，教士Constable Geikie在给加拿大学院做的一次演讲中首先使用了"加拿大英语"一词。Geikie是苏格兰裔加拿大人，他认为只有那些英国来的移民讲的英语才是纯正的，而加拿大英语是一个"污染了的方言"。Geikie反映了当时在加拿大盛行并延续100多年的盎格鲁中心观。

其他人一批接一批地从美国东部海岸地区移居到加拿大。50年间，大约到1826年左右，加拿大东部人口已经达到10万多人。这些定居者讲的是带有美国宾夕法尼亚口音的18世纪新英格兰方言。这种方言在当时和所谓的标准英国英语几乎没有相同之处。

此后在1910年和1960年分别有两次移民高峰，它们对加拿大英语的影响要小一些。这四次移民潮使加拿大成了一个文化多元的国家，为在今天全球化的浪潮中吸纳外来语言奠定了基础。

移民无疑是引发语言接触的一个重要因素。另一个对加拿大英语造成重大影响的因素是与其毗邻的超级大国美国。由于地理、气候等原因，加拿大的经济发达地区集中于从太平洋到大西洋与美国接壤的狭窄地带，不少美国人也定居在这一带，而且两国人可以自由往来，无需签证。再加上美国强大的平面和立体媒体的力量，美国在意识形态、社会、文化、经济、教育等各个方面都深刻地影响着加拿大和加拿大英语。加拿大英语的词汇构成在相当大的程度上要归因于这类语言接触。

其实，早在英美人和其他移民进入加拿大之前，印第安人、爱斯基摩人等极地民族早已在这块土地上生养栖息。加拿大原住民的语言早就对来自欧洲的语言产生了影响。

语言接触导致语言在各个结构层面上发生变化。下面我们从拼写、词汇、语音、语法和语篇等几方面探讨一下加拿大英语的特点。

拼写

40多年前，我在加拿大学习英语的时候，单词的英式拼写占有主要地位。每当我到中小学参观时，许多老师强调学生要使用英国英语的拼写方式，因为当时人们认为英式的拼写更具有权威性。因此，20世纪70年代我在加拿大学习的几年里，我们的作文中就充满了以字母-our结尾的单词，比如colour, labour, honour, neighbour, humour或harbour等等。但是到了90年代，当我再次参观访问加拿大的小学和中学时，老师们在课堂上对学生们讲不要只用-our，也可以使用-or的拼写形式。40多年前，加拿大的老师要求学生必须遵循英国英语的-re拼写形式，例如centre, fibre, metre, theatre；而自90年代起，我和加拿大朋友们的通信、传真、电子邮件中就经常出现-re和-er这两种拼写方式了。

加拿大英语的拼写不像大家想象中的那样单纯和统一。地区（如各个省）之间有差异，作为语言"执法者"的编辑们意见也不一致。政府提议编辑们遵循*Gage Canadian*

后 记

Dictionary 词典首选的拼法，但该词典的质量并不尽如人意。1984年"加拿大自由编辑协会"（现称"加拿大编辑协会"）对出版业人员、学者、编辑及作家等做了一次调查，发现如下结论（百分数指的是占被调查人总数的比例）：

- colour或color？约75%的人喜欢用-our。有关使用-our还是-or有过一场旷日持久的争论，目前是趋向于使用-our。
- centre或center？89%的人中意传统的-re，如centre和theatre。
- cigarette或cigaret？85%以上的人喜欢较长的拼法，如cauldron，而不是caldron。更喜欢axe，catalogue，cigarette，moustache和omelette。但是，人们喜欢短的program，而不是programme。
- deffence或deffense？约80%的人中意-ce，而不是-se，如名词defence，practice，pretence；但是同意把-se留给动词，如practise the piano lesson。
- aesthetic或esthetic？约75%的人使用双元音(ae或oe)，如aesthetic，archaeology和manoeuvre，但人们对medieval还是mediaeval意见有分歧。
- organize或organise？加拿大编辑反对英国英语拼法-ise，而喜欢美国英语拼法-ize。
- cheque或check？许多这样的同音词的拼写视其意义而定，不能一概而论，包括mould/mold，cheque/check，racquet/racket。如：One uses a cheque to pay for a dipstick with which to check the level of oil in the tank.
- enroll或enrol？约90%的人喜欢双l，如enroll，fulfill，install，marvelled，marvellous，signalled，skillful，traveller和woollen。在加后缀时，加拿大人有自己的偏好，如果一个单词以一个元音和一个辅音结尾，加后缀时辅音一定要成双。而美国英语规定，只有在单音节或最后一个音节重读的情况下，辅音才要成双出现。

该协会没有调查到的还包括：

- adviser或advisor？首选advisor。
- co-ordinate或coordinate？加拿大人喜欢加连字符。
- gray或grey？加拿大的拼写是grey。
- sulfur或sulphur？加拿大人喜欢用sulphur，尽管标准术语是sulfur。

从上面大部分例子可以看出，在加拿大英语中仍保留了部分英国英语的拼法。然而从整体上看，加拿大英语的拼写和美国英语基本一致，如tire和curb，而英国英语是tyre和kerb。

加拿大英语拼写的特点与加拿大的贸易史有关。cheque的用法可能与加拿大与英国一度在金融机构方面的重要联系有关。而加拿大的汽车工业从一开始就受到美国公司的影响，这就是为什么包括tire在内的汽车部件名称都用美国英语的拼法。

词汇

与英美英语相应的词汇：

加拿大英语使用的词汇，情况比较复杂，既有美国英语的又有英国英语的，还有自身独创的词汇。一般说来，社会、经济、科技、日常生活方面多使用美国英语的，但政治机构、政治体制方面，加拿大英语使用英国英语词汇，如"政府首脑"用Prime Minister，不用President；"众议员"用Members of Parliament，不用Congressmen；"参议院"用House of Commons，不用Congress。

如下列出了加拿大英语、美国英语和英国英语相对应的一些例子：

加拿大英语	美国英语	英国英语	汉语
ABM	ATM	cashpoint，cash	提款机
bachelor	efficiency	bedsit	单间公寓
beater	clunker, junker	banger	破车
beauty parlor	beauty parlor	ladies hairdresser	美容院
berry sugar	superfine sugar	caster sugar, castor sugar	精制白砂糖
Billion—a thousand million (1,000,000,000)	Billion—a thousand million (1,000,000,000)	Billion—a million million (1,000,000,000,000)	［加、美］十亿,［英］万亿
bus depot	bus station	coach station	公交车站
chesterfield	sofa	couch, settee	沙发
child benefit, baby bonus	child tax benefit	family allowance	育婴补贴
chips potato	chips potato	crisps	薯条
cling wrap	plastic wrap, Saran wrap	cling film	保鲜膜
coin laundry	laundromat	launderette	自助洗衣房
depanneur	convenience store	corner shop	便利店
driver's permit	driver's license	driving licence	驾驶执照
elevator	elevator	lift	箱式电梯
EMT, ambulance technician	paramedic	ambulance man	医疗技师，救护人员
fire hall	firehouse	fire station	消防站
flat tire	flat	flat tyre, puncture	爆胎
first floor	first floor	ground floor	一楼
funeral chapel	funeral home	funeral parlour	殡仪馆
gas	gas	petrol	汽油
housing development	tract housing	housing estate	居民点

后 记

（续）

加拿大英语	美国英语	英国英语	汉语
main floor	first floor	ground floor	一楼
offence	offense	attack	攻击
parkade	parking garage, parking ramp	multi-storey car park	停车库
phone, call	call	phone	（打）电话
pogey	unemployment, welfare	dole, income support	福利补贴，失业救济
postal code	zip code	post code	邮政编码
puckster	hockey player	ice hockey player	冰球手
Revenue Canada, RevCan	International Revenue Service, IRS	Inland Revenue	（加拿大）国家税务局
riding	district	constituency	选区
runners	sneakers	trainers	运动鞋
serviette	table napkin	serviette	餐巾纸
social housing	public housing	council housing	政府为低收入者所建的住房
stagette	female bachelorette party	hen party	女士聚会
statutory holiday	legal holiday	bank holiday	银行假日
street busker	street entertainer	busker	街头艺人
tap	faucet	tap	水龙头
university	college	university	大学
vacation	vacation	holiday	假日
video lottery machine, VLT	one-armed bandit	fruit machine	老虎机，赌博机
washroom	ladies' room, men's room, rest room	ladies, gents, lavatory, loo	厕所，洗手间
welfare cheque	welfare check	giro (cheque)	失业津贴支票

加拿大英语特有语汇：

加拿大英语特有的语汇（Canadianisms）很多。首先是加拿大独有的词语和谚语。加拿大词源学家Bill Casselman的著作*Casselmania: More Wacky Canadian Words & Sayings*收录了500条有典故和来源的加拿大词语和谚语。（Casselman, 1996）此外，在*The Canadian Oxford Dictionary (2nd Edition)*收录的3万个词条中，真正属于加拿大特有语汇的有2200多条。（Barber, 2004）然而，现已收入一般英语词典的词汇，有的词源可追溯到加拿大。还有的词在加拿大英语中词义已有所变化。如上述书名中的wacky，在美国英语中本是"怪僻的"或"怪异的"（wacky person，wacky outfit）的意思，而在该书名中显然是"有趣的"（interesting）的意思。

与加拿大环境、职业等有关的加拿大英语特有词汇和表达：

sin bin（冰球受罚球员席），slap shot（冰球猛击），hockey stick（冰球球棍），rink rat（冰球义工），rot hole（冰窟窿），frost boil（路面冻得崎岖不平）。

这些词或词组在一般的英语词典中都找不到。比如后两个词组是奇怪的组合。这些词与加拿大大部分地区冬天冰天雪地、冰冻期长、冰球运动发达有关。

再比如，skidroad（〈伐木场的〉滑木道，拖横木的一组牛和马），skidder（滑道建造者，集材工人），hit the skids（〈习语〉身无分文），be on the skids（失业或彻底失败），put the skids under（使倒塌或失败），grease the skids（使事情进展顺利）。除了最后一个习语以外，其余词和习语在《新英汉词典》中都可以找到，但未注加拿大来源。

来自原住民语言的词汇：

加拿大英语中有一些源自印第安语、爱斯基摩语的词语，这是它的词汇的一个显著特点。例如：muskey（沼泽地），caribou（驯鹿），moose（加拿大驼鹿），parka（派克大衣），mukluk（爱斯基摩海豹皮靴），tepee（印第安人圆锥形帐篷），kayak（兽皮独木舟），umiak（兽皮舟），igloo/iglu（用冰块造成的冰屋）。除了muskey和kayak外，《新英汉词典》都收录了，但其中一半词未注出加拿大印第安语的词源，而且igloo被解释为"爱斯基摩人的圆顶茅屋"，联系爱斯基摩人冰天雪地的环境，该解释似有误。

来自原住民语言的加拿大地方英语打招呼语有：aksunai/auksuai（来自因纽特语言），bo-jo bo-jo（来自印第安语言），chimo（来自因纽特语言，亦作祝酒呼号），klahowyah（钦努克印第安语言），nitchie/niche/nee-chee/neejee/nidge（来自阿尔冈基亚语言），wachee/wacheya（来自印第安克里语）。打招呼词语，以及土著语言的山川、湖泊和地名，将留在占支配地位的语言中，成为语言接触的见证。

加拿大英语特有语汇举例：

以下例子是 The Canadian Oxford Dictionary (2nd Edition) 收录的一些加拿大英语的特有语汇。

词汇	释义
Allophone	讲英语和法语以外的魁北克人
Anglophone	以英语为母语的人
biffy	室外蹲式厕所
Canuck	加拿大人的自称，无贬义
chesterfield	沙发，双人沙发

（续）

词汇	释义
click	kilometre 的俗称
concession road	南安大略和南魁北克殖民时期修建的老路，这些路把地分隔成固定面积的方块。在安大略省，许多道路至今叫做 lines
First Nations	美洲印第安人
fishway	水坝上让鱼回游的设置；鱼道
Francophone	以法语为母语的人
garburator	洗涤槽下的杂物切割器
hoser	粗鄙的酒鬼
humidex	湿热指数
Inuit	爱斯基摩人
joe job	收入低的工作
keener	用功的学生（隐含贬义）
loonie or loony	加拿大一元硬币，复数形式 loonies（口语）
Métis	原住民和法国人结合的后裔
muskeg	厚苔沼
Newf or Newfie	纽芬兰人，略带贬义
outport	海边孤屋
parkade	停车库
pogey	福利或失业保险（略带贬义）
poutine	加拿大名吃：加奶酪和肉汁的法式炸土豆条
pure laine	法裔加拿大人（源自法语单词"纯毛"，略带侮辱性）
runners	跑鞋：sneakers
ski-doo	雪地车，可做动词，原先是商标名
sniggler	抢占停车位的人
sook or suck	发牢骚者，形容词 sookie 或 suckie；sook 与 hook 押韵，可用于一般场合，但 suck 不可
stag and doe, buck and doe	婚前单身聚会，相当于 bachelor party 和 bachelorette party 的结合
toboggan	一种雪橇，平底，一头翘起，两侧有扶手
toonie	两元硬币，根据 loonie 造词
tuque	冬天戴的帽子，与 kook 押韵
wedding social	婚礼前亲友为准新郎和准新娘举行的筹款聚会，款项通过入场费、卖饮料和抽奖收入筹集，在安大略省西北部等地流行

200多年来，加拿大人凭借自身的智慧和经验，创造出了许多具有加拿大特色的词

汇、格言、谚语等，从而丰富了加拿大英语。笔者在加拿大不同地区收集了一些方言，在这里仅举几例有关天气方面的谚语。温哥华的四月经常下小雨，因此那里的人们常讲：April showers bring May flowers.（四月雨催五月花。）多伦多冬天雪大，那里的人们常说：A year of snow, crops will grow.（大雪普降，丰收在望。）但美国纽约人也这样说。温尼伯草原蚱蜢多，人们常说：When the grasshopper sings near, the weather will be hot and clear.（蚱蜢唱得欢，迎来艳阳天。）

语音

Kinloch & Avis（1989）详细分析了加拿大英语和英国英语的异同，值得注意。

两位学者把加拿大中部英语的发音作为比较的对象，是有道理的。他们认为，加拿大中部英语，指安大略省以西广大地区使用的通用英语，亦称加拿大普通英语，是加拿大大部分地区受过教育的人使用的英语，很受推崇。（Avis, 1973）这一点很重要。原来，安大略省以东地区为魁北克，为法语区或法语、英语混用区，剩下来的只有面积较小的新斯科舍省和纽芬兰省。按上面说过的美国保皇派大量涌入的哈利法克斯地区就在新斯科舍半岛上，这些人受英国口音（具体来说是宾夕法尼亚口音）影响很大，因而不能算作加拿大普通英语的语音；至于纽芬兰地区，由于跟广大的魁北克省接壤，英语口音已经不纯。

根据上述两位专家的材料，可以归纳出加拿大英语与英语标准发音（英国英语）的异同。

二者的辅音系统相同，但/r/、/č/和/š/，和/k/、/hw/中的/h/、/t/等发音要注意，即有变化。

/r/在所有的环境中（即词首、辅音后、元音之间、辅音前、词末位置）都要发音，这跟美国英语相似，而跟英国英语不同。

/t/的表现比较复杂。在大多数位置上，加拿大中部英语/t/的表现跟英国公认的发音很相似，然而，/t/在元音之间弱浊辅音化，甚至变成齿龈嗒音，乃至完全浊化的/-d-/。笔者就曾听到把butter读成budder、later读成lader的例子。也有些学者报道说，加拿大儿童把首都渥太华（Ottawa）写作Oddawa，把petal写作peddle。

元音系统的不同点是：英国公认标准音的/iə/、/ɛə/、/uə/、/ɔə/、/aiə/、/auə/中的/-ə/，加拿大普通英语都变成/-r/，如/iə/变成/ir/，余者类推。

元音中的合并现象也很突出。例如：英国英语中/e/和/ei/合并成加拿大普通英语的/e/，/o/和/əu/合并成/o/。英式发音为/ɑː/的场合，美式发音为/æ/，加拿大英语的发音介于/ɑː/和/æ/之间。

可以说，合并是加拿大英语音变的重要途径。Labov说，创新的加拿大英语音变，都是由合并引起的。

语法和语篇

语法与组合有关，语篇是较高层次组合的结果，因此放在一起来讨论。一般认为，与词汇相比，语法的变化较慢、较少。然而值得注意的是，语法变化一旦形成，就成为语言变体引人注目的标志。（Heine & Kuteva，2006）综合前人的研究成果和笔者个人的观察，加拿大英语的语法和语篇方面的主要特点如下：

情态动词will和shall的用法。要表达"我不会告诉别人"这样的意思时，加拿大英语的表达法与美国英语相同："I won't tell anyone."而不用英国英语表达式："I shan't tell anyone."

定冠词的有无。加拿大英语与美国英语一样，倾向于在有些介词词组的名词前用定冠词，虽然该名词不一定是定指的，如in the hospital和to the university；而英国英语则不用定冠词，如in hospital和to university。

数词和集体名词的单复数形式。加拿大和美国英语用单数形式，如six million，而英国英语用复数形式，如six millions。类似的例子还有staff，family，crew，press，audience等等。（Bock，2006）

虽然加拿大人创造出多少具有加拿大特色的词汇及用法，而且在英语使用上试图和美国英语保持距离，但是在大多数情况下，加拿大人还是基本上遵循美国英语的习惯用法，而不跟随英国。虽然加拿大英语/美国英语使用的词汇与英国英语不一样，但表达的意思相同。

加拿大英语/美国英语与英国英语比较：

加拿大英语/美国英语	英国英语
I won't tell anyone.	I shan't tell anyone.
He is in the hospital.	He is in hospital.
I'll see you over (on) the weekend.	I'll see you at the weekend.
Did you look out the window?	Did you look out of the window?
There were six million.	There were six millions.
Let's give it another try.	Let's have at it again.
She is now making some good money.	She is now making a good penny.
Watch your head.	Mind your head.
I didn't get the grades.	I didn't receive marks.
We seldom take our kids to a candy store.	We seldom take our children to a sweetshop.

Eh?

"eh?"的用法多义化、多功能化。加拿大英语最具特点的是"eh?",它已成为当代加拿大英语的标志。Casselman 认为:"'eh?'之于加拿大人,犹如干草之于骏马,不可分离。"(Casselman,1996)也就是说,加拿大人说英语,口不离"eh?"。"eh?"甚至被新移民认为是体现加拿大人身份的象征。(Casselman,1996)

"eh?"可用来说明意见(Nice day, eh?),表示感叹(What a beautiful night, eh?),陈述事实(It goes over here, eh?),表达批评(You took the last piece, eh?),表达请求或发出命令(Think about it, eh?),等等。"eh?"还用于固定的搭配中,如"I know, eh?""Thanks, eh?"。

Gold (2004) 调查了"eh?"在加拿大英语中的10类用法。笔者根据他的研究,将这10类用法按常用程度降序排列如下:

意见	Nice day, eh?
感叹	What a game, eh?
熟语	I know, eh?
批评	You took the last piece, eh?
祈求	Think about it, eh?
陈述	It goes over here, eh?
致歉	Eh? What did you say?
斥责	You're a real snob, eh?
疑问	What are they trying to do, eh?
叙述	This guy is up on the 27th floor, eh? Then he gets out on the ledge, eh?….

上表说明,"eh?"所起的作用有时相当于反意疑问句的后半截,有的用法与汉语中的"吧"等句末小品词相似:

- Nice day, eh? [isn't it?]
- It goes over here, eh? [doesn't it?]
- Oh, you're still here, eh? [aren't you?]

我们还可以看出,"eh?"常表达说话人对所述事物否定的态度。除了"You took the last piece, eh?""You're a real snob, eh?"表达不快和斥责以外,wh- 疑问句"What are they trying to do, eh?"事实上也表露了说话人的不满,甚至是谴责的意思。

其实,eh在中古英语中用得已相当普遍。乔叟在《坎特伯雷故事集》中已用过这个形式,不过那时拼写成ey。《韦氏新世界美国英语词典》中注解为:eh为感叹词,表示惊奇、怀疑或询问。《新英汉词典》加上了"表示同意"。这些也是加拿大英语的基本用法。《加拿大牛津词典》认为，eh在其他英语变体（英国英语、美国英语）中也使用，唯一属于加拿大英语的用法是"探察听话人是否理解或同意说话人所说，是否对所说仍有兴趣"。例如，"Nice day, eh?" "This guy is up on the 7th floor, eh?.... then..." "It's four kilometres away, eh? So I have to go by bike." 在最后这个句子中，"eh?"用来确认听话者仍在听，并期望对方做出mm、oh或okay的回答。

由于历史和地理位置的原因，美国和加拿大边境一直是开放的。两国公民一直是自由出入，不需签证。90%的加拿大人居住在距离加美两国边境300公里以内。由于美国各方面的长期影响，加拿大人逐渐形成了看美国电视、听美国音乐和广播，学校里大部分用的是美国人编写的课本。加拿大Janet Morchain在她的 *Sharing the Continent* (《共享新大陆》) 一文中指出，"每年约有9千万册的期刊杂志进入加拿大"。最终，加拿大英语吸收了许多美国英语的词汇和用法。"加拿大报纸使用的英语语言和美国报纸的语言基本相似。"（见David Crystal, *English Language*, 1990）据多年与加美朋友接触，我发现，越来越多的美国人在cot和caught发音上具有加拿大英语特色，两个词都发成/ɔ/，而现在许多加拿大人也不像以前那样把leisure只是念成/ˈleʒə/，把schedule念成/ˈʃedjuːl/，倒是向美国人学习，也念成了/ˈliːʒə/和/ˈskedʒjul/了。

我认为，随着美国人和加拿大人如此频繁地接触，加之两国200多年来是最亲密的贸易伙伴，而且两国公民有着千丝万缕的亲戚关系，加美两种风格的英语会在两国人民不断交往中交融。正如一位加拿大作家描述的那样，如果一个美国人从天而降，正好落到了加拿大境内时，人们很难从他的发音和用词上辨别出他是美国人还是加拿大人。

Index
索 引

A
a bird's-eye view
a far cry from
a pain in the neck
a tough / hard / long row to hoe
a while back
add insult to injury
alive and kicking
(It's) all in a day's work
answer for
as / so far as
as the crow flies
at ease (at one's ease)

B
baffle someone (or be baffled)
be breathtaking
be captivated by
be crazy about
be fed up
be frozen stiff
be hard on (something or somebody)
be high on
be in a dilemma
be in / get into a rut
be in good / bad / great / terrible shape
be in one's shoes / boots
be nosy
be snowed under with work
be tired out
blow a fuse
boggle the mind
brush up on something
bug someone
bury oneself in something
buy it / that

C
can't beat something with a stick
can't get a word in edgewise (edgeways)
can't make head / heads or tail / tails of (something)
catch on to something
catch-22 (situation or position)
clue someone in
come down with (an illness)
come in handy
(something) come to someone
coop up
cope with
cost a mint
cover a lot of / much ground
crack up
crop up
cut short
cut through the red tape

D

dish up

do one's bit / part

do some browsing

do someone good

do / work wonders for

double check

down in the mouth / dumps

draw a blank

draw / bring someone out of one's shell
   (come out of one's shell)

draw in (on someone)

drop in (on someone)

E

eat / drink one's fill

F

fast

feast one's eyes on (something)

feel / be on top of the world

feel / be self-conscious

feel up / equal to

few and far between

fill someone in on the details

find a happy medium

follow suit

for the birds

frame of mind

full of vitality

G

get a load of

get a move on (get a wiggle on)

get along in years

get along with someone

get away from it all

get / go to the bottom of

get / go to the heart of something

get / have one's work cut out

get into

get into the swing of (something)

get lost

get off to a flying / good start

get someone down

get someone wrong

get to someone

get two left feet

get wind of

give someone a break

give someone a piece of one's mind

give someone/something time

go about (doing something)

go on / run errands

go out for a spin

go out of one's way to do something

go over big

go over / through something with a fine-
   tooth comb

go the extra mile

go up

goof off

gripe

grow on someone

H

hard up for

have a head for

have (a lot of) nerve
have it in someone
hear something through the grapevine
hit the ceiling
hit the road
hit-or-miss (hit or miss)

I

If my memory serves me right...
I'm right behind you.
in a bind
in store (for someone)
in the nick of time
Isn't it a small world?
It goes without saying

J

jot down (something)
jump at
jump / climb on the bandwagon
jump in with both feet
jump ship

K

keep an eye on (something or someone)
keep one's fingers crossed
keep one's head above water
keep one's shirt on
keep someone posted
kill two birds with one stone
knock someone out

L

land / light on one's feet
last but not least
lay off (someone)

lay / put / spread it on thick
lean / bend over backwards
leave someone alone
leave something up to someone
like a fish out of water
little by little
look into
look / feel / get run-down

M

make good time
make sense
meet someone halfway
mind one's own business
miss the boat

N

no sweat
not half bad
not know the first thing about (something)
(every) now and then

O

off the beaten track
off the cuff
off the top of one's head
on display
on speaking terms
(go / be) on the blink
on the fritz
on the job
on the road
on the safe side
on the same wave-length (on the different wave-length)

on the spur of the moment
on the tip of one's tongue
out of one's hair
out of the blue
over / above one's head

P

paint the town red
pay lip service to
pay off
pep talk
pick out
pick someone up
plug away (or keep plugging away)
pry into
pull off
put / lay one's finger on
put in
put two and two together

R

rack one's brain
rat race
read up on
re-run
right off the bat
ring a bell
roll up somebody's sleeves
rub someone the wrong way
(a) rule of thumb
run
run a temperature
run away (from something difficult, unpleasant)
run someone ragged

S

scratch the surface
seasoned traveler
see eye to eye (with someone)
sell like hot cakes (sell like T-shirts)
serve one's turn / purpose
set (great) store on
shake a leg
show off
shower someone with something
sleep on it
slip one's mind
smooth things over
spill the beans
stand / be / come face to face with someone
stand for
stand out
start from scratch
step in (to do something)
stick around /about
straight from the shoulder
stumbling block

T

tag along
take a back seat
take a dim view of something
take advantage of
take after
take heart
take in

take pains/trouble

take pride in

take someone up on (something)

take something for granted

take something with a grain/pinch of salt

take the words out of one's mouth

talk (something) over

talk down on someone

talk shop

tell (two things) apart

tell someone off

the best bet

the ins and outs

the lights went out

the pot calling the kettle black

the cream of the crop

throw someone

tight-fisted

time on one's hands

to say the least (of it)

top-notch

try one's hand at (something)

turn someone down

turn someone on

use / take a breather

wait on somebody hand and foot

wait on / upon

with the best of intentions

work against

You can say that again! (You said it!)

You've never said a truer word.